'Highly readable . . . hugely informative . . . everyone's dream of the good life without sentimentality or unrealistic expectations'

Country Life

'Entertaining, accessible and sincere'

Rory MacLean, *Guardian*

'Webster offers both the humorous depictions of local traditions and idiosyncratic figures that we might expect, and a more searching Sebaldian perception of historical events that have shaped society'

Irish Times

'Webster has the endearing writer's knack of making us laugh and weep along with him . . . written in the sympathetic tradition of Chris Stewart's best-selling *Driving Over Lemons*, but is even better'

Sunday Telegraph

'If you've read any of Webster's books on Spain you'll know he has a natural empathy for the people and their culture. In *Sacred Sierra* he describes a year living in the rural heart of the country. He and his girlfriend bought a run-down farmhouse and tried to build the perfect retreat. They knew nothing about farming but, with a little local help, managed to cultivate olives, almonds and truffles. It was back-breaking work, but Webster makes it sound utterly seductive'

Mail on Sunday

SACRED SIERRA

Jason Webster was born near San Francisco and brought up in England and Germany. After spells in Italy and Egypt, he moved to Spain. *Duende: A Journey in Search of Flamenco* was described as 'a great book' by the *Guardian* and 'mesmerising' by the *Sunday Times*, while *Andalus: Unlocking the Secrets of Moorish Spain* and *Guerra: Living in the Shadows of the Spanish Civil War* were also critically acclaimed. He has appeared in several TV documentaries on Spain and written for the *Observer*, *Sunday Times*, *Guardian* and *New Statesman*. He lives in Spain with his wife, Salud, an actress and flamenco dancer from Valencia.

JASON WEBSTER

Sacred Sierra

A Year on a Spanish Mountain

ILLUSTRATED BY LAETITIA BERMEJO

VINTAGE BOOKS
London

Published by Vintage 2010

4 6 8 10 9 7 5 3

First published in Great Britain in 2009 by
Chatto & Windus

Vintage
Random House, 20 Vauxhall Bridge Road,
London SW1V 2SA

www.vintage-books.co.uk

Addresses for companies within The Random House Group Limited can be found at: www.randomhouse.co.uk/offices.htm

The Random House Group Limited Reg. No. 954009

A CIP catalogue record for this book
is available from the British Library

ISBN 9780099512943

The Random House Group Limited supports The Forest Stewardship Council (FSC®), the leading international forest certification organisation. Our books carrying the FSC label are printed on FSC® certified paper. FSC is the only forest certification scheme endorsed by the leading environmental organisations, including Greenpeace. Our paper procurement policy can be found at www.randomhouse.co.uk/environment

Printed and bound in Great Britain by Clays Ltd, St Ives PLC

A Salud, con todo mi amor

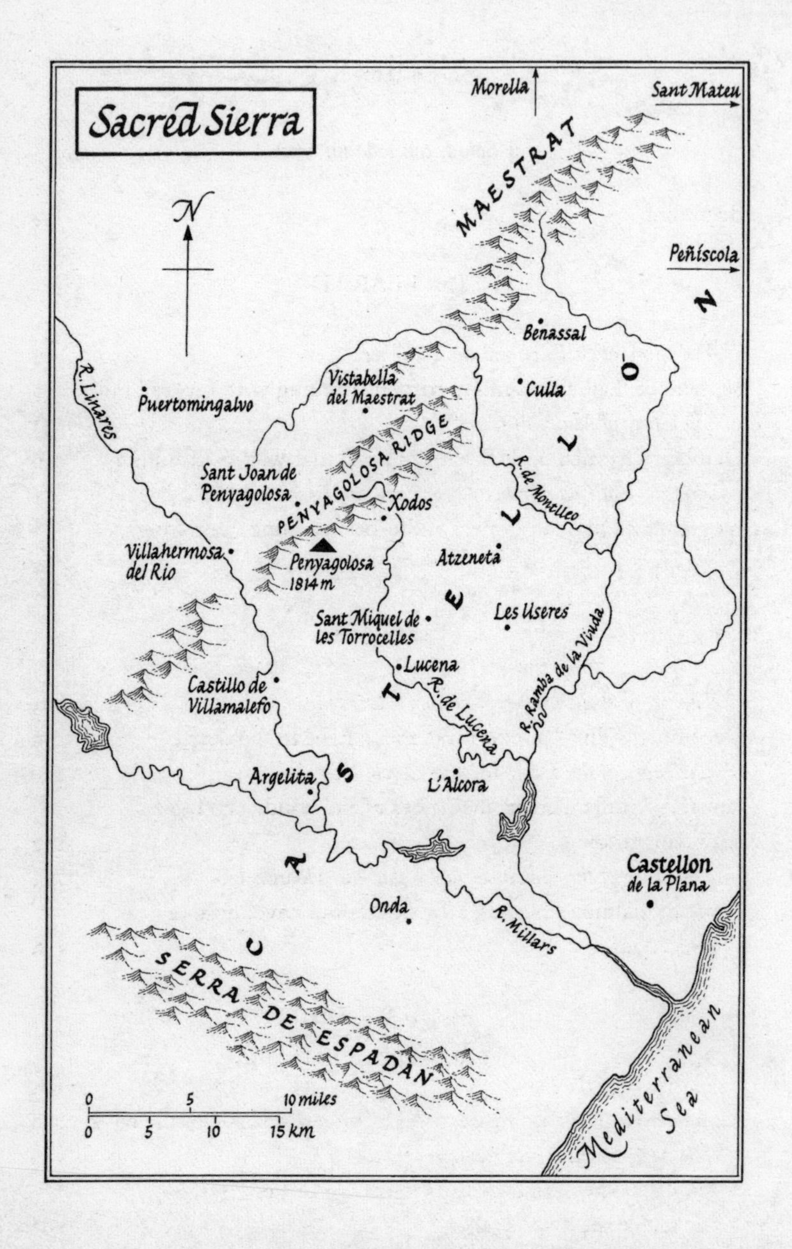

Sacred Sierra
N
Morella
Sant Mateu
MAESTRAT
Peñíscola
CASTELLÓN
Benassal
Culla
R. Linares
Puertomingalvo
Vistabella
del Maestrat
PENYAGOLOSA RIDGE
Sant Joan de
Penyagolosa
Xodos
R. de Monlleo
Villahermosa
del Rio
Penyagolosa
1814 m
Atzeneta
Sant Miquel de
les Torrocelles
Les Useres
R. Rambla de la Viuda
Lucena
R. de Lucena
Castillo de
Villamalefo
Argelita
L'Alcora
Castellon
de la Plana
Onda
R. Millars
SERRA DE ESPADAN
Mediterranean
Sea
0
5
10 miles
0
5
10
15 km

Contents

Note on Language

The area of Spain described in this book is linguistically complex, being essentially bilingual, with speakers of both Castilian Spanish and Valencian. Nonetheless, there are important variants within Valencian from valley to valley. Depending on context, names and key words, are usually given in the local Valencian dialect, but in some instances it has been more appropriate to use 'standard' Valencian, while in others the Castilian word or phrase is given.

I have tried to remain as neutral as possible with regard to the relationship between Valencian and Catalan.

Today is your day! Your mountain is waiting. So . . . get on your way!

Dr Seuss

De medico, poeta y loco
todos tenemos un poco.

'we all have a bit of a doctor, poet
and madman in us.'

Spanish proverb

BEGINNING

The old farm was a mess. Some of the roofs had fallen in and thick brambles had taken over most of the garden. There was no electricity and the nearest water came from a spring a ten-minute walk away on the other side of a deep gorge. But a magnificent three-hundred-year-old oak tree shaded the front patio, while the south-facing view down the valley, with a whitewashed Spanish village perfectly framed in the distance, was the kind I had only dreamed of. There were more than a hundred almond trees and a small olive grove – enough to produce a few litres of oil.

I was no farmer and nor was Salud; both of us were more used to city life, and neither her life as a flamenco dancer nor mine as a writer had really prepared us for something like this. What would we do with forty acres of steep, rocky land? Crumbling dry-stone walls would need repairing; whole fields needed clearing of thick, prickly gorse and a dozen species of weed I couldn't even identify. Could we really take this on?

I turned the question over in my mind as we headed slowly back to the house, convincing myself it was a crazy idea. The elderly farmer selling the place paused and looked up at a large outcrop of rock rising above us and I followed his gaze. Wild fig trees dotted its slopes, the orange and grey cliff-side reflecting the mellow light of the evening sun. Swallows were darting in and out of its crevices in search of insects, while ancient terraces climbed almost to the top, like steps, just visible behind a blanket of wild vegetation after years of neglect, then stopped where the slope had became too steep to build any more. It was a beautiful sight, multi-textured shadows lengthening across its craggy face.

'The farmhouses where we're standing are at seven hundred metres,' the old man said. I did a quick calculation in my head: over two thousand feet. '*Eixa*,' he went on, pointing up at the cliff with his gnarled walking stick, '*es la vostra muntanya*. That is your mountain.'

And suddenly the choice became no choice at all.

*

This is the tale of two mountains: one a sacred peak near the Spanish Mediterranean coast, a place of legends and stories, of ancient kings and popes, home to great pine and oak forests and the birthplace of life-giving rivers. And another much smaller mountain, a fold in the rock on the edge of the first, barely warranting a name, which became our home and the setting for a new life, and a garden that we slowly tried to cultivate around us. It is a tale of how we learned about the earth pressing between our fingers, both its workings and its mysteries, its dangers and the gifts it offered. And of how the mountain became part of our lives.

The original idea was simply to find a quiet bolthole in the country to do some writing. The city where we lived was hot and noisy: I wanted somewhere cooler in the hills to escape the suffocating summers on the coast.

Spain was at the centre of my life. After fifteen years living here I'd written three books about my experiences and exploration of it, from the dreamy pull of the Alhambra in Granada to the passion and other-worldly exoticism of flamenco. I'd fallen in love with Spanish food and wines, its music and art; the language, with its graphic, usually scatological swearwords, had penetrated deep into my psyche and become the common idiom of my dreams. Even the darker, crueller side had fascinated me, leading me to travel around the country investigating the deep wounds remaining from the civil war.

Now I was settled in the city of Valencia, on the east coast, the home town of my partner, Salud, a flamenco dancer and actress. We had a small flat where my books filled every wall space, with a tiny area left over for her to rehearse, padding the tiled floor wearing thick socks so as not to annoy the neighbours downstairs. Valencia was a sunny, lively place, set on the Mediterranean. The people were proud of their own culture and language and usually ready with a smile and talk of the paella they would be making for the family lunch that coming Sunday.

But for all its charm, Spain had changed since I had first moved there. Back in the early nineties the country was still at the tail end of the party that had broken out when the Franco regime had finally been removed and democracy took root. Sleep was something reserved for the elderly or infirm: you were expected, almost as an article of faith, to go out and dance, drink, laugh, eat and consume substances of questionable legality until dawn at least, and often beyond. And that was just on the week days. Simply stepping outside your door felt like an adventure, a journey into a wild, creative playground. There were few rules or regulations: everyone smoked, as though their lives depended on it, from the fishmonger at the market, dropping his cigar ash on to the freshly caught monkfish on his ice display, to the girl sweeping up the street, and the car mechanic, bending over oily and highly explosive engine parts with the dull burning glow of his Ducados inches away from sending him and his garage to kingdom come. There was a healthy disrespect for authority: many of my friends had been driving for years without ever having a lesson, let alone passing their test. After decades of strict autocratic rule, cheating your way through life was looked upon as something worthy and respectful. The deep-rooted anarchic individualism of the Spaniard blossomed during those years. It was the time of the first Almodóvar films; the great flamenco singer Camarón de la Isla was still alive; and Freddie Mercury and Montserrat Caballé were booming out *Baaarcelona* for the Olympics. Everything was on the up. Booze was cheap. Life was good.

Almost imperceptibly, however, this had begun to fade. Spain, a unique, special country, happily semi-detached from the rest of Europe, was beginning to conform. It began with small, seemingly insignificant things: there was a shop round the corner from us that had only sold potatoes. I used to marvel that such a place could exist; this was no specialist potato boutique: it only sold one variety – the ones dug out of the owner's plot of land the morning before. Yet still, there it was. One day, though, it didn't open. And the shutters stayed down for months until an estate agent opened in its place. Other odd little shops soon followed suit: the haberdasher's, the knife-sharpener's, a shop which only sold dried pulses, all closed within the space of a year or so. In each case the owners were getting on and their children didn't want to take over a loss-making, anachronistic concern. And each time what had once been a unique little corner was turned into a bank, or an estate agent, or a hairdresser's – lining the streets with their blandness.

The change in bar opening hours was what alerted me next. Spain was often lauded as the bar capital of the world. It had a healthy twenty-four-hour drinking culture, with none of the bingeing you associate with some countries. Suddenly, though, where once you were regarded as either strange or unwell if you headed home before five in the morning, we were being turfed out at half-past one. No one was quite sure how this had happened, but people mumbled darkly about new European Union legislation before trundling off into the shadows. The world was changing and Spain was being dragged along in its wake, but nobody could explain why.

The realisation that something was truly wrong came when people started to talk seriously about a possible end to bullfighting. It is impossible fully to understand Spanish culture without knowing something about *los toros*. Even if most people in the country don't even watch it, bull-lore is part of the country's DNA. Life itself is viewed as a variant on the *lidia*, each person facing the world and what fate throws at him like the torero in the ring staring down the deadly beast sent to challenge him. The language of bullfighting peppers everyday speech, while bull-running is the most important fiesta of the year in thousands of towns and villages. That bullfighting should cease to exist was unthinkable: it was the country's great in-built defence system against the safety culture that was slipping in from across the Pyrenees. How could 'health and safety' ever become an issue in a place where throwing yourself into the path of a horned animal weighing over half a tonne was an honoured national pastime? But there it was: audience figures were down; certain ministers in Madrid were talking in private about 'modifications' to the bull fiestas; the city of Barcelona was toying with an outright ban.

The strangeness of Spain had always attracted me. I'd often felt it had something of a fairy-tale air about it, as though by living here you came as close as it was possible actually to stepping inside a magical world of spirits and ghosts, of evil monsters and wise old kings. There had always been an earth-wisdom about the people and the place, a sense of what was truly right or wrong in any situation, beyond superficial judgements. It was a country where to be 'well-educated' referred to polite and correct behaviour towards other human beings, not whether you'd read more books than the person standing next to you. And I loved all this about it. Yet now it felt under threat. Urban, modern Spain seemed to be losing the very charm that had made it different. The spark was dulling; it was losing its rawness and becoming ever more regimented – something I had come here to escape.

Up there in the hills, though, I was sure, the tide was being held back – just.

Salud needed to stay fairly close to the city for her work. So, not wanting somewhere too far away, our search took us north and inland into the neighbouring province of Castellón, one of the last undiscovered areas of Spain. So far, only a relatively small section of the province's thin strip of coastline had been developed for tourism, but few people ever made it past the ceramics factories behind the beaches and up into the magical mountains that lay beyond. To do so was to enter a land of hilltop villages, hidden monasteries and thick pine forests. It was a world of myths and legends, of medieval knights and bizarre heretical sects, the last refuge of the Cathars, and a heartland of the ancient and mysterious Iberians.

The area was a complex patchwork of former counties and ancient fiefdoms, each with their own character and dialects, strengthened by the poor communications between them and by the difficult terrain. The central axis of the region was Penyagolosa, the highest mountain in the province. Much of the area around it was at mountain height – over 2000 feet, or 600 metres – but the peaks were still quite low, perhaps around 1000, or 1200 metres at most. Penyagolosa – the sweet-toothed, or hungry mountain, as its name suggested – rose above this, however, and sat much like the mountain of a child's drawing, a triangular peak stretching above the rest to over 1800 metres – just under 5500 feet. It wasn't an Everest, or even a Mont Blanc, but here, as the highest mountain around, it was greatly loved. It was the furthest reach of the East Iberian Mountains, the chain that gave the backbone to the Iberian Peninsula, snow-capped in winter and baked dry in summer, its broken triple peak – like a crown – slashed sideways by a red clay deposit sandwiched between its pale limestone layers. Viewed from some angles it looked almost like a hawk taking off in flight. Penyagolosa was what made the land, what gave it its special *encant*, or magical charm.

To the south of it lay the area known as the Alcalatén – from the Arabic meaning 'the Two Castles' – while the pine forests of the Gúdar and Alt Millars stretched out to the west. To the north sat the harsh plains of the Maestrazgo, or Maestrat in Valencian. The name originated from when the area was first conquered from the Moors, back in the thirteenth century. King James I handed the region over to two orders of Knights – the Templars and the Hospitallers – in gratitude for their assistance during the campaign. As the head of an order was known as a *maestre*, or 'master', the area under their control became the *maestrat* – the 'land of the masters'.

Nowadays the Penyagolosa area is a rough, unspoilt part of the country, sparsely populated, with a few small towns dotted here and there – many unchanged for centuries. It is the kind of place where turning any corner might bring you to a deserted medieval village, or else a monastery or hermitage tucked away in some forgotten corner, perhaps shaded by an ancient elm or yew tree.

The legacy of the traditional, rural way of life is still visible across the countryside in the thousands of small farms – *masos* – often grouped into little hamlets of half a dozen or so houses. Most have been abandoned as the rural economy suffered during the 1960s and 1970s. Many of the farms you encounter when out walking stand as the last occupants left them, with clothes hanging from wooden pegs on the wall and newspapers or copies of *¡Hola!* dating from the time lying scattered on the floor. The weather has taken its toll, and many buildings are slowly falling down, or in some cases lying in ruins.

The *mas* culture was the pillar of the rural economy that had once flourished in these hills. *Masos* were scattered over the entire countryside, on almost every slope or peak. Dating back hundreds of years, most could only be reached by foot or mule, often a day's walk from the nearest village along tortuously steep and dangerous paths.

The people who had lived in them – the *masovers* – had been poor, hard-working, independent people who barely scratched out a living by ploughing and tilling the thousands of terraced fields cut into the hillsides. Most of these terraces were overgrown now, the dry-stone walls that held them up slowly crumbling away with every rainstorm, but occasionally you caught sight of some well-tended patches amid the wilderness – an old farmer, perhaps, no longer living in a *mas*, carefully looking after land passed down to him from his father and grandfather.

I had long been attracted to the area, and the idea of finding a *mas* of our own. Life here followed an older rhythm: the air was clean and cool, in contrast to the choking humidity and pollution in Valencia; the roads were narrow and winding – some farmers still pulled their carts along with horses or mules; and the people seemed possessed of qualities that appeared ever more 'real' in an increasingly virtual world. I wanted a life that hit me in the face every morning and told me I was alive: you couldn't retreat into the cocoon-world of a cosy flat with an Internet connection when wood needed chopping for the fire, or snow was blocking the front door. After another record-breakingly hot summer in the city, we decided the time had come.

The only problem was finding a *mas* that someone was willing to sell. After many years in Spain I had learned that seemingly straightforward procedures rarely were so. Rather than going to an estate agent with a few of these places on his books, local wisdom dictated that the best bet was to hit the bars in a particular village and then try to ingratiate yourself with the regulars. Then, and only then, might you get the inside word on some empty farmhouse in the area for sale. The problem was that the locals often spoke only Valencian, which I understood, but still wasn't entirely at ease with; and they were notorious for being the most closed, difficult bunch of people around.

'Don't bother trying to talk to people from Castellón,' Salud's father, a farmer himself, had once said. 'They're a bunch of greedy peasants.' He only lived sixty miles down the road.

Still, we decided to give it a go: it seemed the only option available to us. And at least Valencian was Salud's mother tongue.

'It's a strange dialect up there,' she said. 'Not sure if I'll be able to understand everything they say.'

In the end we found our bar, in a whitewashed village high up in the hills at the foot of Penyagolosa, a long way, it felt, from the concrete coast.

'You'll wanna talk to Vicente,' the child serving beer said when eventually we told him what we were looking for. The place gave me a warm glow: anywhere that a twelve-year-old could be paid to pour alcoholic drinks had to be pretty sound.

Vicente, it turned out, was the man in the cowboy hat standing at the end of the bar. He looked about fifty, clean shaven, with a pearl-white smile and throaty laugh.

'Looking for me?' he said.

After establishing that he might be able to help us with our search, Salud dived in.

'We want something south-facing, not too high up or too cold, with a spring or well for water, drains, spectacular views, no neighbours, a good amount of land for working on, and no more than five miles away from the nearest village.'

There was a pause. We'd talked in rough terms about what kind of thing we'd be looking for, but it seemed reasonable to think we'd have to look around a bit before we found something of such an exact description. Vicente put his knuckles on the bar, leaned in towards us with a furrowed brow, and made a whistling sound.

'You mean the *Mas del Barranc*,' he said in a low, conspiratorial voice. 'You've heard of it already?'

Vicente drove us out of the village and up a green valley cut by a fast-flowing river. It was lush and alive, small farms dotted along the banks of the river, tall poplars shading their thick stone walls from the worst of the summer heat. Old mill houses and olive groves with red clay soil rushed by as we wound down the windows, the air mercifully clear and cool enough here for us not to need the air conditioning of his four-wheel drive car. It seemed so different from the scorched landscape I had grown accustomed to; it felt like the hidden secret valleys in the Himalayas I had read about as a boy.

We turned a sharp corner and there was a sudden bump.

'That,' said Vicente, 'was the end of the road.'

The tarmac had finished and we were on a dirt track. Vicente raced on at the same speed, a cloud of fine light-brown powder blowing up behind us from the back wheels.

'There's no one else up here,' Vicente said. 'Those houses back there are the nearest neighbours.'

We drove on for mile after mile, climbing up hills and then back down into the valley once more. For a moment we started to wonder if the place actually existed at all.

Then we saw it, through some pine trees, high above us: a small group of about four whitewashed farmhouses in the distance, huddled on an outcrop under a steep cliff-face. Vicente laughed: he could see the expressions on our faces.

Agustí was the old *masover* thinking of selling the place. He didn't live there any more – it was too much work for him now, so he spent most of his time in a flat down on the coast. He'd come up that day to check up on a few things: we'd been lucky to catch him.

'Used to make walking sticks in my spare time to earn some money,' he said once we'd been introduced. Vicente hovered in the background, smiling. Agustí had taken hold of Salud's arm almost as soon as he'd caught sight of her and leaned on her like a daughter as we slowly shuffled around. 'We used wood from the *llidoner* – the nettle tree. But they were all burnt down in the forest fire fifteen years ago.'

The farm had a perfect view down the valley we had just driven up. Yet apart from the almond and olive trees, and the odd pine and oak here and there, it felt denuded somehow, as though there should be more trees, more greenery in this ancient spot. Agustí's remark seemed to explain why.

'They used to call this the *pinar* – the pine-wood area,' he went on. 'Pine trees as far as you could see – all the way down to the village there.' He pointed to the town we had just come from in the distance. 'They reforest other areas after a fire, but not here. We're not important enough. Just a few old *masovers*. No one cares about us.'

He'd tried, he said, to get his children interested in the place, but they just weren't bothered.

'It's a beautiful place, this,' Vicente said from behind us, keen to be part of the sell.

Agustí gave Salud and me a wink.

'That gorge,' he said, pointing down into the gulley that separated the houses from the spring, 'is what gives this place its name: *el Mas del Barranc* – Hollow Farm.'

Salud turned to me. 'I could dance. No neighbours.'

Agustí looked at her steadily for a moment. There seemed to be a tear welling up in Salud's eye.

'You two would do well here,' he said.

*

For over a year after finding the farm we worked with family and friends on doing up one of the houses to create a proper living space. As well as the mountain – called, we were told, La Cantera Motxá, although the name didn't appear on any map – and forty acres of land, we had two main houses – centuries old – one of which was half ruined and would need considerable work further down the line, and two outhouses, one half a mile down the mountainside near the spring. We were almost at the top of the valley. Apart from the occasional goatherd or elderly farmer checking his almond trees nearby, our only company was the herd of ibex that used to skip down the rock face at dusk, or the wild boar that scoured the earth for food at night. Gradually, almost imperceptibly, as I got used to the place – mentally and emotionally adapting to what we had taken on board as we spent greater amounts of time up there – my ideas began to shift from it being a simple country retreat into something more. Water was piped up from the spring, solar panels installed, an extension built, a new bathroom and the beginnings of a proper kitchen put in. I enjoyed the experience immensely, relishing the challenge of having to learn new building and carpentry skills – such a change from my normally sedentary life. But in the back of my mind, the work on the house was always going to be a first step towards what I now knew and saw clearly would be the main project on our mountain: the creation of a garden and planting of a forest.

The thought had come all too easily, but I didn't really have a shining track record with gardens. As a boy, 'gardening' had usually been my mother's code for 'weeding', a dull business which had only served to stop me climbing trees or reading – far more exciting activities as far as I was concerned. A garden was something to run around in, not spend hours fiddling about with, and the wilder the better. Years later, in my late twenties, when I found myself trapped in a desk job, my appreciation of gardens had begun to grow. Hounded by sociopathic middle managers and starved of natural light and air in a large 'open-plan' office, in idle moments I found myself dreaming of gardens, and they increasingly became means of achieving a temporary imaginary release from the uselessness of what I was supposed to be doing. At that time I used to drive every day past an arboretum, and would look up at it with longing from the road: healthy, lush trees with exotic blossom in the spring, or fiery, dynamic colours and shades in the autumn. It had seemed to beckon me towards a calmer, better world. Caught up in either getting to or getting away from the office, though, I never once stopped to go in and visit. Yet the concept – a dream – of this garden-forest somehow planted itself in my brain, as though seeds of thought had wafted through my open window as I wheezed past. Years later I would be surprised to find myself saying to people with absolute certainty, 'One day I will plant an arboretum', despite having little actual knowledge of what such a thing was, or what planting one would entail. So do we carve out our lives, our minds often several steps behind what our imagination has long seen clearly.

But I was stuck at the desk job for the moment, and such a project had seemed – at best – a very long way into the future. Although I might, for the time being, at least try my hand at growing some flowers and vegetables, I thought. The prime years of my life had been mortgaged to a soulless corporation, but that didn't mean I couldn't prepare for better times to come.

The only problem was that the flat I was living in had no garden. So, with a couple of friends, I decided to rent an allotment. For about three pounds a year we would have a plot of land on which we could do pretty much what we liked. And the allotment, in our minds, quickly became the key to solving everything that was wrong with our lives. Tired of eating tasteless supermarket vegetables that glowed in the dark? No problem, we'd grow our own – potatoes, lettuce, tomatoes, everything. Need some colour to brighten up a grey morning? How about a bunch of chrysanthemums? A patch of lawn where you could sunbathe, get away from the city noise and simply potter about for the afternoon? Hey presto! It was ours. We even had a garden shed where we could keep deckchairs and a few tools. The potential for fun and adventure away from the overcrowded, overregulated world outside seemed endless. We could dig a well and have our own water supply. We could plant an orchard of strange and exotic fruit trees. We could do our bit to save the planet by cultivating rare species of orchids or endangered Amazonian hallucinogens. From being a small patch of land on the banks of the Thames, before we'd even done any work on it the allotment had became, in our minds, a kind of anarcho-gardening collective that was going to change the world.

There were, however, a few minor problems standing between us and our dream. Firstly, the eldest of us, despite being a huge asset as the only one with any idea about gardening, was half blind and the wrong side of eighty. She might just be able to tell a rose from a horseradish, but catching the number nine bus from her home to our miniature New Jerusalem proved more problematic. Meanwhile, the other friend had just become a father for the first time. Sleep deprivation, plus the fact that he appeared to have 'black' fingers where plants were concerned – rather than the more useful 'green' variety – meant his contribution beyond the ideas level was limited.

Then there was the fact that, not having actually been 'gardened' by anyone for some time, our allotment – one of the ones at the back, the kind no one else was stupid enough to take on – had become the weed capital of the world. Weeds had taken such a foothold there some were competing with nearby trees. Left to their own devices for so many years, others seemed to have mutated and to be experimenting at crossing from the plant into the animal kingdom.

'Old carpets' came the surreal advice from one seasoned veteran with an allotment nearby. 'Place some old carpets on them for a couple of years – starves them of light and kills them stone dead.' The problem was we didn't have a couple of years, and the weeds standing between us and our planned earthly paradise looked like the kind that ate old carpets for breakfast. Napalm was ruled out as a solution on the grounds of being non-organic. And none of us could afford the heavy machinery which alone could deal with the problem. Dreams of gardening our problems away were evaporating before our eyes. Two weeks later, the Thames burst its banks and flooded the entire allotment field. We never went back.

I had sworn, though, that if ever there was a next time, I would not make the same mistakes.

Part I
Earth

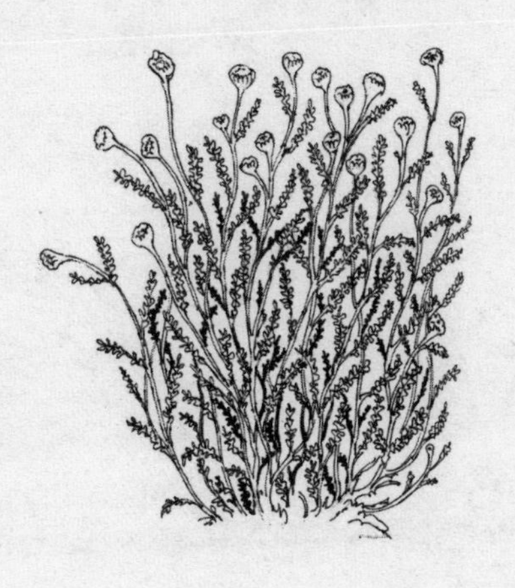

The Story of St Peter and the Fig Trees

Aixó diu que . . . Once upon a time, many years ago, Jesus was taking a walk through these mountains with St Peter. And as they passed through the fields and crossed the valleys, Jesus asked St Peter which was his favourite fruit.

Now Peter had a think before answering. The fact was that his favourite fruit was the grape. But he thought that if he told Jesus this, he might work out that what he really liked about it was the wine made from it. And once he discovered this, Jesus might make all the grapes on the vines wither and dry out. So he thought of his least favourite fruit: the fig.

'If I say figs, and he makes them dry out, I won't really mind,' thought St Peter. So he turned to Jesus and said:

'Lord, my favourite fruit is the fig.'

'I didn't realise you liked figs so much,' said Jesus. 'Well, if that's the case, for your sake from now on I shall make fig trees produce fruit twice a year: black early figs in June, and green figs in September.'

St Peter kicked himself when he heard this.

'Just think,' he thought to himself. 'If I'd said "grapes" we could have had two harvests of grapes a year, and there would be twice as much wine!'

And he was so angry with himself he almost died of rage right there on the spot.

But that is why, to this day, fig trees produce two crops every year: one at the beginning of summer, and another at the end.

SEPTEMBER

Farmers consider the first season of the year to be autumn, which is made up of three months: September, October and November. September *is the Latin name of the first month, which in Syriac is called* Ailul, *in Persian* Mehrmah *and in Hebrew* Iilul. *It is made up of thirty days, and during this time the days are equal to the nights, it being the autumnal equinox, after which the days begin to wane and the nights grow longer.*

Almond trees are planted in the mountains, as they are lovers of the cold, and in soft soil they grow big and produce abundant fruit. Other writers say they should be planted only on slopes facing the sun at midday. According to Democritus, the time to harvest almonds is when their outer shell begins to open: they are placed in salt water and then under the sun, after which they are dried. By this method they become white.

Figs ripen at this time of year. They should not be eaten while drinking wine, as the two do not mix well together in the stomach. A stick from a fig tree placed in a pan will make the meat there cook more quickly.

Ibn al-Awam, *Kitab al-Falaha,* The Book of Agriculture, 12th century

Dawn here has a rare and unusual power. In the city it passes unnoticed, drowned into insignificance by the street lights, the noise: just another hour – one of many – that makes up the day. But on the mountain, where we can hear silence, I feel it before I am even awake: a restlessness, nervousness, wrenching me away from sleep. Eyes closed, I can sense its coming, like a pulse in the landscape: a pale-blue cloak of the first promise of daylight, a shock of cold intake of breath. A current seems to spark under the surface of the earth, surging through every rock, up every tree and blade of dry grass. A first bird gives a waking cry – perhaps a great tit or a wren – then a second, and a third, and soon the valley is awash with song. The sun is coming, light is coming; the stars fade and disappear with the veil of night.

I drift on until daylight reaches out to shake me from slumber until, with a jolt, my eyes open, staring incredulously at the rising, stretching world outside my window. Sleep, so easily my early-morning master, is cast aside like a dry, unwanted skin. I find myself up and moving through the house as though possessed of a different energy, one that comes from outside my normal self. I am surprised by it at first: the experience is a change from my ordinary habits. But as the days and weeks go by I grow more accustomed to this new rhythm. There is something cold, something harsh about it, but I am content to let it follow its course, and watch the change this landscape is bringing over me.

The day progresses, and as we work on the house and the land I keep one eye fixed on the slow, patterned transformation of the world around us. As the sun traces across the sky and the light passes from colour to colour, so the valley stretched out before us and the mountainsides rising up like hands change and alter: vast waves in a slow-moving sea. A feature like a copse or a broken rock hanging tentatively from a cliff-face may be invisible in the morning, only to come into view with the gentler light of late afternoon. As the days pass I see more and more *masos* like our own, abandoned on the hillsides. Before, these were simply not there, and, even now, when I know where they are and could point to them with ease, they only really exist at their appointed time of day, when the landscape offers them up for a few hours before shrouding them from view again.

The morning is best for making out details to the west of the house, as the sun rises over the Talaia mountain to the east and drapes its first rays over the steep gorge, near the spring. Rising a little more, it catches the water of the spring and brings the trees there into focus, their shadows stretching long and high up the slope behind them. Driven by the surge of dawn, the birds are still singing by this point, but by eleven, or midday, when the sun is high over the valley and the light becomes a flattened white, blanching everything beneath it into near non-existence, they fall silent. In fact nothing seems to move during the few hours when the sun is at its zenith. We are not far from the beginning of autumn now, but except for the marked shortening of the days there is still little sign of it: the sun still burns and drives every living thing to seek shelter. By four or five o'clock, though, when the sun is moving closer towards the peak of the Picosa to the west, and the colours are softening, the heat no longer so punishing, a second chorus, like a second dawn, can be heard. Gentler this time, with fewer participants: perhaps a cuckoo down in the valley. Not long now and they will be migrating south for winter. This has always been my favourite time of day, but here evening takes on new textures. I look out once more, our work for the day finished, at the slowly moving, slowly transforming landscape laid out in front of us like a magic carpet. By now the ibex have usually emerged from their midday hideaways: they skip their way down the rocks to the spring to drink, or trot along the track that leads past the house, their grey-brown coats, black tails and vast horns standing out against the pale white of the stones. They appear to have grown used to us, watching us from safe distances, daring to approach the houses when they think no one is here. Their sharp whistle, which they use when startled, has become another part of our acoustic landscape.

I watch the shadow run towards us as the sun finally passes out of view. Sunset here comes relatively early, but we are recompensed with an extended dusk. In the half-light we sit and look out towards the village at the bottom of the valley, catching the last of the sun's rays. Its whitewashed walls glow yellow and orange, like a jewel: close enough to feel accessible, far enough away to feel apart, separate and on our own. We have not left the world, we're simply watching it from another vantage point. There's life enough here under the rocks and trees: perhaps, I sometimes wonder, even more than in the city we have – for the time being – gladly left behind.

⋆

Once the bulk of the building work on the house had been done, we moved into the farm on a more full-time basis, with plans to turn our attention to the land and to start slowly trying to transform it. The beginning of our new life coincided with the tail end of the fig season. Much of our time in these early days was still spent plastering, painting, replacing and securing some of the terracotta tiles on the older sections of the house, collecting firewood for the months ahead. But in the late afternoon and early evening we would make time simply to wander about the mountainside, slowly familiarising ourselves with the complex terrain. We had to pump water up regularly from the spring to a deposit, an *aljub*, near the house, so we'd head down to the gulley where it lay, scrambling over the rocks, trying in vain to identify some of the thousands of plants that surrounded us. Salud would dip her fingers in the small pool where the water collected after spilling out from the mountainside, while I fiddled with the pump, trying to wrest it into life so that we could wash and clean over the coming few days. Often the pipe leading back up to the house would split or crack, and I spent a lot of time patching it up, quickly having to learn basic plumbing skills so that we wouldn't run out of water. Each time I managed to pump some up successfully – perhaps two or three thousand litres a go – I felt a great sense of achievement: now when we turned on the taps we knew exactly where the water had come from and the effort that had gone in to getting it up to the house.

When not working on the pump, we'd head on to the terraces and seek out isolated fig trees among the long grass and bushes to collect the last of their delicious fruits. By now figs were rotting on the branches, or had been sucked dry by wasps or ants, but there were still enough ripe ones left for us to fill a dark wicker basket Salud had found lying inside one of the ruined houses. They were almost bursting, their sticky red insides wonderfully sweet and soft. The trees grew randomly across the terraces: some grouped near the house, others by the almond trees, and yet more scattered over the wilder areas of our land, sprouting up spontaneously, it seemed, with long spindly finger-branches and broad green leaves. Most were quite short, and looked more like bushes than trees. I wondered if they, too, had fallen victim to the forest fire and had since revived and grown in this chaotic fashion. Still, walking around the fields with handfuls of rich fruit in our grasp gave us the feeling of children living in a blessed semi-paradise.

One afternoon, as we were exploring the land on the east side of the house, sitting by an oak tree, we caught sight of a car driving along the dirt track below us. We had quickly grown so used to being alone up there, with nothing but mountain goats to keep us company, that seeing another human being always came as something of a surprise, as though it broke a trance or a dream state into which we had fallen. After a few moments the car – an old dark green Land Rover – stopped on the edge of an orchard that lay some way in the distance and a man got out. He went to the back of the vehicle, picked out some tools and then walked over towards the trees. From where we sat, it seemed he was picking something off the branches.

'That,' I said after a lengthy pause, 'is our neighbour.' It was a strange word to use in such an uninhabited place: the nearest houses with people actually living in them were at least four miles away, down the valley towards the village. But the behaviour of the man working away in the fading light below us made it clear that while the other farmhouses dotted around the hillsides might have been abandoned, some fields were still being tended.

'Perhaps,' said Salud after another pause, 'we should go and say hello.'

Fifteen minutes later, after scrambling down crumbling terrace walls and fighting our way through thick and not always friendly plant life, we were standing in front of a short, elderly man of stocky build, dark blue slippers on his feet and sharp yellow eyes that squinted through narrow folds in the hardened, tanned skin of his face. He gazed steadily at us as we approached and I thrust my hand out towards him, introducing ourselves as the owners of the next-door farm.

He hesitated for a moment and then placed a rough, relaxed paw into mine.

'Arcadio. They told me someone new was up at the place,' he said. His voice was uneven, rough-edged, as though it might fail him at any moment. His age was hard to guess: he could be anything from sixty to eighty, I thought. For a moment it looked as though there was nothing more to be said, but a hint of a smile was just visible on his thin, downturned mouth. I looked around at the trees surrounding us: short, stunted, with sharp-looking branches; they seemed to have been made in his image.

'You'll be wanting to harvest your almonds,' he said. So that's what they were: the green, felt-like fruits hanging in clusters from the branches actually contained nuts. 'You've got a hundred and thirteen almond trees up there: could bring in a nice load.'

I tried to hide my concern that he knew more about our farm than we did. 'About a hundred' was all we had been told when we got the place. What else did he know that we didn't?

'Is that what you're doing here?' I said. 'Harvesting?'

His face creaked into a wry smile.

'How do you do it?' Salud asked. 'Just pick them with your hands? Or do you have to beat the tree to make the almonds fall down?'

I'd been hoping she'd already know this, that she might have picked it up somewhere from the general stock of farming knowledge of her childhood. But oranges, it seemed, had been the only fruit in her household: anything to do with any other type of crop was a black hole.

Arcadio was smiling again, not entirely pleasantly, I thought.

'I'll come up tomorrow and harvest them for you,' he said, pointing to our almond trees with his thumb. 'You can watch.'

'That man,' I said as we walked back up to the farm after saying our goodbyes, 'is going to run rings round us.'

At eight the following day I was alerted to his arrival by the sound of his Land Rover heaving its way slowly up the mountain road. We just had time to bolt down some breakfast before stepping outside to meet him on the flat piece of ground that lay just above the house.

There was no 'hello', barely a greeting of any kind, just a nod of the head and a low, barely audible kind of animal call: '*Iéeah*.'

He pointed at the ground beneath our feet. 'This is where we used to bring all the produce from the terraces,' he said.

I looked down, not quite grasping what he meant. 'This is the *era*,' he explained. 'Everything that was harvested was brought here and placed in a big pile before being taken to the village, to the market.'

With all the steep slopes and narrow terraces that surrounded us, I had always been struck by this rare flat stretch of land which acted as a kind of plaza for the tiny hamlet that was now our home. We used it as a convenient place to park the car or to store building materials, but it seemed it was no accident in the landscape, and had played an important role at the heart of the communities that had once lived up here. I glanced around at it with a new-found respect: we would have to clear it up and make something of it. Right now it was a bit of a dump.

'Right,' I said. 'We'd better get started.' I looked over towards the east and the peak of the Talaia: the rising sun was just clipping the top and scattering its light over the farm: we only had a few hours before it would become uncomfortably hot to work.

Salud nudged me in the ribs.

'Would you like some coffee first?' she asked Arcadio with a smile. For some reason she didn't share the slight unease I had about the man.

Arcadio gave a cough, although I quickly realised it was a sort of strangled laugh.

'Don't drink coffee,' he said, and from a shapeless bag he carried over his shoulder he pulled out a soft leather gourd with a little black spout which he proceeded to lift above his mouth and then squeeze, forcing out a thin red liquid into his mouth.

'Ah,' said Salud, 'you've brought your *bota* with you.'

'Only drink wine,' Arcadio said. 'Want some?' And he thrust it into my hand.

I'd seen Spanish men often enough drinking from a *bota*. There was a trick in squirting the liquid directly into your mouth and then timing it so that you pulled away and closed your mouth without spilling a drop. There were even some who could just keep pouring the stuff down their throats seemingly without pausing for breath, swallowing continuously with upturned head. Try as I might, it was a technique I had never quite mastered, but that morning I didn't care: a shot of wine at eight in the morning seemed an eminently sensible way to start the day. So I squirted, and drank – and the working day began.

Arcadio was all tuts and mumbling as we walked down from the *era* towards our almond trees. We had spent so much time working on the house, there'd been little time for doing anything yet on the land. Now, simply by walking beside him, I felt I was looking at it all with new eyes. Weeds were growing neck-high in places, while the almond trees, far from being neat and stunted like the ones on his land, were stretching branches high into the sky: too high, I now saw, to be able to reach for harvesting. I could see that pruning fruit trees was a skill I would have to master if things were going to move forwards up here. I looked over at Salud as we trotted behind Arcadio: from the expression on her face I could tell she was thinking the same thing.

'We'll just forget about those ones up there,' Arcadio said pointing to some terraces climbing up the mountainside. With a shock I realised there were more almond trees up there as well – and I'd never even noticed. The path to them was completely blocked by a bramble bush that had spilled out from behind a pine tree and was threatening to take over most of the terrace itself. I quickly counted – there must have been around twenty trees up there, now out of reach. It seemed absurd that we should call this farm our own: our lack of knowledge about what was actually here, about the very crops and plants that had been cultivated, was embarrassing. There was a vast amount to learn.

Arcadio was carrying a basket, while Salud had picked up a canvas sack. Seizing one of the branches roughly with his left hand, Arcadio pulled it down towards the ground and started grabbing handfuls of almonds, tossing them into his basket. His aim was fairly haphazard, with more than a few missing the target and getting lost in the weeds and grass around the base of the tree.

I was expecting some kind of farmer's insider knowledge on how best to harvest almonds, but all it seemed to involve was grabbing the things with your hands and pulling them off with a sharp tug. Salud gave me a look and we went off to a neighbouring tree to start harvesting ourselves. I waited for a moment, watching Arcadio just to make sure I wasn't missing anything, then went over to join Salud.

The green skins wrapped around the nutshells were soft and velvety to the touch, with a coating of fine hair, but the branches of the tree were sharp and gnarled, with little thorns poking out at irregular intervals.

'Wild boar love this,' Arcadio called over as we started filling our sack. 'Pull your trees down if they could to get the almonds. Already done some damage.' And he pointed at another tree further down the terrace: one of the branches had fallen to the ground and was hanging by a thread from the main trunk; the leaves had died and the earth where it lay seemed to be scuffed.

'Had a feast with that. Be back for more.'

Until this point 'wild boar' had only been a concept for us. We knew there were some roaming around the mountains, and had heard that they might pop over our way occasionally, but this was the first time we had evidence of their actual presence – and it wasn't a pretty sight.

'The wild boar did that?' Salud asked incredulously, indignation and fear in her voice.

'They're after food,' Arcadio said. 'Almonds are easy for them: rip the branches off and then eat all they want. Got whole families of them living up there.' He pointed towards the upper section of the gulley that cleaved the side of our mountain, a dense dark-green area thick with trees and bushes.

There was a pause as we took this in. I had two mental images of wild boar: one as frightened, harmless creatures that always ended up as banquet material in *Asterix* comic books; the other as fierce, territorial beasts that could charge and kill a man. I had the feeling the comic-book version was not entirely accurate.

'Shooting them's the best thing,' Arcadio said. 'Hunters'll come up once the season's started. Nothing but trouble, those boar.'

Wild man-eating beasts, and now the prospect of armed men wandering around our land taking potshots at them: rather than a farm in Spain, it was beginning to feel more like some kind of safari park.

We carried on stripping the trees of their fruit as the shadows shortened and the sun rose higher in the sky, Salud and I carefully picking each almond and placing it in the sack, Arcadio ripping them off in handfuls along with clumps of leaves and bits of twig and tossing them carelessly into his basket. By the time we had had finished one tree, he was already on his fourth.

'Perhaps there *is* some trick,' I said.

I heard a sharp intake of breath from Salud and a soft, muffled '*¡ay!*'. From the tone I knew something was wrong: she was never one to scream or make a fuss. I looked round and saw her holding one hand tightly while blood was oozing out from between her fingers.

'Bloody thorns,' she said.

The cut had stretched along her finger and looked deep, lips of skin parting and exposing the bloody mass underneath.

'I need to sit down,' she said quietly.

'I'll go to the house and get some iodine.'

'Wait,' said Arcadio. He had walked over and was kneeling down to take a look at Salud's hand.

'Almond thorn?' he asked. She nodded. The blood was still flowing thickly, dripping over her clothes and drying in ugly brown stains. Arcadio walked towards a nearby terrace wall and bent down as though looking for something. Then he knelt, pulled up part of a plant he'd found, and stuffed the leaves into his mouth to chew. For a few seconds of confusion we watched him masticating like a cow. It had seemed he was about to do something to help the cut on Salud's finger, now I started to wonder if he'd changed his mind and was simply having a hillman's snack.

Finally he spat a dark green gob into the palm of his hand, looked at it for a moment as though to gauge its usefulness, then walked over towards Salud again. Taking her hand he started spreading the gunge on to her bleeding finger.

'Should slow it down,' he said. 'Might take some of the pain away as well.'

I watched his spittle mix freely with her blood.

'It's stopping,' Salud said. 'It feels sharp, as though it's drying up.'

Arcadio stood up.

'Should be fine by tomorrow,' he said. '*Bruguerola*. Makes it heal quicker.'

Later that night we sat at the kitchen table next to the remains of dinner and an empty bottle of wine, a large sack of almonds on the floor beside us. We'd bandaged Salud's hand up, but barely a drop of blood had appeared since Arcadio's intervention.

'Something in the leaves must make the bleeding stop,' Salud said. I wondered what it might be, and how Arcadio had got to know about it. What other medicinal treasures were we walking over every time we stepped out of the front door? The grasses and weeds choking up the mountainside started to appear in a different light.

We'd carried on all morning, stopping only for a short break at midday before picking almonds late into the afternoon. It wasn't a strenuous job in itself, but had become so after several hours, when my arms and hands began to complain from so much lifting and grabbing.

Salud had slowed down a bit after cutting her hand, only collecting the almonds that had fallen to the ground.

For a while we stared down at the enormous pile of nuts at our feet, the inevitable question 'Now what?' hanging wordlessly in the air. What on earth were we supposed to do with them all? Sell them? Where? Who to? How much should we charge? The complexities of a simple task farmers all over the world had been carrying out for several millennia held us paralysed for a moment. One of us should have asked Arcadio, but it had slipped both our minds.

'What does your father do with his oranges?' I asked Salud.

She thought for a moment. 'The local co-operative takes them from him and then gives him money depending on quality, weight, that kind of thing.' She pushed her hair back behind her ear. 'They rip him off. In the shops they sell for over ten times the price he gets for them. Sometimes he ends up just giving them away.'

So here we were with a pile of almonds we had nowhere to take, and even if we did find anyone to buy them they'd probably only give us a pittance for them. Farming was looking less attractive as a way of life by the minute. We should stick to planting trees, I thought.

'Whatever we do with them,' Salud said, 'we can't just leave them like this. We'll have to break them open, get rid of the shells.'

She stood up, walked over to where I kept the tools, picked up a couple of hammers and then came back to the table. I looked down at the overflowing sack with a renewed horror. This was going to take a very, very long time.

'Here,' she said, thrusting the hammer into my reluctant fist. 'Get cracking.'

It was four o'clock in the morning when I woke up, my head resting on the kitchen table, a small pool of dribble forming from my half-open mouth. Salud had collapsed on the sofa. Beside me was a large bowl of shell-less almonds. I smiled, before looking down and realising there was an even bigger pile of unshelled almonds still waiting for us in the sack. I gave a groan and went to pick Salud up and take her to bed.

Arcadio returned the next day unannounced. Our bodies ached by now from sitting bent over the table trying to crack open the almonds without breaking what was inside. I had about a 50 per cent hit rate; Salud was doing only slightly better. We were, however, at least managing to get close to the bottom of the sack.

Arcadio looked unimpressed when he saw how many almonds we had. 'Bad year,' he said enigmatically. I thought we'd done rather well. 'Too much rain last spring,' he said by way of explanation. 'Affects the blossom. Almonds don't grow right.'

And he bent over to pick up the bowls of nuts we'd shelled and started pouring them into a bag.

'Er . . .' I started.

'Be back this afternoon,' he said. And with that he was gone, our almonds now sitting in the bag tossed over his shoulder.

'What the hell's going on?' I said. Had we just been robbed under our very noses?

'It's all right,' Salud said. 'He'll come back. Just watch.'

I had no choice but to trust her instinct.

Some time after lunch we heard the sound of Arcadio's car chugging back up our road. Salud smiled.

'Let's see what story he's got to tell,' she said.

Moments later the old farmer was back in our kitchen.

'Here,' he said, holding something out in his hand. 'It's all I could get for them at the village co-op. As I said, it's a bad year.'

He pushed the money forward again and Salud eventually reached out with her bandaged hand to take it from him.

'Hundred euros,' he said. He pronounced the word strangely – '*ebros*' – as though still not quite used to this weird new currency that had been around now for six or seven years.

I looked into his small, yellow eyes and somehow knew that he was telling the truth: he'd gone and sold the almonds for us and this was exactly the amount of money he'd got for them: no secret cut for himself.

'Thank you,' said Salud.

'Brought you this,' he said, and he pulled out a small jam jar from his jacket pocket with a creamy-brown paste inside.

'For your hand,' he said to Salud.

'Is it – is it herbal, like the stuff you used yesterday? Salud asked.

'Made it myself,' he said nodding. 'You can use that for anything –

any skin problems,' he said. 'Just rub it on at night.' He paused and looked at me. 'Helps the healing.'

*

Understanding of the scale of my ignorance is growing by the day. Planting trees seems such a simple operation at first: get tree, dig hole, put tree in it, then wait twenty or thirty years. Do this several hundred times and you'll end up with a wood, or a small forest. But there are endless questions before you can get to this stage. Which trees? Will they be suited to the soil? The altitude? The weather conditions here? This is a Mediterranean climate, which means long, dry summers, so anything I plant has to be drought-proof. Which seems simple enough, until I realise there are all kinds of sub-categories of 'Mediterranean' with prefixes like 'meso' or 'supra'. Some trees will be all right in one, but not another. But I don't even know which one we're in! And then there are the winters to consider: it gets cold here – I'm sure temperatures regularly drop to around minus five in late December and early January. So anything we put in the ground has to be able to cope with that as well. All of which makes me start wondering how anything grows up here at all.

One place to start would be to look around at what's already here, but again I end up running into more brick walls, not least the fact that I can barely identify a single plant species on our land. I know which are the almond trees, but only because they were the first ones to be pointed out to me, that plus the fact that we've got about a hundred of them. Show me an almond tree elsewhere, though, and I might be stumped to recognise it.

And then there's all this business about mulching and pruning and God knows what. In desperation I've turned to Ibn al-Awam, the only complete book on agriculture I've got on my shelves. Although it remains to be seen how much help a medieval Andalusian farmer can give me.

The *Kitab al-Falaha* – The Book of Agriculture – is a Moorish masterpiece from the twelfth century, sometimes described as 'the greatest of all medieval treatises on agriculture'. A two-volume work by a Sevillian gentleman farmer, Yahya ibn Muhammad Ibn al-Awam, it was rediscovered in the mid-eighteenth century in the Escorial library just north of Madrid, having lain forgotten for hundreds of years. The book was a detailed manual for running a farm, with tips on everything from irrigation of the land to keeping horses and even bees. It was written in a surprisingly technical, almost scientific style: 'I establish no principle in my work that I have not first proved by experiment on repeated occasions,' the author asserted. This didn't prevent him from adding all kinds of eccentric ideas about farming and land management, however. (*If you want to grow coriander without sowing any seeds, take the testicles of a goat and plant them in the earth and water them. Later you will see coriander grow up where no seeds had been planted.*) And it was filled with quotations and tips from his Greek- and Latin- as well as Arabic-speaking predecessors. One of the interesting things one could gleam from his writing was how the weather had probably changed since his time: one of his recommendations, for example, was that almonds should be picked in August, an indication, perhaps, that the month hadn't been quite as hot then as it is today.

Apart from the fact that he lived in the Aljarafe district of Seville – a city four hundred miles to the south-west of our farm, significantly hotter today than where we were – little was known about Ibn al-Awam himself. He was mentioned only by two other authors of his period, Ibn Khaldun and the geographer Al-Qalqashandi. Yet his book, sometimes described as a 'mosaic' made up from works by previous agriculturalists, was one of the best-known and best-loved works on farming to have been passed down from the golden age of Spanish gardens – the Moorish period, which lasted from the early 700s to the end of the fifteenth century. The standards of agriculture were so high during this time they were not surpassed until the nineteenth century, with the development of modern chemistry. During the Enlightenment, the Spanish authorities became so worried about the decline of agricultural standards that they commissioned a translation of Ibn al-Awam's work. So in 1802 José Banqueri brought out the first edition in a European language. A copy of this, bought on a whim years before, had been gathering dust on my bookshelves, waiting patiently, it now appeared, for me finally to notice it, take it down and delve into the rich, detailed natural world it set out, page after page. Ibn al-Awam was a wonderful observer – in many ways a man before his time. Or was it simply that our view of his time was misjudged? Certain words and phrases dated him – I didn't have a team of labourers – or slaves – to hand, as he obviously had, to carry out the operations he described, nor would his observations on how to use a lance and shield on horseback prove particularly useful, despite making fascinating reading. Yet I often had the sense of dealing with a near contemporary, a fact highlighted by the absence of reminders of the 'modern' world around us on the mountain. It would be wrong to describe him as a friend – there is a formality and distance in his writing which prevents such a degree of intimacy, despite his very personal musings on topics such as the curative powers of rue for epilepsy or the use of squills for warding off lions and wolves – but as time passed and I dipped into him more and more, his presence grew. He became almost like a kindly guardian to whom I might turn in times of need for quiet, gently guiding advice drawn from hard-won personal experience.

The farmer's year, I was delighted to learn from him, began in September. I was virtually clueless about what I was doing, but had managed to get something right, even if unawares. I decided to follow his advice where I could: fate, it seemed, had already done much to bring us together at the opportune moment.

*

If I was going to plant trees up on the mountainside, I would have to start preparing the land. Regardless of the question of which particular trees might thrive in which particular area, there were huge swathes of weeds which had to be dealt with first. And unfortunately they weren't the usual kind of plants for which the word 'weed' seems adequate or even appropriate: 'toughs' might have been a better name for them, given that I was dealing almost exclusively with brambles and gorse bushes. There were several hectares of the stuff to be got rid of – and given the difficulty of the terrain I was going to have to do it by hand: no tractors or large weed-destroying machines could make it up to the terraces, and we were against the idea of using herbicides or any weedkillers.

'Probably wouldn't do much to them anyway,' Salud's father had said when the subject came up once. 'Too well established. Either that or you spray a sulphide which'll make all the goats miscarry.'

So hand-weeding it had to be – on a massive scale. The brambles were the easier to deal with: I'd found a big scythe-like tool with a sharp cutting edge which I set about them with. It was exhausting work, but you could slice through quite a large amount in a fairly short time. The problem was with the gorse: the bushes were growing about eight feet high in places and had trunks as thick as a man's arm. It took a huge amount of effort, and no small number of scratches and cuts from the incredibly sharp needles to fell just one of the bastards – and there were several thousand of them to dispose of.

There was no choice: I was going to have to get tooled up – with the one piece of machinery I could manage to get up on to the terraced fields: a heavy-duty brush-cutter.

When you're not used to them, heavy power tools can produce a mixed sense of awe, fear and excitement. Excitement at holding something so powerful in your hands; awe at the sight of what it can do in such a short time; and fear of what it might end up doing to you if you get it just slightly wrong. We were lucky enough in that one of Salud's cousins had a shop selling exactly what we needed, supplying me not only with a man-sized strimmer I could barely lift, but the helmet, face mask, shin protectors and ultra-thick gloves I would also require if I was to come out of the experience of using it alive. I was also given a crash course in the workings of it and what to do if we had any problems – vital information when you're stuck at the top of a mountain an hour's drive from the nearest mechanic.

'Don't worry too much,' Salud's cousin said as he saw the expression of incomprehension on my face. 'If it starts playing up just call me and hold the phone next to the strimmer: I should be able to tell you what's wrong with it just from the sound it's making.'

Fully kitted out, I set out from the house the next day looking like a rejected extra from *Mad Max*, stiff, with my extra thick protective trousers making it even more difficult to climb up the narrow, rocky track to the gorse-infested terraces. Brambles tore at my arms from the sides, as though aware of what was about to happen and trying to force me back. I brushed past them as nonchalantly as possible: this was my land and it was about time I started showing them who was boss. The reign of weed terror was about to come to an end and a new dawn of clear fields and freshly planted trees was about to begin. The battle was going to be long and fierce, but I had my mighty brush-cutter in my hands and no one was going to hold me back.

I fired up the strimmer and it roared into life. Clipping it to my harness, I closed the face mask on my helmet and stood to face the first gorse bush: a monster a yard and a half wide and a foot higher than myself, daring me to take it on. I pressed the accelerator, raised my weapon high and then brought it down on the fearsome beast. A shuddering pulsed up my arms as the spinning blades made contact with the gorse, then in a flash all was flying needles and spraying vegetation as the machine descended almost of its own volition in a zigzag motion down the entire height of the bush, chopping and cutting mercilessly, until moments later I was looking down at a pile of mulched gorse at my feet, the sorry stump of its once proud trunk poking pathetically out of the ground until, with another swoop, that too was gone and the gorse was no more. I took my finger off the accelerator and paused for breath. The whole process had taken less than thirty seconds and this once menacing foe now lay defeated beneath me. I was covered with debris from the kill, but was exhilarated at my victory. Man over vegetable: there was no holding me back now. The other gorse bushes seemed to cower before me as I approached them, aware for the first time of their own mortality. With a bloodthirsty grin I pulled on the accelerator once more and dived into the fray.

After two or three hours, I had managed to clear one terraced field: a once impenetrable corner of the farm was now accessible, perhaps for the first time in years. There was still a seemingly infinite amount of land to clear, but I had made a start, and, most importantly, I now had the necessary tool to carry out the job.

In my excitement and concentration, I hadn't realised in all this time that it had started to rain. Clouds of humidity were rising off my overheated body as, tired but happy, I turned to look over what I'd done and head back to the house to dry off. I switched the strimmer off and crunched my way over piles of dead gorse bushes. I was still quite amazed at how the machine pulped them like this. Rather than simply cutting them down, it reduced them to virtually nothing. I looked up above the wall running by my side to the next terrace to be dealt with: I would return here the following day and continue.

The rain was falling quite hard now and I dropped my head to protect my eyes: the wind was blowing up and starting to whip the droplets into strange whorls which flew into my face. For a moment I lost my sense of direction as I turned my head away from the rain: if I could just get to the shelter of the nearest pine trees I would be all right.

But suddenly my heart was in my mouth – the earth gave way beneath my feet and I was falling. Before I knew what had happened, I landed with a hard crack on my side, the strimmer crashing on top of me. I gave a low groan, the air kicked from my lungs. The helmet, still on my head, had bashed against a stone; the sound rang inside my brain like a bell. In the split second that followed I gave thanks I was still wearing it and that the strimmer blades, now resting gently against my shins, were mercilessly motionless.

I picked myself up with a cough, quickly checking that everything was working. I was lucky to have got away with nothing worse than a shock. Looking up against the rain I could see that the dry-stone wall holding up the terrace I had been walking on had simply crumbled away, and pieces of it were now lying around me in a pile. The gap in the tract of land I had just cleared seemed to stare defiantly: one minute the terrace had been there, and now it was gone, its remains lying in a heap of rubble around my feet.

With a sigh I trudged off back in the direction of the house, sore and getting wetter by the moment. The nagging thought in the back of my mind was that the very gorse bushes I'd been so happily chopping down had actually been holding the terrace up in place. And now, with the rain, in a moment a huge chunk of it had been washed away. At the very least it looked as though I was going to have to add dry-stone walling to the increasing list of skills I had to master if I was going to manage the land with any degree of success. Steps forward and steps back. I pushed it all from my mind, thoughts of hot showers and a cold beer leading me home.

*

Arcadio is coming round more regularly, popping over for an hour or so every few days. We are slowly getting used to each other, and he's beginning to teach me the names of some of the trees here. He only knows them in Valencian, so I have to look up the Castilian and English names once he's gone (and sometimes the Latin, while I'm at it). Slowly, very slowly, I feel the land is becoming less of a nameless, mysterious wilderness. But as is so often the case, the more I pick up, the more I realise how much there is to learn; knowledge, when it comes, only does so in small, less than satisfactory, bursts. I have bought a few books on plants and wildlife to help me along, but I find I can pick up a huge amount just by wandering around with Arcadio for half an hour. The mountainside is home to several types of oak tree, it appears: the ordinary type, such as the one overhanging the patio, and holm oaks, or holly oaks, which are evergreen and very well suited to the Mediterranean climate. They have small, round, prickly leaves, like holly, and were used for making ships, according to Arcadio. I told him I'm interested in planting trees, in trying to recover something of the forests that grew here before the fire. He mentioned the pine trees that had previously covered these hillsides.

'But planting more pines is like planting matches,' he said. 'Burn like buggery. Better off with more oaks. Harder, denser wood – not that you'll ever get to see them fully grown in your lifetime, though,' he laughed. 'Perhaps not even your children. Grandchildren maybe.'

⋆

There was hardly a sound. The street lights had been switched off and a hush fell on the crowd as it huddled around the edge of the village square, waiting. I saw a gap at the top of one of the wooden scaffolds nearby and climbed up to watch next to a couple of teenage boys with wild, energised looks.

'*Ahora viene*,' they said as I lifted myself up beside them. 'It's coming.'

A single light was now shining down on the empty stage below, while in the middle of the sawdust-covered floor a small metal cage, just big enough to accommodate possibly two people inside had been erected. It was painted red, but large ugly scratches up and down the thick, solid bars bore witness to the hammering it had received on previous occasions. Doubtless it had saved countless lives over the years.

Some of the boys on the other side of the square were already breaking away from the relative safety of similar cages lining the edge in anticipation of the spectacle to begin. Naked from the waist up, they held their T-shirts in one hand and darted sharply in and out, as though practising their moves for when the moment came, with cheers of encouragement from their friends and girlfriends behind them. For a second I wondered about going in myself, feeling the intense thrill of mortal danger, but held back: I would wait and see how my body reacted once the bull finally appeared: which would be the stronger emotion – excitement or chilling fear?

'Are you going to go down?' I asked the boys beside me.

'*Claro* – of course.'

It was, I told myself, a teenagers' thing, not something someone in his late thirties should be getting involved in. Until I saw a man clearly the other side of fifty suddenly dash out of his cage and back in again, just as the young boys were doing, his paunch bouncing like a medicine ball above the thin leather belt holding up his trousers.

September had drawn to a close and the village was celebrating the feast of its patron saint, the Archangel Michael, marking the end of the harvest period. The centre had been cut off and fenced in for the big event. Our first proper month on the farm had ended, but already it felt as if we had been there far longer. I was confident we could manage with what we had taken on, but had niggling doubts nonetheless. The problem with steep learning curves, I thought as I looked out at the ring, was exactly that – they were steep.

At that moment the bull charged suddenly into the square, catching us all unawares. There was a scream and a surge in the noise of the crowd as it darted out from a side road into the open. It was smaller than the half-tonne animals used in professional bullfights, but it had the same dull, deadly expression, the same powerful body that could toss a grown man high into the air, and the same smell of dung, sweat and blood about it. What was different, though, was the presence of great torches on the end of each horn above his head, their fiery light illuminating the bull's face and reflecting from his black, empty eyes. A *bou embolat* – a 'fireball bull'. It was the most terrifying sight: in the heart of the blackened night here was this ancient symbol of fertility, like the sun bursting out in a proud, violent blaze looking for new blood to help irrigate the barren land.

Memories of what I'd read about the ancient symbolism of bulls and bullfighting flew from my mind as the creature started crashing wildly about the square, enraged by the flames bursting from the ends of its horns, and by the young men buzzing around it like flies. I stood transfixed on the scaffold as it was quickly surrounded by six or seven of them darting and dodging in front of it and then flying back as fast as their legs could carry them to the safety of the cages. Two boys were already inside the central cage, leaning out and waving their T-shirts at the bull, trying to catch its attention, and then whipping their bodies back as it turned sharply and charged at them. CRACK – the bull's head crashed against the heavy steel bars and for a moment one of the torches got entangled round it. There was another scream as the crowd realised the bull was caught and would almost certainly bring the cage crashing to the floor with its incredible strength, before, with a jerk, it set itself free and started hurtling again through the crowd.

There was a sudden collective intake of breath as its golden horns brushed inches away from a young lad, arching his back as far as he could from danger as he sped towards the barriers. An ancient, sobbing fear masked his face as he ran, distorting his features into a harrowing grimace, only for a great smile to break out once he'd dodged his would-be killer and rejoined his group. Within seconds he was back in the ring, but this time making doubly sure, I noticed, to keep his distance.

After watching for a time, the teenagers beside me were now preparing to climb down the scaffold to get inside the square themselves.

'What do you think of the bull?' I asked them as they started swinging their legs over the top.

'Watch him on the right,' the eldest one said. 'He pulls round quickly to the right once he's finished his charge.'

My legs didn't move, frozen. I watched as the boys descended.

The bull tossed and whipped its head from side to side as they leapt into the square and started to run in parallel towards the other side. The flames were sickeningly close to their exposed skin and I stared, not wanting to see, as the elder boy pushed away at the fire with the T-shirt in his hand. With a ducking motion he was quickly inside the cage and safe, but I saw him hold up the cloth to his friends: it was smoking; they laughed. The man with the beer gut, however, was standing on his own in a corner of the square, egging the bull on with loud, hoarse shouts, to come and charge at him. It seemed suicidal. For a long while the bull ignored him, more preoccupied with the swift, eye-catching movement of the youths than the heavy ranting of the older man behind. But a lull came unexpectedly, and in that moment the bull turned swiftly on the spot, pawed at the ground and charged full-speed at him. The space the man had put himself in was virtually a trap, with a wall cutting him off on the left, and only a small gap for him to escape on the right. He stood for a second, arms outstretched as though daring the beast to impale him, and then threw himself in a dive towards his one exit point. But the bull seemed to anticipate him, and as soon as the man was dashing towards the safety of the cages, he pulled his head round, checked his run, and in a flash was beating the man's bare back with his forehead. The man fell to the floor, the bull scraping with his flaming horns at his prostrate body lying in a pile in the dirt by one of the cages. The light from the torches on the bull's horns lit up the faces of the villagers inside, their expressions frantic as those closest tried to pull the man's body towards them. I felt my body go cold, unable to look away.

Some boys from the other cages ran out and tried to draw the bull's attention away from the man on the floor. For a moment he seemed to ignore them, then with a start lifted his head from his victim and started charging at his new tormentors. No sooner had he moved away than the fat man was on his feet, as though nothing had happened, and was running like a terrified toddler into the nearest cage. I gave a thankful sigh. Miraculously it looked as though he was all right: after a few concerned words from the people around him, he was now back at the front of the cage, shouting abuse at the bull. There didn't appear to be a scratch on him.

I climbed down the scaffold and walked away from the crowd, my feet scuffing the gritty soil underneath. For a second I looked back, as though searching for a reason for not hanging around and giving it a go. The flames from the bull's horns were flashing through the silhouettes of the people pressed inside the protective cages. I was glad that this festival still seemed to be alive and strong up here, but personally I'd seen enough: the image of the fire-beast had been engraved on my mind for good.

I found Salud chatting to Mariajo, the forty-year-old village punk who ran the grocer's store. Like the rest of the villagers, Mariajo was virtually legless.

'Did you have a go?' Mariajo asked with a smile. I shook my head. 'You're better off,' she said. 'It's for young boys and old men, all that. They're crazy – *bojos*. It's as if they need to *prove* they're men. Can't understand it.'

Salud nodded vigorously.

'We've got plenty of challenges of our own to deal with up on the mountain,' she said squeezing my arm and leading me away. 'You don't want any of that.'

The sound of the crowd and the screams from the bull-running gradually faded as we walked away from the square, an enveloping silence seeming to flow from the narrow, empty houses lining the streets.

'I've been thinking,' Salud said as we headed towards the car. 'Living up here on the mountain . . .' She paused.

'If we get through this, if we're still together in a year's time,' she said. 'Maybe we should . . . get married.'

The Story of Mig Cul Cagat

Once upon a time, in a *mas* not far from here, there lived half a chicken called Mig Cul Cagat. None of the *masovers* knew who he belonged to, as he appeared one day as if from nowhere. But they gave him food and let him live with the rest of the chickens. One day, as he was picking around the *era*, Mig Cul Cagat came across something hard and shiny on the ground. He blew on it and saw that he'd found a coin.

'Aha!' he thought as soon as he realised what it was. 'With this I can go and marry the King's daughter.'

And without a second's thought he left the *mas* and set off to the royal palace to seek his fortune.

As he was walking along the road he came across a great ants' nest, blocking his way.

'Where are you going, Mig Cul Cagat?' the ants asked him.

'I'm off to the palace, to marry the King's daughter,' he replied.

'Only if we let you pass!' cried the ants.

But Mig Cul Cagat wasn't going to let them get in his way.

'Ants!' he said. 'Climb up into my backside.'

And as if by magic, all the ants suddenly found themselves inside the half-chicken.

Mig Cul Cagat carried along his way, until he came across a big hammer.

'Where are you going, Mig Cul Cagat?' asked the hammer.

'I'm off to marry the King's daughter,' he replied.

'Only if I let you pass!' said the hammer.

But Mig Cul Cagat simply said: 'Hammer, get into my backside.'

And so it did.

Mig Cul Cagat carried along the road, and soon he was getting close to the capital city, and the home of the King. But in order to get there he had to cross a river.

'Where are you going, Mig Cul Cagat?' asked the river.

'I'm going to the palace to marry the King's daughter,' he replied.

'Only if I let you pass!' said the river.

And Mig Cul Cagat said: 'River, climb up into my backside.' And the river disappeared inside him and he walked across and into the city.

Now when he reached the King's palace he knocked on the door and a guard appeared.

'Where are you going, Mig Cul Cagat?' he asked.

'I'm going to marry the King's daughter,' Mig Cul Cagat replied.

The guard went to tell the King. But the King just laughed and ordered that the half-chicken be thrown in jail for his insolence. And he had a vast amount of food placed in the dungeon with him.

'You can only have my daughter if you can eat all that food before dawn,' the King said.

When the King and guard had both gone, the chicken called to the ants.

'O ants! Come out, come out. There's work to do.'

And the ants climbed out of his backside and Mig Cul Cagat told them what had happened.

'Don't worry,' said the ants. 'We'll fix it.'

And they set about eating all the food that had been put in the dungeon, and by morning it had all gone.

The King was furious when the guard told him the news.

'You can only marry my daughter,' he cried, 'if you break out of the dungeon.'

But when he had gone, Mig Cul Cagat called out: 'O hammer! Come out, come out. There's work to do.'

And the hammer came out of his backside and Mig Cul Cagat told him what had happened. So the hammer started bashing the dungeon door, and within a few moments had broken it down and Mig Cul Cagat was able to walk free.

Now the King saw the half-chicken walking around the yard, and decided to finish him off once and for all. He ordered the guard to grab Mig Cul Cagat, saying: 'Light a fire. We're going to use this chicken to make a paella!'

So they tied Mig Cul Cagat down and they placed him in a huge paella pan on top of a burning fire.

But Mig Cul Cagat called out: 'O river! Come out, come out. There's work to do.'

And the river came out of his backside and doused the flames and saved him.

By now the King realised there was nothing he could do, and so he finally allowed Mig Cul Cagat to marry the princess. The wedding was held straightaway, and all the ladies of court cried tears of sadness as they saw the newly-wed princess walking back down the aisle with half a chicken as her groom.

That night, when the couple retired to their bedchamber, the princess started stroking Mig Cul Cagat, for although she had hoped for a better husband, she was not unkind. But as her fingers passed through his feathers she felt something unusual. Looking closer she saw that it was the end of a needle, a needle of gold. Mig Cul Cagat said nothing, and so she pulled at it and suddenly there was a bang. A bright blue flame filled the room, and where there had once been half a chicken, there now stood the handsomest young man. The princess gave a cry.

'Do not fear,' said the young man. 'For I am in fact a prince, and you have broken the charm that was placed on me. And I am still your husband, if you will have me.'

The princess fell in love and threw herself into the prince's arms.

And they lived happily ever after.

OCTOBER

October, *as it is called in Latin, is known as* Tishrin al-Awal *in Syriac and is the first month of the year for the Syrians; the Persians call it* Abanmah. *In this month the cold grows stronger and sheep, which are now full with milk, suckle their young. This is the time for gathering fennel seeds, anis, onions, saffron, violets and pistachios. Green olives for pickling are also harvested now, before they become full of oil and start turning yellow. It is said that wood cut after the third of this month will not become infested with woodworm.*

Ibn al-Awam, *Kitab al-Falaha*, The Book of Agriculture, 12th century

October came, like a new spring after the half-life of summer. The hillside was awash with colour as the gorse bushes burst into bright yellow bloom, quickly followed by the pale blue of the rosemary flowers and the deep mauve of the *bruc*, a kind of heather. The birdsong seemed to grow louder and last longer through the day rather than passing a lull and silence during the hottest hours. But still, although it was usually one of the wettest months, it refused to rain. Pale blue skies stretched endlessly out over the valley, the temperatures regularly reaching the mid-twenties in the afternoon. The oak by the house, one of the few deciduous trees on our land, refused point blank to give any sign that autumn was in the air, its leaves lush and green as though it were the beginning of May. Pleasant though it was, there was something abnormal about it, as though by taking so much time the change in season was coiling itself like a spring: when it finally came it would be let off like a gun.

The new flowers had brought an influx of bees. Salud, never happy with insects of any kind, was frantic at the invasion but I was fascinated by them, watching as they buzzed around the garden and darted in and out of the house through the open windows. They were honeybees, I was certain, which meant that not far from us there must be some hives. Sorting through some of the wreckage of the other *masos* nearby I'd come across one item that looked very much like an old hive of some sort: pieces of thick cork bark tied together to form a kind of cylinder. It was bent out of shape now, but if I was right about what it was, it suggested beekeeping had been a traditional activity up here.

I couldn't remember how far bees would fly to collect nectar, but it couldn't be more than a few miles. One clue came from the way the bees would always get stuck on the east window – one we rarely opened – when they entered the kitchen. It was as if they knew that 'east' meant home. Wherever the hives were, I reasoned, they must be in that direction.

One afternoon I decided to go down and investigate, heading over the terrace fields and towards the dirt track that led to Arcadio's almond groves. It was another hot day and I was wearing just an old pair of holey jeans and a T-shirt. A straw hat kept the worst of the sun's intense rays from the top of my head.

Strips of plastic were hanging mysteriously from the almond trees when I reached Arcadio's fields, but there was no sign of any beehives. However, I noticed that the sound of the bees, that wonderful background hum of life and energy, was several decibels higher than up at the house. The almonds weren't in bloom, so it seemed I might be on the right track.

I carried on, pushing my way through the grass, trying to let the sound of the bees itself lead me to their hives. Finally I caught sight of something above my head. I walked up to the terrace wall and stood on tiptoe: there in front of me were at least fifty beehives, wooden boxes painted grey, with thousands upon thousands of bees hurrying in and out of tiny holes at the base of each one. My eyes widened as two thoughts simultaneously crossed my mind: firstly of the enormous amount of honey that must be produced right here under our noses; and secondly that I mustn't breathe a word of this to Salud. It was bad enough with all the spiders, wasps and sundry beetles and flying bugs that disturbed her up here in the mountains; if she discovered the presence of a vast bee colony this close she might leave and never come back.

At that moment I heard the familiar sound of Arcadio's old Land Rover driving down the track behind me. Soon he had pulled up and was walking over with his usual crusty half-smile.

'These hives yours?' I asked him as we shook hands. He glanced over at the bees, then back at his car, then finally looked me in the face.

'Forty-five euros each,' he said. A series of thoughts passed through my mind in the space of about a second: what was he talking about? I wasn't asking how much they were. But then maybe in the back of my mind I *was* interested in having some hives of my own. Why else was I down here investigating in the first place? The old man knew perfectly well what I was after, more than I did myself. But what on earth was I going to say to Salud? Yes, but think of the honey we'd have! Surely she'd grow to love them once we'd lined the cupboards with jars of our own honey.

'I'll take two,' I said.

But Arcadio didn't want me to take two of the hives from down here: he wanted me to have a couple from some other hives he had higher up the mountainside, on the slopes of Penyagolosa.

'We'll go and pick them up now,' he said. 'Shouldn't take long.'

We set off in his hard, utilitarian vehicle down the mountain and along the dirt track that led to the village. The hives were, at least according to what he'd told me, in the opposite direction.

'Only way to get there,' he said. 'Stone's throw away from your place, but this is the only track available.' After several miles of the normal road, we were quickly back on the dirt variety after he took a sharp turn. Despite bumping along in his Spartan, suspension-lite car, it felt good somehow to be back trundling along rocky paths – Arcadio, with his leathery skin, thick-fibre clothes and flat cap looked out of place anywhere but in this rough landscape.

Penyagolosa came into view as we emerged from behind a cluster of pine trees and turned a hairpin bend on the edge of a steep incline. Our land was on the edge of the Penyagolosa massif, but the peak was hidden from view unless we climbed high up the other side of the valley. Despite its modest height, it was a magnificent mountain, strong and powerful, towering over the other hills and summits below it, the red, rusty stripe running diagonally through its exposed rockface like war paint.

'They say it's magical, that mountain,' Arcadio said as he negotiated the deep trenches and dips in the track. 'Dragons and stuff.'

We carried on driving for what seemed an age before Arcadio eventually brought the car to a halt outside an abandoned *mas* just off the track. We stepped out and he trotted over purposefully towards the broken buildings. There didn't seem to be bees anywhere. I looked out over the horizon: we were higher up now, and the air was sharper and cooler. The grass looked greener, darker, as though more rain fell here than back down on the farm, while the pine trees were shorter, their trunks blacker than the pale pines we had. Many of them seemed virtually stripped of needles and had mysterious white fluffy balls hanging in the branches, not unlike candyfloss.

I heard footsteps behind and Arcadio emerged again holding something brown and hard in his hands.

'Cow dung,' he said victoriously. 'Dry cow dung: we burn it and it calms the bees down.' From my paltry knowledge of beekeeping I recalled images of people in white outfits calmly puffing smoke out of cans on to the hives before extracting honey. But were all those genteel amateur beekeepers in the Home Counties really using cow shit?

'Arcadio,' I asked, 'what are those fluffy lumps on the trees?'

'*Procesionaria*,' he said. Parasitic insects, he explained, that walked in long processions – hence the name – and infected the trees and almost killed them by building their nests in them.

'Big problem,' he said. 'Nothing you can do. Sometimes hunters just shoot them out of the tree.'

He got back in the car and fired up the engine: we had to get going. I looked mournfully at the dying trees for a second and then climbed in to join him.

After another ten minutes we reached an overgrown terrace. Arcadio pulled the car over, scraped it through some thick bushes and then brought it to a stop. Along the edge of the terrace, up against a wall, were half a dozen hives. They looked more like old fruit boxes that had been converted into bee homes, with a simple metal sheet nailed on to the lid in an attempt to make them waterproof. Meanwhile the hole at the bottom where the bees flew in and out looked as if it had been carved with a penknife, and even then only as an afterthought.

Forty-five euros each, I thought to myself. I should have haggled.

Arcadio opened the back of his car and pulled out an old canvas sack stuffed with a couple of dirty old beekeeper's jackets complete with protective hood.

'Try this,' he said. 'Used to be my father's.'

I put it on: it was four or five sizes too small.

'That's all there is,' he said. I noticed that he'd kept the better-looking outfit for himself. 'Put some gloves on and you'll be fine.' The sleeves barely reached past my elbows.

I had no idea how we were now going to proceed, but assumed Arcadio, as the master beekeeper, would have a master plan for transporting the hives back to the farm, one that doubtlessly involved as little stress – both to the bees and to ourselves – as possible. But I was wrong.

Placing a lighter under one of the lumps of cow dung, he got it smoking a bit, waved it for less than a second at one of the hives and then called over to me: 'Right,' he said, 'take that one to the car.'

Just like that, with no more preparation? Weren't the bees going to be slightly annoyed by me simply picking up their house and putting in the back of an ancient Land Rover? Didn't he have some kind of protective sheet, perhaps, that he could throw over the thing to keep all the bees safe – from us?

I walked as calmly as I could to the hive he had indicated and went to pick it up. The first thing I noticed was that it was heavier than I had anticipated, so I found myself immediately straining and going red in the face as I lifted it up and started stumbling towards the car. The second thing I noticed was that the bees, quite predictably, were less than amused by the catastrophe besetting their quiet abode and were starting to fly and circle around me with a particularly aggressive sounding buzz. And the third thing I noticed was that these upset and naturally violently disposed bees had discovered a convenient hole in my trousers – in my crutch.

I have never pulled my trousers down so quickly. Quite how I got the hive back on the floor beforehand to free my hands I can't remember. All I do remember was exposing myself on the mountainside in front of an elderly farmer as a swarm of killer insects realised that my Achilles heel wasn't on my heel at all. My body seemed to react faster than my mind could possibly ever do, survival of my procreational capacity suddenly overriding all other processes in my biological machine. With my trousers hanging down around my knees I hopped and skipped as far away from the hive as I could, my hands flicking and swatting like rotor blades to remove the deadly foe from their intended target. No bee was going to sting me down there, no matter what.

The bees, though, were smarter than me, and simply changed their military objectives: as I swiped and cleared them away, an advance party was crawling up the inside of my shirt looking for new targets.

With a shriek I felt two of them sting me simultaneously on the belly. The pain was incredible, like searing hot needles pressing deep into the skin. With a gasp I fell to the floor, beating out the other bees and gripping my stomach. Arcadio stood over me, the smoking cow turd still in his hand. The bees seemed to vanish as soon as he appeared.

'You better pull your trousers up,' he said. 'They might be coming back for more.'

An hour later we were back at the farm, two hives somehow sitting in the back of the car. The stings hurt so much I'd thought I was going to be sick during the return journey, jolting around on the bumpy road. Good job I wasn't in the army, I thought, if a couple of beestings could almost do me in. There wasn't even any blood. Arcadio drove straight to the house and called out for Salud.

'Bring some olive oil,' he said. Moments later Salud was dabbing oil on a couple of mounds that had developed on my belly. I was in too much agony to wonder why, but almost instantaneously the pain disappeared, as if by magic. It was so surprising that I sat up with a start.

'Did the oil do that?' I asked incredulously. Arcadio nodded.

'Swelling'll take a day or so to go down. By tomorrow you'll have forgotten it.'

And he started to recite:

La Verge Maria
quan pel món anava
amb oli de cresol
tot ho curava.

When the Virgin Mary
Walked the Earth
She cured all illnesses
With the oil from her lamp.

'Used to use olive oil in their lamps, see,' Arcadio explained. 'It's good for lots of things.'

I felt ashamed at how feeble I'd been. A couple of beestings!

'Better set them up, then,' he said.

'You're putting those hives here?' Salud asked.

'I'll explain later,' I said, and rushed out of the door.

We drove Arcadio's car down to a patch of land below the house, next to a white stone outbuilding. Picking up a couple of pallets I'd found lying around, we laid them down next to an olive tree and then carefully carried the hives out and placed them on top. Arcadio, I noticed, was careful to smoke them more thoroughly this time. I wondered if we'd brought a particularly vicious strain of bee into our lives. That would take some explaining . . .

'Turn them round so the entrance faces the east,' Arcadio ordered. I did as he said, while he placed a heavy stone on top of each hive to keep the lid firmly down.

'They like to wake up facing the sun,' he explained. It seemed such a happy image – cute little bees getting up in the morning and heading off to spend the day mooching around the flowers. It was easy to forget for a moment how nasty they could be. I rubbed my stomach gently: the lumps were still delicate and swollen. Bees were the source of all that was sweetness and light, they used to say: sweetness from the honey, light from the candles made from their wax. Right at that moment, though, I never wanted to see another one of the little sods again.

★

Salud and I had been together for almost seven years. Marriage, for me, was really more about a state of mind than a ritual performed by a celibate man in a frock, or, even worse, a piece of paper signed by a civil servant. Salud, as far as I was aware, felt more or less the same, and we'd been calling each other husband and wife for some time. Who else could really know the truth of the commitment between us more than we ourselves? God? Perhaps, but I suspected there was little connection between Him and the clergy. The state? The idea was risible.

And yet Salud's comment struck a chord. I had never been a great one for rituals: I was never baptised or christened, never confirmed, and missed the graduation ceremony after leaving England for Spain when I finished my degree. I even failed to have a TB jab at school – another minor rite of passage. I didn't mind any of this: not going through the official bit of 'getting married' just seemed a natural continuation of a long trend.

But something about being on the mountain was changing me. Here I was experiencing a world entirely bound by natural rhythms, where the beginnings and ends of earthly cycles were carefully marked and registered: symbolic doorways through which one passed from one world into another: from summer into autumn, from harvest time to sowing time, dry seasons to wetter seasons. I had known all this at an intellectual level, but now I was beginning to develop a different sense of what these rituals might mean – an understanding that had nothing to do with rational understanding. It was emotional – rituals spoke directly to your feelings with their colour and pageantry – but it was something else as well, something I was struggling to define, something about being connected to the land, about being earthed in some way.

Marriage – before I came here I could scarcely have thought I would ever do something like that. Now, though, the concept was beginning to feel less alien to me. The earth itself, in a gentle, undemanding sort of way, seemed to be taking us there.

★

The twelfth of October – El Día del Pilar, Spain's national day. It has been fairly quiet here – most of the festivities take place either in Madrid, with a massive military parade, or in Saragossa, where the 'Virgin of the Pillar' resides in the cathedral. It marks the proper beginning of autumn, though, and the approach of winter – the sun is already setting behind the Picosa at around six these days.

Salud received a telephone call from her mother. 'Should be getting busy up there soon,' she said. Salud didn't know what she meant. 'Hunting season officially starts today,' she explained.

Mountainsides all over Spain, it seems, are now crawling with armed men. There's plenty to take a potshot at up here: a family of partridges has taken up residence in the ruins of the lean-to next door. Birds can be shot anytime, Salud's mum says; wild boar can only be hunted on Thursdays and Sundays. Today is a Thursday. I look out of the window but can't see anyone. If the boar have any sense they'll have taken off further up the mountain looking for sanctuary. From what little I know, the laws on hunting are complicated. I've got the horrible feeling that hunters can wander all over our land without us being able to do anything about it. God knows I've found enough spent shotgun cartridges lying about.

⋆

It finally felt properly autumnal for the first time that day, with thick, heavy skies and damp earth, from the overnight showers. Something must have clicked in Salud's mind, for she suddenly smiled and uttered the word '*rovellones*' over breakfast, and declared we would head out and spend the morning looking for this highly prized wild mushroom. *Rovellones* are saffron milk caps – aptly named *lactarius deliciosus* in Latin – and tend to grow on and around pine trees.

After a quick unsuccessful sortie around the few pines growing near the house, we headed out along the dirt track leading past the bend in the gulley and up towards the ruins of the old shepherd's house. Arcadio had told me they had found the old guy dead up here a few years before, no one having seen him for about a month. He had lived on his own with a few animals, and judging by the chaos of remains left rotting in his house he seemed to have spent most of his time eating tins of tuna, praying to the Virgin Mary and looking at porn magazines – there was some vintage 1970s stuff lying around: black and white photographs and all the men with big bushy moustaches.

A stand of pines nearby seemed to have survived the fire, although they weren't easy to reach: we had to cut a path through the wilderness, jumping down from terrace to terrace like mountain goats in order to get to them. It was fascinating to see how, in such a short distance from the house, there was a subtle but noticeable change in the flora – the trees seemed more luscious, somehow.

We spent about an hour looking for the *rovellones*. I'd never seen them in the wild before – only ever at the markets, all bright orange with green spots – and Salud had to point them out to me, bunched up around the base of the pine trees and hiding under tufts of grass. For some reason they didn't look quite so brightly coloured out in the open. We only managed to half-fill her basket, so we pushed on further, forcing our way as best we could through the gorse, looking for more groups of pine trees, or just the remains of those that hadn't survived the fire. Salud had some kind of sixth sense for them, and we eventually came across our biggest haul on the slopes of a hill where there appeared to be no sign at all of any trees. But we found some blackened stumps, and there they were growing by the dozen.

And so we had *rovellones* for lunch. The traditional way of cooking them, with fresh green garlic, is as follows.

Pour a few drops of very good olive oil in a frying pan along with a sprinkling of salt. The *rovellones* should be washed, dried and cut into strips about half a finger's width. Chop the spring garlic finely, along with the green stalks. Place this first into the frying pan, with the heat turned up high. After about thirty seconds add the *rovellones* and cook until soft. Add more salt if required. When done, sprinkle with chopped parsley and eat immediately. The garlic and parsley help bring out the delicate flavours of the *rovellones*. Works well with chunks of fresh bread as a starter.

⋆

At eight o'clock one Sunday morning I was woken by the sound of gunfire very close to the farm. One of things we'd had to deal with living so far out in the countryside away from any towns or villages was an urban fear of isolation, so often expressed in subconscious images of wild axemen coming in off the hillside to do you in. '*On a mountain no one can hear you scream . . .*' Typical horror-movie stuff. But these nightmares almost invariably took place in a night-time setting. I had never expected bloodthirsty killers to show up at this tranquil time of day.

Dragging myself tentatively out of bed, I threw on my overalls and searched for something I might use to defend myself. Nothing came to hand – all my tools were downstairs, out of reach. The only 'weapons' available were a couple of books, a pair of slippers and a bright orange collapsible umbrella Salud usually kept in her handbag. Cursing my luck, I realised I had no choice but to head out anyway: Salud was pulling the bedcovers up under her chin and looking concerned. It was my manly duty to go out and find out what was happening, armed or not.

I poked my head out of the door and saw nothing. The gunshot had come from the direction of the old oak tree behind one of the other ruined houses. It was there that I had to go.

Bleary-eyed, I tiptoed my way over, unsure if this sunny, clear Sunday morning was about to become my last. After we had bought the farm, a friend from Valencia told us that when he bought a similar place, out in the middle of an empty valley a few miles further south, the local police had paid a visit and told him simply to shoot and bury anyone if they came round giving him trouble; they wouldn't want to know. A feeling of the Wild West about the area was growing stronger by the day, and I felt like a cowboy about to get into a gunfight. The only problem was I had no gun.

I turned the corner round the back of the ruined house and the oak tree and patio beneath it came into focus. Rubbing my eyes, I saw a group of men standing next to half a dozen four-wheel-drives, shotguns and rifles clearly and nonchalantly tucked under their arms. By their dress and manner – all dark-green clothing and an air of cockiness that seems to come over most people once you put a gun in their hand – I understood they were hunters, out for a jaunt with a view to taking out a few wild boar and perhaps the odd partridge or two.

The chances were they hadn't come with murderous intentions – at least not towards humans. But as I began to breathe more easily, I realised there was another problem to deal with. These men were treating our patio as though it were some public square. And they were about to go hunting on our land, something I wasn't entirely keen on them doing. But how on earth did I go about telling a group of armed men to clear off? I had no idea. Unsure as to the protocol, I decided to go in softly.

As I walked towards them, some of them spotted me out of the corners of their eyes and turned away guiltily, like naughty children caught out by the headmaster. One or two faces were familiar: they were local men, thickset, with short limbs and closed faces. I caught the eye of one of them, an old man with close-cropped white hair, and approached him. He had what looked like a twelve-bore shotgun in his hands, while a couple of grey hunting dogs were sniffing the ground near his feet.

He smiled nervously and started talking before I even said a word.

'Those wild boar are ripping up your trees,' he said with a forced chuckle. 'Causing a lot of damage.' And he pointed over towards our almond grove.

I understood: he was doing us a favour by bringing his hunting chums out here on a Sunday morning and waking us up with his gunfire. I'd seen the trees he was talking about, and the damage was considerable, but nonetheless I wasn't too happy about encouraging him. I'd come across hunting types before – you gave them an inch and before you knew it they'd built a lodge on your land and were shooting at all and sundry.

By this point, though, the others in the group had circled around me and were staring intently. After an initial sense of guilt, they now realised they had some kind of upper hand. I wanted this to be resolved amicably, if possible. They'd obviously been hunting here for years. And they were the nearest thing we had to neighbours. I didn't really want our relationship to get off on the wrong foot. Then there was that little thing about them having guns.

It was an impossible situation. If I wanted peace and harmony, it seemed I'd have to back down. Perhaps, I told myself, it would only be this once. There was plenty more mountainside for them to go shooting on. Let them do their hunting today, then they'd go and, I hoped, never come back.

I heard myself wishing them luck and returned to the house, totally defeated, Salud waiting anxiously for me upstairs.

An hour or two later, after we had properly risen and had breakfast to the sound of more gunfire, I headed out to do some chores. The hunters were still huddled under the oak tree, talking to others who were milling about among the almond trees speaking into walkie-talkies. Catching sight of them I grumbled. I had been beaten – in my own castle – and it hurt.

As I pottered about, however, a scream suddenly came from inside the house. It was Salud. In an instant I sprinted up towards the front door and arrived just in time to see the two grey hunting dogs come running out, pieces of what looked like raw chicken hanging from their mouths.

'*Los perros!*' Salud shouted, seeing me speechless in the doorway. 'What are they *doing* here?'

It was the excuse I realised I had been waiting for. A line had been crossed and I saw red. Pruning shears in hand, I ran towards the oak tree where the dogs had disappeared with their spoils. If they hadn't managed to catch any boar or grouse that day, I was damned if raiding our larder was going to be some kind of consolation prize for them.

The old, white-haired man was still there, along with three or four others. This time, though, I didn't see the guns, or the fact that I was heavily outnumbered. They'd simply gone too far and it was time for them to leave.

I filled my lungs in preparation for the bollocking I intended to give them. Just as I was about to launch into my barrage, though, I heard a voice shouting from behind me.

'What the hell do you think you're doing? Get away with you! All of you. *Fuera!*'

I turned and saw Salud barking like a sergeant major, her normally slim dancer's body now pumped up to make her appear almost doubled in size. Without my realising, she had followed me for this moment of confrontation. Standing on slightly higher ground than the rest of us she looked daunting and commanding.

'And take those damned dogs with you!'

For a second the hunters looked stunned. It seemed they had never been talked to like this before, let alone by a woman. Within seconds, though, they were shuffling around, collecting their gear, mumbling under their breath and calling the others in from the mountainside. It seemed hard to believe, but they were clearly about to head off.

Minutes later we watched their convoy of 4×4s driving away down the road. Salud was still raging inside, but I sensed a growing pride in her. She was surprised by the strength of her own reaction. Heading back inside the house, I poured us both a congratulatory mid-morning brandy.

'You've got more *cojones* than me,' I said. 'Always said you had.'

★

I have been cutting down about half a dozen abandoned almond trees which lie in the area above the track where I want to start planting some oaks. They won't be dry enough for firewood for this winter, but probably for next year. I bumped into Arcadio in the village and he said you must always make sure you cut wood after the 'change of the moon', i.e., after the full moon has passed and it has started to wane.

'Still got some wood stored away that I cut ten years ago,' he said. 'Did it during the waning moon and it's still fine. Cut another lot during the waxing moon and within six months it was useless – rotten right through.'

He didn't know why the moon had such a powerful effect, but said everyone in the past had always insisted it was true, and he'd managed to prove it himself.

Later, I checked the phase of the moon – we're just in the waning phase. It seems I got it right, albeit unwittingly. I wonder if there's a particularly auspicious time for planting trees according to the moon as well. Although I'm not entirely sure whether to believe it all. Is it just the moon? What about the planets? Do they affect plants as well? How far can you take this? I can already envisage a lengthy, complicated process of star-gazing and chart-drawing before you even cut the grass at this rate.

'Best way to carry firewood back to the house is with a rope or string and then fling it over your shoulder,' Arcadio said. 'Don't go trying to carry it in your arms: too heavy. Simplest is best.'

Sometimes I feel like a child taking remedial lessons for life in the country.

★

We had to collect our mail by driving into the village early in the morning and visiting the office of the postman in the town hall before he set off on his rounds: he only did the village and a few outlying houses; our *mas* was well beyond his range.

Jordi, the postman, was a small, intense, chatty man of about fifty, with short grey hair and a neatly clipped grey beard covering his pointed chin. Reading glasses were propped on the end of his nose, exaggerating the glare of his expression as he bent his head down to look over the top of them. He was also an anarchist militant.

'Down with Capital!' screamed the colourful posters plastered around the walls of his tiny, windowless office. 'Worker! Do You Know Your Rights?' It felt like a museum of propaganda from the Spanish Civil War. Jordi was still fighting the good fight of 1936, or so it seemed from the inevitable barrage I received whenever I popped in to check if we had any letters.

'Have you seen what's happening in Baghdad? Look at the newspaper! We're organising a march next weekend: climbing Penyagolosa and planting a peace flag up there. We're demanding an immediate withdrawal of Yankie troops and reparations to be paid. Oh, and we want a committee to be set up to examine the repercussions for the postal sector of the new pensions law.'

'The Spanish pensions law? What's that got to do with Iraq?' I asked.

'If we bunch together a few local issues – you know, closer to home – we reckon we can get a few more people involved, let them know about US imperialism and the danger it poses to the whole world. Wanna come along? I can get you a ticket half price.'

'People have to pay to go on the march?' I said.

'Got to cover costs somehow. World peace doesn't come cheap, you know.'

'But I thought –' I checked myself. Wasn't this guy an anarchist? It made no sense, but I knew that if I asked him to explain I wouldn't get out of there till at least midday.

'I was wondering if there was any mail for us,' I said.

He peered into a little wooden pigeonhole, pulling out a large wad of letters bound together with an elastic band. He flicked through them quickly, the names half-whispered through his open mouth as he did so, his bottom lip glistening under the strip lights from beneath his grey whiskers.

'Nothing today,' he said with a smile once he'd finished. 'These are all for the other *masos*.'

'Are there many with people living in them?' I asked. Up our end of the valley, I knew there was no one except ourselves – all the other farms nearby were well and truly abandoned. But was that the case everywhere? Perhaps there were other people like us, quietly living in the countryside, doing up old houses and working on the land. It might even be a good idea to meet some of them.

'Used to be a lot more,' Jordi said, 'before the farmers all left to come and live in the village, or down on the coast. In the days of the Republic, see' – it seemed we were in for another lecture about the 1930s after all – 'the government built schools all over the countryside, trying to educate people, eradicate illiteracy and all that. Built about half a dozen just around this village. It was good for the kids, 'cause they got to read and write, and good for their parents, 'cause they were still around to help on the farm.'

In the sixties, though, Jordi continued, Franco – he spat the name out contemptuously – had decided to shut down all the rural schools and build a big central one in the village instead. All the children had been forced to go to the new school, and board there during the week, as it was too far to travel to every day. So they were no longer helping on the farm, and the farmers couldn't cope with the sudden labour shortage. And by the early seventies most of them had upped sticks and gone – abandoning their *masos*.

'Within a few years new people had moved in, though,' Jordi went on. 'This village became famous for all the communes that were set up – Indian gurus and all that stuff. Said there was something magical in these mountains – good for meditating or something. Reckon it was just the quality of the *maría* up here – the grass. Perfect conditions for growing. Bloke got busted a few years back. Fields of the stuff. They send detector helicopters round every now and again with sniffer technology. Bloody 'copter nearly stopped dead in its tracks when they flew over his place – metres and dials went off the scale. Got fifteen years, they said.'

'What happened to all the commune people,' I asked, not a little unconcerned: the last thing I wanted to learn was that there was an ashram on our doorstep.

'Oh, they all left,' he said. 'Sex scandal of some sort.' My eyebrows rose. These quiet mountains we had come to live in were perhaps not so quiet after all. 'Some of them still meet up here once a year, though. Get transformed into animal spirits – eagles and bears, that kind of thing: shamans.

'Is that what you're up to at your *mas*?' Jordi asked earnestly. 'Setting up a commune, then?'

I disabused him of the idea.

'Tell you what,' he said, undeterred. 'There's a party tonight at a *mas* of some friends of mine. It's a couple of valleys over from your place. Why don't you come along? Nice bunch of folk. I'm sure you'll like them. Bring Salud.'

⋆

It was clear from the start that the inhabitants of the *mas* were not 'country folk' in the ordinary sense: not people who had been born and brought up here. They were what were sometimes called *neorurales* – city folk seeking a new life in the mountains. A different aesthetic, a different eye had been employed in the overall look and feel of the place. It was neat and well kept, in a relaxed and easy-going kind of way: the grass at the edge of the dirt track had been clipped, flowers in brightly coloured pots sat proudly on the windowsills and lined the tidy stone steps leading up behind the farmhouse to the garden. A painted sign with the name of the *mas* hung over the door, decorated with a crescent moon and stars. Another painted sign in the window made a reference to the *duendes* of Penyagolosa – the earth spirits of the mountain on whose slopes this farm, like our own, had been built. Colour had been added to the house as well. The usual style for *masos* in the area was either to leave the stone in its natural state, or else to whitewash the outer walls and then paint the insides of the windows a bright, clear blue – this was said to ward off either evil spirits, or mosquitoes, depending on who you spoke to. This *mas*, though, had eschewed the traditional style and painted each window with a different colour: one red, the other yellow, another purple and another orange. The effect was light and gay, and I quickly found myself warming more to the idea of meeting the people who lived here.

'Look, honeysuckle – *madreselva*,' Salud said as Jordi led us to the front door: a large, well-kept creeper had been trained to cover most of one side of the building.

We walked in through the front door without knocking, pushing our way past a blue and yellow woollen curtain hanging on the inside to keep out the draughts. The hallway had been painted a deep blue, while the floor was made up of well-worn terracotta tiles.

'Through here,' Jordi said, passing into an adjacent room.

A fire was blazing in an open grate with a black metal hood catching the smoke. The room was dimly lit by a couple of table lamps, the walls reflecting a thick heavy lemon colour. Two middle-aged women were lounging on a long, dirty sofa of uncertain shape, their arms wrapped around each other. From the kitchen behind them came the sound of dinner being prepared.

'Jordi!' One of the women on the sofa freed herself from the other's embrace and stood up to kiss the postman on both cheeks.

'And you've brought some new friends with you!' she cried, a wide, beaming smile lighting up her heavy, greasy face. '*Hola, hola.*' She leaned forwards to kiss us. 'Concha,' she introduced herself. 'Jordi told us some time ago there were new neighbours in the area. Come in, come in.'

She had a compact body, hard and stiff, her hair short and wiry. Her knees rubbed together slightly as she toddled back towards the sofa and gave her hand to help lift up her friend.

'This is Marina,' she said. 'Watch out – she's a witch!'

Marina was almost the same height and age as Concha, but her hair was longer and softer, and dyed a deep shocking green. She seemed shyer than Concha, her lips struggling simultaneously to smile and cover up her crooked teeth.

'Hello,' she said, in a deep, thunderous voice. 'Looks like Jordi's brought us a special delivery.' She gave a wheezy laugh and punched her chest to dislodge the phlegm. Only now, as she stood up, did I realise she was almost twice Concha's size, her flesh seeming to roll out horizontally in endless folds.

'We've just cracked open a bottle of *orujo*,' she said with a grin. 'Want to try some?'

After a few moments a young man and woman who'd been in the kitchen came out to meet us.

'Pau,' said the man, wiping his hands on a cloth and then leaning over to shake my hand firmly. His beard and balding head made him look older than he probably was, I thought. But he had a strong bearing and straight, proud back. 'This is Africa,' he said, pointing to his girlfriend next to him. I felt two soft, almost substanceless kisses planted on my cheeks. There was something watery about her, her eyes glancing down at the floor when she spoke, her limbs like waifs', thin and fragile.

'El Clossa should be arriving soon,' Concha said. It was a strange name, obviously an *apodo* – a nickname: it meant 'the crutch'. As if on cue, a car pulled up outside.

The front door burst open and a couple of metal sticks poked through from the hallway while someone fiddled with the latch on the door before turning round and coming inside.

'Jordi, you lazy anarchist bastard! You haven't brought me any mail for weeks. Stop agitating for strikes and start doing your job.'

El Clossa was a short man with short, grey hair and a protruding nose. Perching himself on a couple of crutches, his weak, semi-useless legs swung from beneath a powerful, compact torso. His eyes, light-blue and glaring, were pointing in the direction of the local postman, still sitting on the sofa from which Salud and I had just got up.

'Where's my copy of *Walkers Monthly*? I haven't received anything from the stone masons' guild for weeks. And my local history magazine – the *Boletín*?'

'Perhaps you forgot to pay the subscription,' Jordi said weakly.

'Like fuck! You just can't be arsed to pull them out of your pigeonholes and bring them round.'

'Dinner,' Pau said with an air of disapproval, 'is ready. If you'd like to come through to the kitchen.'

The night slowly slipped into a golden haze of excess. Within minutes of finishing the meat stew, and slurping the last drops of wine in his tumbler, El Clossa was slumped half asleep on the table in front of him, while Concha had started singing endless folk songs that all sounded the same.

Pau got up and started to clear away some of the dishes.

'We should tell them what's going on here,' he said, nodding towards Salud and me. 'Not just pretty songs.'

'They'll find out soon enough,' Concha said, knocking back her drink in one and reaching for the bottle again.

'What Pau means,' Marina started gently, 'is that these mountains, all this beautiful countryside that you've started to explore, isn't going to be around for very much longer. At least not in the way we all know it.'

I'd had too much to drink to think clearly and for a moment felt very confused. What was she talking about?

'The government,' Pau started. 'The government doesn't care about the things we care about. It doesn't care about the woods and forests, and the rivers and the wildlife – at least not if it can't make any money out of them. That's why they're slowly destroying this area.'

'You have to explain properly,' Concha said, reading the expressions on our faces. 'Have you heard of Marina d'Or?' she asked.

For the next hour and a half a picture of The Threat was chaotically and colourfully painted for us. By the time they'd finished it appeared that perhaps there really was something to be concerned about.

The Spanish *costas* had become a byword the world over for the worst kind of tourist development. Castellón had managed to survive some of the ugliest assaults of the 1960s and 1970s, but speculators, teaming up with local officials, were doing their best to make up for lost time, it seemed. The centrepiece of the new development was a purpose-built resort being constructed along a relatively untouched stretch of coastline: Marina d'Or – the 'Golden Harbour'. According to Concha, in addition to the already constructed tower blocks providing beach apartments and hotel space for the tourists, they were planning to build 'Europe's largest holiday city' there, with three golf courses, three casinos, a dry-ski run right next to the beach, and a scaled-down version of the Eiffel Tower. The city was going to occupy almost two thousand hectares of what was now mostly orange groves and wetlands, with a resident population of 200,000 people. Offices promoting the resort and offering to sell properties there at 'once-in-a-lifetime' prices had been opened in major cities, including London, New York and Beijing.

Unfortunately, the development wasn't restricted to just one area. A further eleven golf courses were under construction or being planned for the rest of the province – many of them inland, away from the coasts, while clones of Marina d'Or were being pencilled in for the future.

And when it wasn't tourism, Concha went on, it was heavy industry: the ceramics factory owners made up a powerful lobby – they were the biggest employers in the province – and they wanted more clay. The existing quarries were almost exhausted; there was no choice but to open more. Lorries drove from as far away as Russia to pick up deliveries here – it was a big money earner. The only problem was that it was eating up the very land on which it stood.

What's more, Pau added, the ceramics factories pumped out arsenic as their furnaces blazed twenty-four hours a day. There were towns nearby with worryingly high levels of child cancer.

And all this industry and tourism needed more roads, and more water. But the rains that had once irrigated these lands could no longer be relied on: reservoirs where once people went boating in summer were now cracked and dry. And it needed more energy to keep it all going, which was why they were building wind farms on every available mountain top. Landscapes that had barely changed for millennia were now hosts to towers of steel whirring and spinning night and day, frightening away the birds and scarring the ancient views. Once you could walk these hills for days with little to remind you of the times you lived in: an antique land and rural culture – perhaps the last of its kind so close to Spain's Mediterranean coastline – was at your very fingertips here. Now that was endangered, and in some places had gone completely.

The greatest threat, however, was the new airport being built just a few miles away. Every other province on the Mediterranean coast had one – now it was time to fill the gap. Getting here would no longer involve a long drive from Valencia to the south or Tarragona to the north. With the new local airport they'd be able to pour the tourists in from every corner of Europe and beyond. And there was a whole under-developed coastline waiting for them – particularly those jaded by the other stretches of the Spanish coast that had been spoilt by . . . too many tourists.

The site for the new airport was inland, near the picturesque red-stone hill town of Vilafamés, home of one of the longest established colony of artists and painters in the province. Their peace and tranquillity were about to be destroyed by the landing and taking off of scores of planes every day, spreading their noise and fumes over the mountains.

'Change', 'progress' – it was all taking place right here in front of us. They all knew what the result would be: we'd all seen it before so often in other parts of the country. Their language was almost hysterical at times, but they were witnessing the beginning of a process that would eventually see fields turned into parking lots, potholed country lanes become smooth tarmac speedways, the farmer with his horse-drawn cart chased off the roads while his newly rich neighbour kicked dirt into his face from the back wheels of his shining SUV. Soon there wouldn't be a clean, unspoilt vista left in this region, every hillside, every valley marked in some way by the mushrooming spread of holiday homes, flats, villas and hotels. And before long the holiday-makers would be arriving here at the new airport, and many of them would want to stay, meaning more roads, more villas, more golf courses, more concrete obliterating the unspoilt world that still existed – just – in these parts.

Anger and resentment mixed with a fatalistic pessimism seemed to kill the room. This was a cause for them, something to occupy them and bring them together. It was also based on fear – fear of losing the beautiful countryside in which they lived. But there was more than mere cynicism driving them, I felt. More than a desire for it not to happen on their patch. This shouldn't be happening on any patch – anywhere. How many more Benidorms did the world really need? How many more golf courses and bathroom tiles? When did you say: that's it, we've got enough?

And then there was something else, something unspoken, or less clearly expressed, but there nonetheless: not only dread of what lay in the future, but also a sense that something of worth, of real worth, was in danger of being lost. Something fragile, subtle, that didn't belong to the brutal, hungry world invading these lands and imposing itself on them. Something to do with the way local workmen still made cloths, cheeses or espadrilles in the same way they had been made for hundreds or thousands of years. Something to do with the way children still played in groups out in the countryside. Something about old widows dressed in black sitting outside their front doors in the evening crocheting tablecloths and napkins. It was about all this and more: you captured it in moments or visions such as these, but it remained elusive: a timeless, human quality, one that had to be quietly nurtured and protected to survive. None there could give it a name, but I felt sure it lay behind all their talk of 'witches' and 'spirits' – and it was this that faced the greatest danger.

The Story of Old Mother Misery and the Pear Tree

Old Mother Misery lived in a *mas* on the outskirts of the village, where she kept a few chickens running around in a yard, in the middle of which stood a large pear tree. When she wasn't cooking, or cleaning, she used to go out and about sowing seeds of misery wherever she went, making people's lives as wretched as she could – making shepherds lose their sheep, farmers lose their crops, children lose their toys and old people lose their wits. So it was no surprise that she didn't have a single friend in the entire world.

Now Old Mother Misery was getting on in years, and she knew that sooner or later Death was going to appear one day at her door to take her away with him. So one night she sat down to think about what to do and came up with a plan.

The next day she went to Heaven to see God.

'Oh me,' said God when he saw her approaching. 'It's her again.'

'God,' said Old Mother Misery in her high, scratchy voice, 'I need a favour. Little boys from the village keep coming into my yard, climbing the pear tree and stealing all the fruit! It has to stop!'

'Well, what do you want me to do about it?' said God.

'I want you,' said Old Mother Misery, 'to make it so that if ever anyone climbs my pear tree, they won't be able to get down again unless I go up there myself to fetch them. Just to teach them a lesson.'

Now it did seem to God that this was an odd thing to ask for, but Old Mother Misery had given him enough headaches in the past, and it didn't seem like too big a task, so he said, 'If I do this for you, will you promise to go away and leave me in peace?'

'Certainly,' said Old Mother Misery.

'Very well then,' said God. 'Consider it done.'

Now about this time the Devil was down in Hell doing his annual inventory check to see how many souls he'd got and who was expected to be joining them in the near future.

'Death,' he called out to Death. 'Isn't it about time Old Mother Misery was making her way down here? She's certainly getting on a bit. Why don't you go and pay her a visit?'

So Death set off to find Old Mother Misery's *mas*, where he knew she lived.

When he arrived he found Old Mother Misery tending her chickens in the yard.

'Oh Death,' she said when she saw his dark black shadow over her. 'Is that you? Has my time come already? Surely you can spare me for a bit longer yet.'

But Death was implacable. 'Come along now,' he said. 'You've been here far too long already. It's about time we got going.'

'Oh but please,' said Old Mother Misery. 'It's going to be a long journey. Couldn't we take something with us to eat in case we get hungry along the way. I've got some lovely ripe pears up in that pear tree if you'd be so good as to climb up and get some.'

'Good idea,' said Death. 'You're right, it is a long way, and doubtless I'll be wanting something myself during the journey. I'll just nip up and get those delicious looking pears up there at the top.'

And so it was that Death climbed the tree to pick some pears. But no sooner did he have the fruit in his hands than he realised he was stuck and couldn't get down again.

'Hah!' cried Old Mother Misery. 'I've got you now. You're trapped, and you shan't be taking me anywhere.'

Death cried out and cried out, but all to no avail. It looked like he was going to be there for a long time, perhaps even for ever.

Now with Death stuck up Old Mother Misery's pear tree, nobody was dying: builders fell from their scaffolding and survived; sailors were shipwrecked at sea but didn't drown; children went hungry but didn't starve. After this had been going on for some time, back down in Hell the Devil began to suspect something.

'Haven't had any new batches of souls recently,' he muttered to himself. 'Come to think of, we haven't seen Death around for quite some time . . . not since I packed him off to fetch Old Mother Misery.'

So he decided to set off to find out for himself what was going on.

Now up on Earth everyone was dancing and singing and having

fiestas right, left and centre because no one was dying any more, so it took the Devil quite a time to push his way through the crowds before he reached Old Mother Misery's *mas*. There, to his surprise, he found Death sitting up in the pear tree.

'What's going on? Why aren't you working?'

'I'm stuck,' said Death despondently, for he had been there a long time and was feeling very sore. 'I can't get down unless Old Mother Misery comes up to get me.'

Just at that moment, Old Mother Misery appeared. 'Ah,' she said when she saw the Devil. 'I thought we might be getting a visit from you soon.'

'What have you done to Death? I need him urgently. Release him from there at once or I'll drag you down to Hell myself!'

'How dare you talk like that to me!' she said in a shriek. The Devil was taken aback for a moment: he wasn't used to being shouted at. 'This is my house,' said Old Mother Misery, 'and no one will tell me what to do.'

'But I need Death,' said the Devil, more humbly this time. 'Everyone's out having parties all the time, while the fires of Hell need stoking with new souls.'

'I'll only get Death down for you if you promise to leave me in peace and never come back.'

The Devil thought it over for a moment. He wasn't actually sure if he wanted the old witch down in Hell with him anyway, so he agreed. Old Mother Misery climbed up the pear tree and released Death, and within a flash the two of them vanished, and were never seen at Old Mother Misery's *mas* ever again.

And that is why Misery still walks the Earth. Although some say that one day, perhaps soon, Old Mother Misery will get tired of being so old and causing so much sadness in the world, and that she will pop off down to Hell of her own accord, for a long rest.

NOVEMBER

The Latin November *is called* Tishrin el Tsani *in Syriac and* Azarmah *in Persian. It is the last month of autumn and is made up of thirty days. Now is the time for sowing wheat, oats, beans and flax: start sowing from the middle of the month if Allah has made it rain at that time: thirteen days thence around the time of the setting of the Pleiades, what has been sown will already have taken root. November is the month for collecting acorns, chestnuts, myrtle berries and sugar cane. According to the writer Azib, owing to the threat of frosts from this time onwards, the roots of trees and plants should be protected with fertiliser. This is also the time for harvesting saffron.*

The cold begins to reach certain areas, and the first snow falls. Starlings, swallows, pelicans and other birds start to migrate south. It is a good month for planting trees. The writer Abu al-Khayr says the sap in trees settles at this time, causing leaves to fall. In Seville I have seen round radishes and the local lettuce – with pointed leaves – planted, for picking in January, and spinach, for harvesting in December.

Ibn al-Awam, *Kitab al-Falaha*, The Book of Agriculture, 12th century

Four and a half thousand feet up a frozen mountain, I sat shivering in a school hall, waiting for the Third Annual Spanish Truffle Conference to begin. Huddled around an inadequate gas heater were three professors of 'truffle-ology', a handful of local farmers and Salud's nephew and myself. Bizarrely, the tiny village where it was being held – an old Templar territory from the thirteenth century – had its own television channel, and the cameras were there to record this, perhaps the most important event of the year.

'That's Santiago Reyna,' Vicente whispered loudly in my ear as we tried in vain to keep warm: there was no sign of autumn up here, I noticed, late summer having passed directly to midwinter by the feel of things. 'He's the biggest authority on truffles in the whole of Spain!'

I pulled my thin jacket tighter to try and keep in the heat: at that moment the only expert I wanted to see was one on thermodynamics.

I knew next to nothing about truffles, and was not even sure I'd ever tried one. But Vicente, a grinning twenty-year-old with an Afro of bright curly red hair studying forestry science at Valencia University, had assured me in no uncertain terms that this was the future – and an ideal venture for our new farm. Glancing around the hall at the dozen or so other participants, all wrapped up in scarves and hats against the cold, I had my doubts. If he was right, the rest of Spain had yet to catch on.

It appeared as if the organisers of the event were waiting for more people to show up, but after a delay of about an hour, they finally decided to start. Vicente pulled out his exercise book and pen, breathing on his fingers to try and warm them up.

'I want to study with this guy,' he said, his eyes glazing over as Santiago, a well-fed, middle-aged man with an air of authority stood up to address the meagre audience. 'There's nothing he doesn't know about truffles.'

Over the course of the next couple of hours, he and his colleagues helped lighten some of the darkness of my truffle ignorance.

The most famous kind of truffle, I learned, was the white variety – *tuber magnatum* – which was only ever found in northern Italy. This is the one that often makes it into newspaper articles, where *x* (famous person or restaurant) is reported to have spent *y* (ridiculous amount of money) for *z* (tiny morsel of the stuff). It is very rare, being almost impossible to cultivate artificially or farm.

Black truffles – *tuber melanosporum* – sometimes called black winter truffles, are not quite as expensive but are very much sought after and can command impressive amounts of money. They are most commonly found in southern France and here in north-eastern Spain and are not to be confused with Chinese truffles – *tuber sinensis* – which look similar but taste of nothing and are often used by unscrupulous suppliers to bulk out their wares by placing a real truffle at the top of the jar for the smell so that no one can tell the difference. The advantage of black truffles is that – unlike their white cousins – they can, to some extent, be cultivated. Through a process called mycorrhisation, spores can be impregnated into the roots of a baby tree. Often this is a variety of oak, but hazelnut and other species can also be used. Several years after planting – anything up to ten years – they start producing their first yield. Specially trained pigs or dogs are needed to find this elusive crop, which grows a foot or so under the ground and is almost invisible to the human eye owing to its soil-like colour.

Thankfully, the speakers pitched their talks at the relatively ignorant, which seemed to be most of us in the hall. In France, we were told, truffi-culture was far more advanced. The French had set up websites selling this 'black gold', allowing them a huge mark-up on the wholesale price. They even had fluffy truffle toys for the kids of truffle-scoffing parents. Oohs and aahs of respect emanated from the huddled farmers around. Those Frenchies always were a clever, sophisticated lot. Trust them to have thought of something like that.

With that, and a couple more mini-talks on technical aspects of truffle cultivation that sailed right over my head, the conference came to an end. In that sleepy lull that comes immediately after a talk or lecture, I discovered that Vicente was no longer sitting beside me and was already barraging Santiago enthusiastically with questions. I picked up the pack of leaflets that had been handed out and made my way to the door, curious but far from convinced that truffi-culture was something I wanted to get into.

It was lunchtime by now, and we traipsed through the freezing air towards a local bar. Shadowy specks flew into vision from above, and looking up I saw snowflakes like dinner plates – the largest I had ever seen – falling from a blanket-sky. I held out my hand as one fell into my palm, then watched it quickly dissolve and fade into a tiny drop of water. Vicente slapped me on the back as he came running up from behind, sending the droplet flying.

'Time to eat!' he cried. 'See yourself as a truffle farmer, then?'

The bar had laid on a special seven-course truffle-laden meal in our honour. A good thing too, I thought, for people like me who weren't even totally sure what truffles tasted like. We were, after all, at a truffle conference. It would have been absurd to have learned nothing more than its scientific name and a few suggestions about marketing it on the web. This being a Spanish group lunch on a weekend in a tiny mountain village in late autumn, the wine flowed liberally and we were two bottles in before the first dish was served – salad with shaved black stuff on it.

'That's truffle,' one of the professors intoned, and we all nodded. *That* was truffle? We piled in and I was one of the lucky few to find a piece of this exotic tuber stimulating my taste buds along with a slice of tomato and some lettuce. At first I assumed the professor, despite his obvious advantage over us in these matters, had got it wrong. The gritty substance grinding between my teeth bore an uncanny resemblance to ordinary common-or-garden soil. I was certain because it wasn't the first time soil had made it into my food. Indeed, in my early twenties, before I realised you had to wash vegetables before cooking them, it used to make quite a regular appearance.

I paused, though, before dismissing the whole truffle business out of hand as I noticed that the others around the table were in raptures, while some were digging around the communal salad plate for more of this rare delicacy. It was then that the initially hostile flavour trigger in my mind was switched off and something of the real flavour began to register. There was more to this, although quite what was difficult to say. Something about the smell of it, perhaps. I noticed my mouth salivating unusually as I brought another forkful of the stuff up to swallow. But why? Chewing on, I started to detect something, an earthy tang – not just soil: far more – that was at once exciting and almost dream-like. In fact, I realised with surprise, it was curiously erotic: my hormones seemed to be reacting in ways I didn't normally associate with food. Diving in for more, I decided this was indeed a strange and wondrous thing, both delicate and appetising. I could see now why the first reaction was to think 'soil', but beyond that I was amazed to discover a whole range of other tasting notes, from 'nut' to 'fruit' to 'mushroom' and much more.

An hour and a half later, having waded through truffle pasta, truffle pie, hake with truffle and wild boar with truffle sauce – and God knows how much wine – pudding arrived: vanilla ice cream topped with flaked truffle. I decided to skip that course and headed out into the snow and fading early afternoon light to clear my head, barely able to move after our truffle banquet. I leaned against a railing and took deep breaths, a truffle-flavoured mist streaming into the air from my open mouth as the abnormally large snowflakes settled on top of my head. I looked out over the fields beyond the village, across dry-stone walls to whitened oak forests barely visible in the distance. Right at that moment I might have killed anyone who offered me another truffle or dish laced with the damned things, but the meal – and the conference – had now set me thinking and the seed of an idea was germinating. There was something mysterious and powerful about the taste and flavour of truffles. It was surprising to realise that from virtual indifference I had rapidly shifted through mild curiosity to glowing enthusiasm. Perhaps Vicente was right after all. Perhaps the future – in part at least – did lie in truffles. I thought it through for a moment: a truffle forest would tie in well with our ideas for the farm, for planting trees – especially oaks – up there. It would be a long-term project and we wouldn't get our first crop for years to come. More reason, then, to get going right away.

I shivered and headed back inside the bar, snow crunching underfoot. It looked as if we weren't going anywhere for the time being with weather like this. Which meant more wine, more food, more stories, more truffles. My stomach rumbled at the thought, but the image of that distant oak forest stays stubbornly in my mind.

⋆

Today I saw a scene repeated that I've come across time and again recently – a sparrowhawk chasing away an eagle six or seven times its size. I imagine the eagle is trying to pick up the sparrowhawk's eggs or chicks. There is a slow arrogance about the way the eagle saunters in, but it is easily chased away – the sparrowhawk screams outrageously as it dives at it and harries it off – much like a fighter plane attacking a heavy bomber in a dogfight, perhaps. The eagle quickly gives up, the sparrowhawk goes back to its nest to protect its young, and the eagle, catching a thermal surging up from the mountainside, circles high into the sky before drifting off nonchalantly in search of easier prey.

⋆

Despite being disabled and having to move about mostly on crutches, El Clossa was difficult to keep up with. He skipped nimbly down a steep grassy bank to a ford in the stream below, jumping and hopping his way along. Within moments I had lost him amid all the mud and thick bushes lining the waterside and had to follow by listening out for the clattering of his crutches against stones and rock as he worked his way up the other bank.

'This way,' he called as he raced along. The sky overhead was grey and rumbling, great rolls and waves of pregnant cloud threatening the empty, windswept landscape. The earth felt scarred – a high plateau unprotected against the freezing air hurtling down from the north: austere, rocky, yet green and dramatic. It was hard to imagine the destruction that was about to be unleashed here.

'The electricity company is going to build a massive new sub-station in a valley north of Penyagolosa for all the wind farms they're putting up everywhere,' Concha had told me over the telephone a couple of days earlier. 'El Clossa's found something there I think you'll be interested in. You should go over with him and have a look.'

El Clossa, it turned out, was a stonemason, but, ever a lover of mystery, Concha refused to give me any more clues. She'd arranged a place and a time for me to meet him and that was that.

Our evening at Concha's *mas* had continued until dawn, sitting out in the cold night air outside the front door looking up at the stars. A connection of sorts had been made, and, hesitantly, we allowed ourselves to be drawn in for a time, but always with a view to a possible exit.

'They're interesting – lots of crazy ideas,' Salud said. 'But there's something a bit cultish about them.'

Today, I'd come out on my own, Salud having to head down to Valencia for a couple of days.

I managed to catch up with El Clossa as we passed a small medieval building set on the banks of the stream, with perfect semi-circular arches. It looked to have been a hermitage of some sort, miles from the nearest village yet somehow suited to this romantic location. The poplars lining the stream and the small hillside rising up behind it gave it some protection from the strong winds. It was locked up, now, forgotten.

I wanted to stop and find out more, but I had to hurry to keep up. There was a danger of being left behind.

'Just up here. Not far now.'

We pushed past more thick bushes and low-hanging branches. Whatever path we were following had fallen into disuse and been lost to the reclaiming forces of nature, but every now and again I caught a glimpse of what might be an ancient walkway.

From odd scraps of conversation I was beginning to learn that this landscape was crisscrossed with traditional paths and routes dating back to at least the Bronze Age. Most had been lost now, but many had been in regular use until the previous century, employed mostly by migrant, or transhumance, farmers moving their cattle and sheep between summer and winter pastures.

'This area used to be incredibly rich hundreds of years ago,' El Clossa called back. 'Made their money on merino wool.'

Merino wool, the source of so much of medieval Spain's wealth, had been a closely guarded asset for centuries: it was forbidden to take the animals out of the country on pain of death. But eventually the outside world got hold of them and Spain's monopoly was broken. Today most merino wool – named after the Merinids, a Berber group who settled in Spain during the Moorish period – comes from the southern hemisphere. During the late Middle Ages Tuscan merchants had been particularly keen to get their hands on this king of wools – warmer and more water-resistant than other varieties – and had set up offices in nearby towns to export it.

'Sheep farming was big business round here from the fourteenth century onwards,' El Clossa said.'All these big stone houses you see in the villages in this area?' he said. 'All built by wool merchants. Fifteenth, sixteenth century, that kind of time.'

The routes the farmers had used to move their livestock around, and then to take their wool down to the coast, were the same paths we were now walking on ourselves, and the same you sometimes saw stretching over the hills and valleys.

Man had been crossing this region for thousands of years, yet modern, tarmac roads were still relatively few and far between.

We climbed over some boulders, El Clossa scaling them effortlessly, and came down to a rut in the hillside, shaded by a large oak. This seemed to be it.

'There,' El Clossa said triumphantly.

He knew a lot about the local history, and his ability to race over the hills on his expertly managed crutches was astounding. Now, though, as I stared down into what appeared to be a puddle of mud, I wondered about him for the first time. Was this some kind of wild-goose chase?

'Where?' I asked.

He looked annoyed: I was being slow. He crouched down, laying his crutches to one side, and pointed.

'Here.'

And then I saw it: over a yard and a half long, slender and straight, yet almost the same colour as the ground it was lying in. El Clossa saw the expression on my face.

'That,' he said with a smile, 'is the perfectly preserved, ossified thigh bone of a sauropod.'

For a moment I stood there open-mouthed. I had only ever seen dinosaur bones in museums – preserved, cleaned, assembled and out of reach. Here I had the real thing lying at my feet. I knelt down and touched 180 million years.

'Reckon the whole animal's here lying about,' El Clossa said. 'Probably just fell down one day and died.'

'How did you know it was here? How did you find it?' I asked. He pushed back his grey hair then got up and scuttled away. The question had made him uncomfortable.

'Just knew,' he said.

I remembered Concha saying that he had a nose for these things. The man spent his life working with stone, walking through the countryside collecting and searching. He had a sixth sense for stone, she said. There was no other way to explain it.

I knelt down and ran my fingers along the brown, dirty dinosaur bone once again. What else, I wondered, might be lying beneath our feet?

'Up here!' El Clossa was now further up the hillside and calling me. I got up and followed after him. Some thirty yards on he was resting against a large flat rock, waist-high. Below me, next to the stream, I caught sight again of the small hermitage.

'Look at this,' he said. I watched closely as he ran his finger over the lichen-covered stone, and as he did so, ancient carvings sprang to life in front of me. Circles and straight lines were etched in rows across the upper face, while deeper carvings, like channels for molten metal in a forge, stretched down the sides. Time and the weather had worn them almost smooth, yet they were clearly man-made and very ancient.

'The archaeologists don't know what they are,' El Clossa said. 'Reckon they must be Bronze Age. But look at these.' He pointed to the rows of little circles and straight vertical lines, like digits. 'That looks like writing, an alphabet of some sort. Yet writing was only supposed to be starting at that point in Mesopotamia.'

I put my fingers into the grooves to trace their mysterious shapes. First the dinosaur, now this.

There was a problem, though. El Clossa looked out on to the valley and sighed.

'The archaeologists will be here tomorrow to examine it and dig up what they can,' he said. 'They've been given three weeks. And that only after a fight.'

He pointed at a flat piece of land just a few yards away at the bottom of the valley floor.

'That,' he said, 'is going to be the site of a big new electricity station.' He swept a crutch out in a wide arc with his powerful arm. 'All this is going to be wiped out in less than a month.'

He gave a cough, then snorted.

'It's all these wind farms they're putting up,' he went on. 'They've got to send all that electricity somewhere. So they're cabling it in here before sending it down to the cities on the coast.'

Now I understood Concha's insistence on the phone earlier on – it was the last chance to see this before it disappeared for good.

'What will happen to the dinosaur bones?'

'They'll dig up what they can, clean them up, perhaps put them in a museum one day.'

'And the valley? Can't something be done?' I said. The place was too beautiful, too magical to be destroyed so thoughtlessly.

El Clossa shrugged before skipping away down the hillside. Time was running short.

★

I simply hadn't thought through what a huge task it would be to plant a couple of hundred oaks. 'I'm heading out to plant the truffle trees,' I said to Salud one late November morning. 'Probably be back by teatime.'

Five trees in, the penny began to drop . . .

Having thought it through a little more, I'd decided to plump for the truffle-forest option, and had picked up the mycorrhised oaks and holm oaks from a specialist nursery in the neighbouring province of Teruel. Firstly I had to get the trees, protectors and bamboo supports up to where we were planting – which meant driving the car, fully laden, along a precarious, overgrown mountain track I still hadn't got round to clearing from the last rock fall. The tiny saplings all fitted into the back of my car. That accomplished, for each tree I had to dig a hole with a heavy, Spanish hoe, the traditional tool for the job. This was backbreaking stuff on such hard, rocky earth, although I'd recently managed to clear the land of all the gorse and weeds. According to Ibn al-Awam, holm oaks preferred this kind of environment, high in the mountains, with dry, sandy soil, although he did recommend watering them in the summer. After digging the hole, I had to crouch down, pull the protective plastic pot from around the roots of the oak sapling, place it in the hole without the root ball falling apart, and then cover it up again with soil, filtering out the stones. Once this was done I then placed the plastic protector around the tree and secured it to the bamboo support. Finally I placed larger rocks around the base of the new tree, so that, when it rained, the water wouldn't evaporate so quickly in the sun. At least that was the theory – and what Vicente had told me to do.

It slowly became apparent that this was going to be a much lengthier operation than I'd anticipated. Two hundred very tiny trees might have fitted into the back of the car, but they seemed a hell of a lot more when you had to go through such a complicated process to plant each one. Allowing – on a very conservative estimate – about fifteen minutes for each tree, I was going to need, I realised after some time-consuming multiplication in my head, fifty hours to plant all of them. Straight. Screw all my ideas about getting it done by teatime, I was going to need weeks. And it was tough, physical work – something I was getting used to, but even so: the earth was very hard and still covered in the remains of all the weeds I had chopped. I cursed myself, the thought 'I must be out of my fucking mind' playing itself over and over under my breath.

As I was getting my head round the scale of what I was trying to do, there was a loud shot. Crouching down to get my hands in the dark, blood-red soil (and I don't like to think what might have happened if I hadn't ducked just at that moment), I heard a cracking, or snap, like an enormous whip, immediately followed by a tumbling sound like quickly moving thunderclouds. As I stood up sharply to see what was going on, it was as if I could almost see the noise from the gunfire bellowing across the valley. We were getting used to hearing shotguns now. A *modus vivendi* of sorts between ourselves and the hunters had been established after the previous run-in. They no longer took over our garden on a Sunday morning, but they still popped up now and then. While they kept their distance I had been happy for things to continue this way. This, though, had been far too close.

I heard the panting of an animal somewhere behind me, in the opposite direction from where the shot had come, and then the scuttling of hooves. A wild boar, almost certainly. There I was planting away obliviously while hunter and beast were playing a lethal game of hide and seek around me.

I started running around, scanning the land for the hunters. Though I was clearly visible in my bright worker's overalls, they were probably dressed in camouflage green, and I couldn't catch sight of them. Perhaps they had realised what had happened and had hidden out of embarrassment. I trudged back to my saplings; tree-planting had never seemed such a dangerous activity.

Half an hour later I saw the hunters – a pair of them – walking nonchalantly down our road, stepping out from the protection of the bush and into full view, albeit a good way off. For a moment I fantasised about having a rifle myself, and taking a potshot at them. Arcadio had said once that out here on the mountain, although it might seem we were on our own, someone was always watching you. I just didn't think he meant through the crosshairs of a telescopic lens.

Some minutes later, once the hunters had left, I was surprised to hear birds singing in the trees. I had only subconsciously remarked earlier that the mountain seemed deathly quiet that morning. Now I began to wonder why. I felt sure the birds kept silent whenever hunters were about, who often took potshots at thrushes and other medium-sized birds. But were they even cleverer than that? Could they distinguish between humans who were a threat and those who weren't? I had a fleeting sense of being accepted by the natural world around me, and its gift was the birdsong that now echoed around my ears.

As I was finishing my fifteenth tree, the sun dipped over the horizon and the temperature dropped. I packed up and headed back to the farmhouse. I had planted less than a tenth of the trees. I was dog-tired and decided to call it a day. I would just have to push on with it over the coming weeks.

★

There is an ebb and flow as I get used to the mountain – growing into it, and then withdrawing, as the scale of what needs to be done hits me, or my confidence or energy levels decrease. It has something to do with identity as well – part of the process of *becoming* the person who lives out here, and who can work the land – not just becoming a farmer, or a botanist, or 'country' person, as opposed to a 'town' person – there's more to it than that: almost an expanding and contracting of the self as it takes on board what this entails. I told Arcadio about my plan to plant a truffle forest on our land. 'We were all beginners once,' he said.

★

'We need to ritually purify your land,' Marina said as she poured herself out of Concha's little van once it came to a halt under the oak tree. 'I can feel something here that needs cleansing, moving on. We'll need four twigs of rosemary.'

It had taken some persuasion to get them to come up to our farm. Not that they weren't curious to see it, but there was always something, some previous engagement or obstacle, in the way. And a reluctance, on Concha's part I thought, to move out of her own domain. A new kingdom meant different rules, and she felt more comfortable ruling over her own. In the end only she and Marina had come along: El Clossa was working, Africa wasn't feeling well and Pau had stayed behind to look after her.

Concha got out of her van and immediately rummaged around in the pockets of her striped woollen cardigan for her cigarettes. Lighting one, she inhaled deeply, looked around at the mountains and farmhouses as though inspecting the place, then smiled broadly.

'This is special,' she said. 'But if Marina says it needs purifying, then it needs purifying. You don't mess with her.'

The sun had already passed behind the Picosa and dusk was falling.

'We'll have to get a move on,' Marina said, 'if we want to get it done before dark.'

Salud and I said nothing, unsure as to what ritual she was intending to perform.

'We need to go to the four corners of your land,' she said.

I tried to explain to her how difficult that would be: there were still huge areas we hadn't managed to get to ourselves – either prevented from getting through by the weeds and gorse bushes, or else unable to scale the cliff-face without some kind of climbing gear.

'Never mind,' she said. 'The nearest we can get to them as possible. It'll still work.'

'Let's start over here,' I said.

'That bush,' Marina said. 'Perfect.' And she trotted over to a slope by one of the ruins to where a handful of rosemary plants were growing, their pale-blue flowers fading in the evening light. Scrambling up the stony path, she broke some twigs off and then came back to join us, a bright red velvet scarf pulled round her neck contrasting violently with her green hair and the dark blue T-shirt stretched over her huge form. Pink blotches formed on her exposed upper arms above her elbow from the cold. Concha blew smoke in her direction.

'Ready, *cariño*?' she said.

'What's the rosemary for?' Salud asked.

'It's a powerful plant,' Concha said. 'Lots of cleansing and healing properties. *De las virtudes del romero, se puede escribir un libro entero* – You could write a book on the virtues of rosemary.' It sounded like a proverb. 'People round here use it for reviving tired muscles. But it's also used for *this*.'

The four of us walked over to a group of elm trees round the back of the house. This was roughly the edge of our land on the northern side.

'Let's stand back a bit,' Concha said as Marina got into position. We stumbled backwards over some brambles and stalks of wild fennel. For a moment my attention was distracted, making a mental note to bring the strimmer round here sometime: the place was a jungle.

Marina was holding one of the twigs of rosemary in her hands and rolling the stem between the palms of her hands. 'Elms?' she said, looking up at the naked trees towering over her: two of the older ones had died some years before and stood like weird skeletons behind her.

I nodded and she raised her hands towards them, as though in greeting.

'Good,' she said. I thought about asking her if it made a difference what kind of trees they were, but she had already started the ritual, circling anti-clockwise, head bent down, arms stretched, the rosemary now in her left hand whizzing through the air in a waving arc. A song seemed to be coming from her mouth, long discordant notes. Then, still spinning, she arched down, pulled her head up, closed her eyes and drew her lips together to make a vibrating sound like a baby. I could sense Salud desperately trying to catch my eye, but resisted turning round. Marina might not manage to frighten away any evil spirits, but at least there was a chance that if any were watching they might die laughing.

Suddenly she stopped dead, silent. Salud gave a jump. I watched carefully in case Marina fell over after so much exertion, but she was stock-still, barely moving. She drew out a cigarette lighter to the rosemary and set in on fire. It was still green and fresh, but surprisingly it sparkled and gave off small blue flames for a second or two before extinguishing and letting off a trail of smoke.

'That's a good sign,' Concha said. 'Blue flame is where the spirits are captured, then they can be released.'

Marina was spinning again, this time the other way around, a faint trail of smoke from the rosemary tracing a circle around her before dissipating into the air. She turned five or six times, then stopped again, breathing heavily. I stepped forward to talk to her, to thank her.

'Wait,' said Concha. 'She hasn't finished yet.'

I stepped back again to my place and watched as Marina bent down and stuck the remainder of the rosemary twig in the ground, holding it upright with a couple of stones. Then she stood up, undid the cord holding up her baggy trousers, pulled them down with her knickers in a swift, efficient motion, crouched over the rosemary and urinated on it. Her huge behind had a pale, almost ghoul-like quality to it in the reduced light.

'That's to seal the spell,' Concha said. 'They can't come back now. Ever.'

'Thank God for that,' Salud said.

It took almost an hour in the fading light to reach the other three corners of our land and repeat the ritual, first Concha, then I – reluctantly – dousing the smoking rosemary as Marina had done the first time

Our last corner to purify was back down the track, where it crossed the gorge. I had always liked this little area: two large old oak trees stood over it giving it plentiful shade, while a great rock, ten metres high and about the same breadth, sat there at the edge of the gulley behind them, a huge presence. It must have fallen thousands, perhaps millions, of years before from the cliff-face above it and come to a final rest here. It was, I thought, a perfect place for boyhood games: climbing and hide and seek.

Again the mad circling and lighting of the rosemary. Salud refused to take part, though, and so I had to jump in at the last minute and piss on the damn thing in her place.

'Wait!' said Marina as we were all about to head back to the house. It was almost dark now. There was a moment's silence as we turned to look at her.

'I can feel spirits here – *duendes*,' Marina said finally.

'Where?' I said.

'Here, underneath these trees. They come from' – she turned around and pointed dramatically – 'that stone.' It was the large rock half shaded by the branches of the oaks.

Duende is a generic Spanish term for spirit or earth spirit – often translated into English as 'goblin', but with a much wider meaning. In flamenco it refers to the ineffable experience of power and other-worldliness that can only be produced in the very best performances, while across the country *duendes* can refer to anything from water nymphs to 'little people' living invisibly side by side with us. It is similar to the Middle Eastern concept of 'jinn'. I had no idea if such things existed, but now someone was seriously suggesting there was a whole community of them living at the bottom of our garden.

'*Duendes*,' I said.

'That,' Marina growled, 'is a Duende Stone.'

'A place through which they can travel from their dimension into our own,' Concha said before I could ask.

'I see,' I said. 'Is that good?'

After dinner was over we sat around the kitchen table chatting for a while, Concha asking about the dinosaur hunt with El Clossa.

'These people have no sensibility, *cariño*,' she said before I could say very much. 'How could you build an electric sub-station on such a beautiful site? Apart from its sheer ugliness and inappropriateness, it will interfere with the energies there.'

It was clear she wasn't referring to the ones that powered your fridge or cooker.

'These things will be lost for ever – they can't be brought back.'

'Talking of energies,' Marina said, 'take a look at this.'

Sitting next to Concha, set slightly back, Marina was hunched over something held in her hand concentrating hard. I leaned over to get a closer look, and saw a tiny pendulum swinging rapidly from her fingers.

'There's someone here,' Marina said with a knowing smile, her head perfectly still over the nervously twitching bead suspended from her fingers.

Salud shuffled in her seat.

'A girl,' said Marina. 'Perhaps ten or twelve years old. She's wearing a little apron, like they used to in the 1920s and 1930s.'

'Where?' asked Salud, getting to her feet.

'Here, *cariño*,' Concha said. 'Right here.'

'Are you saying there's a ghost in this house?' Salud said. I could see where this was going: first the bugs and the bees. Now I was going to have to convince her to cohabit with the spirit of a long-dead schoolgirl as well. *Duendes* were one thing, but now this? Salud could cope with armed men wandering around our land on a Sunday morning – that was fine, it was tangible. But spooky things like spiders and phantoms . . .? I could already see myself sleeping alone that night, Salud driving down the mountain at top speed back to the certainties of the city.

'I can see a tree, right here, behind the house,' Marina went on. 'That's where she is. She died up here and they planted a tree where they buried her.'

Silence, the pendulum spinning, then darting and changing direction. Marina nodded.

'She had TB. After the war. She was sad because her elder brother died fighting at the front. Used to live here with her and her parents.'

We spent most of that night lying awake in bed: me trying to convince Salud there were no such things as ghosts; she trying to convince herself she really enjoyed life out on a mountain.

The next day I went scouting around the back of the house. On her way out Marina had quickly pointed at a tree and identified it as the one under which the girl was supposedly buried. I kicked around the base of it, as though half expecting to uncover a finger pointing out at me or something. The tree could be the right age – less than a hundred years old, I reckoned, but there were a few others planted in the same area of about the same age: nothing seemed to say this was a special spot, a place where someone might have buried their little girl.

Still pondering this, I heard Arcadio's Land Rover pull up on the *era* behind me. The car door opened and he walked over to where I was standing.

'You don't know about some people here in the 1920s or 1930s losing a little girl, do you?' He was certainly old enough, I thought, to have been around then, and would have heard something. 'Died of tuberculosis?'

'Little girl?' he said. 'Don't know anything about that.'

I heaved a sigh of relief. *Duendes*, ghosts. Those bloody witches had virtually lost us a good night's sleep with all their stories. I looked forward to telling Salud when I saw her. Creepy-crawlies were one thing. The supernatural was something else.

'There was a boy, though,' Arcadio said. My smile dropped. 'Son of the farmer who used to live up here.' He looked me straight with his small, intense yellow eyes.

'Sent him to the front during the war. Got killed near Teruel. Family never got over it.'

I tried to speak, but couldn't say anything.

'Terrible thing, war,' he said.

Part II

Air

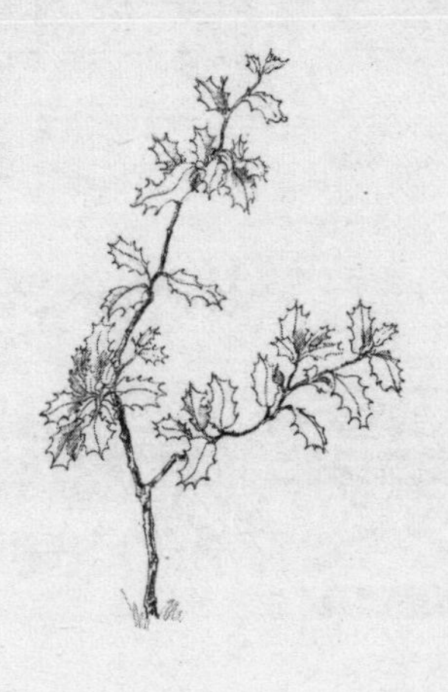

The Story of the Charcoal-burner's Daughter

Once upon a time there was a poor old charcoal-burner who lived in the forest with his daughter. One day, not having anything to eat, the charcoal-burner went to the King to ask for alms. The King was very impressed by the way the man spoke.

'How did you learn to talk like that?' he asked.

'From my daughter,' said the charcoal-burner. 'Poverty and hunger have made her the cleverest in all the land.'

'If that is so,' said the King, 'I shall marry her myself. Here,' he said, 'take these eggs and tell your daughter to hatch them so that we may have chickens for when we are married.'

So the charcoal-burner took the eggs back to his home and gave them to his daughter, telling her everything that had happened. The daughter, though, weighed the eggs in her hands and realised they had been hard-boiled. It was a trick.

'Let me sleep on it, father,' she said, 'and I will come up with a solution.'

The next morning she took a handful of oats and ground them into flour.

'You see this?' she said to her father. 'I want you to go to the King and tell him to sow this so that we might have oats to feed the chickens we shall have when we are married.'

The charcoal-burner did as she said and gave the message to the King. The King was very surprised. But he thought for a moment, and he pulled out a piece of cloth which he proceeded to cut up into tiny pieces.

'Take this to your daughter, and tell her to make swaddling clothes out of it for our first-born child, God willing,' he said.

'How on earth will my daughter get out of this one?' thought the charcoal-burner. And he took the rags back to his home in the forest and told his daughter what had happened.

'Let me sleep on it, father,' she said. 'And I will come up with a solution.'

The next morning she took some branches of wood and broke them into little twigs.

'Take these to the King,' she told her father, 'and tell him to make a cradle out of them for our first-born child.'

The charcoal-burner did as she asked, and gave the message to the King. Once again the King was speechless on hearing the reply. But he thought for a moment and said: 'Take this basket back to your daughter, and tell her to fill it with laughter.'

The poor old charcoal-burner trudged back to the forest.

'He's really done it this time,' he thought. And he tried laughing into the basket himself, ha-ha-ha. But every time he looked inside to see if it was still there the laughter seemed to have slipped away.

When he got back home he told his daughter what had happened.

'Let me sleep on it, father,' she said.

The next morning she told her father to go and catch three dozen small birds and place them inside the basket, and cover them with a cloth.

'Take it to the King when he is sitting down for dinner,' she said, 'and say it is from me, and that he is to remove the cloth.'

Now it so turned out that that evening the King had invited a large number of guests to dinner. The charcoal-burner did as his daughter asked and he placed the covered basket in front of the King. But when the King lifted the cloth, all the little birds flew up into the air and darted around the dining hall. Everyone dived for cover; cups of wine were sent flying, food fell to the floor and in the panic all the guests landed in a heap on top of one another. And they thought it was so funny, they laughed and laughed until some of them couldn't even stand up.

Now the King was aware that the clever girl was getting the better of him, and so he said to the charcoal-burner: 'Right! Go and tell your daughter she is to come and visit me. But she must come neither dressed nor undressed, neither on the road nor off it, and neither riding nor on foot.'

The charcoal-burner returned home with a heavy heart to pass the message on. His daughter slept that night, as usual, and the next morning she said: 'Father, I want you to go up on to the mountain and catch me the wildest goat there.'

When he was gone, she undressed and wrapped herself in a big piece of netting. Then, when her father returned, she got on the goat's back and went to see the King. The goat was as wild as the wind, and it bucked and kicked all the way. Sometimes it stayed on the road, while at others it ran off it. And whenever it managed to throw the girl off its back she simply followed behind before leaping back on again.

So as the King had commanded, she was neither dressed nor undressed, neither riding nor on foot, and neither on nor off the road.

When he saw her, the King realised he was defeated, and he agreed they should be married. But he insisted that it would be only on one condition.

'What is that?' asked the girl.

'That you may never give any advice to anyone else. If you do you will have to return to your father's home in the forest.'

'And may I not be allowed to take anything with me?' she said.

'Well,' said the King, 'you could take one jewel with you.'

'And it wouldn't matter how big it was?'

'Any jewel you like,' he said.

So the King and the clever girl got married and they were very happy together.

Time passed and one day a man came to stay the night at the palace. He had a mare with him and asked where he could stable her.

'In there,' said the King's servants. 'Next to that horse.'

The next morning the mare had had a foal. But the King claimed it as his.

'There was no other animal in the stable apart from my horse,' said the King. 'The horse must have had the foal.'

The servants tried to tell him that the guest's mare had been in there as well that night, but the King wouldn't listen.

'Don't argue!' he shouted.

No one wanted to cross the King, but when the Queen found out about it, she went to find the guest to talk to him.

'Take this fishing rod and go to that dry pond over there,' she said.

'When the King passes he will ask what you are doing. You must say: "Fishing for sardines". When he asks how you expect to fish for sardines in a dry pond, you must answer: "It is as easy to fish for sardines in a dry pond as it is for a horse to give birth to a foal".'

The guest did as the Queen advised and went and sat with the fishing rod by the dry pond. When the King passed he called out:

'What are you doing?'

'Fishing for sardines,' came the guest's reply.

'How do expect to fish for sardines in a dry pond?' laughed the King.

'As easily as I expect a horse to give birth to a foal,' said the guest.

The King was furious.

'Go on, take your foal,' he said. 'And never come back!'

Now the King knew the Queen must have given advice to the guest and he went to find her in the palace.

'You have broken our agreement,' he said.

'So that you would not do our guest an injustice,' she said.

'Never mind that!' cried the King. 'You must leave!'

'Can we not have one last supper together?' asked the Queen. 'And I shall leave tomorrow.'

Now the King had loved his Queen and so he agreed to this last request. But that night the Queen placed a powerful sleeping potion in his wine and he fell fast asleep. When she saw that he wasn't going to wake up, the Queen ordered a carriage and drove him to her father's home in the forest. There she lay him down among all the charcoal, with dust and cobwebs falling on his face.

The King was shocked when he woke up in this small, dark place.

'Where am I?' he cried.

'You are at my father's,' the Queen said, appearing at his side. 'The agreement was that I could take one jewel with me should you ever force me to leave. So I looked around the palace, but the only jewel I wanted was you. And now here you are.'

The King laughed loud and long when he heard this, and he realised the clever girl – his Queen – had outwitted him once again.

And so they went back to live in the palace, and thenceforth the King allowed her to give as much advice to whoever she liked. And it is said they are still living happily together to this day.

DECEMBER

> *After autumn comes winter, which is made up of three months. The first of these is called* December *in Latin,* Kanun el-Awal *in Syriac and* Deymah *in Persian, and is made up of thirty-one days. During this month the days finally stop getting shorter and start getting longer, while the nights begin to wane. It is the time when the* samayemo el-bardi *phenomenon occurs – the cold, so-called Nights of Darkness, which are forty in number: the first twenty coming after the eleventh of the month, lasting until the end, and the second twenty stretching into January. Now narcissus appear, the citrus fruits ripen, and the early almonds blossom. According to Kastos and others, this is the time for laying fertiliser mixed with ash around fruit trees. Azib says in his* Book of Astronomy *that this is also the month for sowing leeks: they should be grown for one year before being pulled up for eating. Finally, this is also when white poppies should be sown.*
>
> Ibn al-Awam, *Kitab al-Falaha*, The Book of Agriculture, 12th century

It is slowly getting colder, but still the sun shines and no rain has fallen since early November. The river, which suddenly kicked back into life at the top of the valley, has dried up once again, only a few remaining puddles hinting at the underground currents that pass along this way. It is always a beautiful sound when the river flows as far as the turning to the house: stopping to open the chain before driving up the final stretch, you hear the gurgling of water just a few feet away on the other side of the pine trees, while in the evening frogs and toads croak along its banks. Water brings life to the area, colours trapped underground bursting forth all of a sudden.

I've finally put my hand to rebuilding some of the dry-stone walls.

Or, rather, I've tried rebuilding one of them, and it's yet to fall over, so I'm judging it a success – of sorts. The stones are heavier than I'd realised, and the blood blisters under my nails pay testament to where I didn't pull my fingers away in time as I plonked them down. It's an intuitive process: the first section looks awful, and I'll probably have to pull it down and start all over again. But during the second half it started to come together. And there were even brief moments when, as if in a state of grace, I bent down and picked up just the right stone for the gap I was looking at. You know when this is happening because the stone makes a very satisfactory *whoompf* sound as it falls into place, and it just stays there, not rocking or moving, looking every bit as though it had been there for years, or even centuries. This is one of the great things about a dry-stone wall: if it's half-decently made, once it's up it has an ancient, part-of-the-land feel about it.

After about an hour the basic idea behind it seemed to make itself clear: the stones need to lean into the bank being built against, while if they have a flat face of some kind this needs to be facing the front. What happens at the back is unimportant, as it gets filled in with rubble and soil. And despite the temptation to place longer stones lengthwise, thus filling more wall space, I quickly learned that the structure benefited far more by laying them across the width of the wall, pointing into the slope. Viewed from above like this they look almost like teeth, and give a sensation of cutting into the mountain and holding the wall together. But building isn't always an easy task with the stone we have here, which is rough and uneven. In other areas, particularly to the north and west of Penyagolosa, there are whole fields full of perfectly flat, smooth rocks that would make this task a doddle. We just have to make do with what we've got. It's a start, though, and I notice now that when I'm outside my eyes instinctively start searching the landscape for dry-stone walls, trying to pick up tips and ideas to improve my technique.

★

With so much concentration on the almonds, and then on the truffle oaks, it was easy to overlook the fact that we had about a dozen olive trees hidden on a terrace below the house. Noticing in early December that other farmers further down in the valley were already harvesting their crops, we decided it might be a good time to have a look at our own. Only four trees actually had any fruit on them, and even then a couple of them only on a few branches. I wasn't sure why the rest of them had no olives, although the lack of pruning and general tending to over recent years probably had much to do with it. It was only now that I gave them a closer examination that I realised they weren't quite the squat, neat trees we saw on other people's land, the olives never more than an arm's reach away. Several of ours had grown quite tall. They probably needed a good feeding as well. Ibn al-Awam emphasised the need to fertilise trees, particularly at this time of year, but I wasn't sure where I could get some good-quality animal dung. Perhaps from the local goatherd, but I hadn't seen him for months.

Still, we spent a couple of days beating, dragging and pulling off what olives there were. I was surprised at the variety there seemed to be: small green ones, *arbequinas*; large black ones, which Salud referred to as *fargas*; and small but longish and pointed half-green, half-purple ones, that grew on the tree in bunches, like grapes – possibly *cornicabras*.

It was a slow affair, picking many olives off individually as a large proportion refused to fall to the ground when we beat the trees with special yellow rakes. Bit by bit the sheets of white plastic we placed underneath filled up with dots of green and black, occasional leaves and twigs joining them. There was a satisfying sound as the rake flew through the air, striking the tree before the olives started to fall. *Whoosh. Thwack. Patter-patter-patter.* It was a strangely pleasing and calming activity.

Salud seemed to have got over the worst of the ghost scare, although I hadn't mentioned to her what Arcadio had told me about the farmer's son. I convinced myself it was because there just wasn't time: our days were filled with endless tasks, from chopping firewood and keeping the house going to all the farm activities and planting trees: in the evenings, when we finally stopped, we were often too tired for much conversation, simply staring deep into the flames of the fire in a trance state before finally collapsing into bed. The real reason, though, was that I didn't want to frighten her again.

In the distance the hunters were back, chasing and shooting at a couple of wild boar, it being a Thursday. We could hear their shouts and cries from across the gulley, while the barking of their dogs sounded like a single beast with innumerable heads.

And yet this time their presence didn't really disturb us. It was as if we had entered a cocoon of our own – the two of us in some kind of communion with the olive trees, as though they themselves had the ability to induce in us a state of relaxation and peace. At one point Salud even started talking to the trees, congratulating them on having so many olives in the first place, despite having been abandoned over the past few years.

In this unhurried, pensive frame of mind, I found myself wondering about the olive branch as a symbol of peace. Perhaps, a thought formed itself somewhere, we were absorbing some substance from the trees through our hands which calmed us somehow. Could this be the reason behind the mythological importance of the olive branch?

'My grandmother always used to drink a glass of hot water with seven olive leaves in it before going to bed,' Salud said when I mentioned the idea to her. 'She said it was to help reduce her blood pressure.'

I recalled how Arcadio had stopped the heavy bleeding in her finger by using a simple weed. Since then I'd started to find out a little bit more from him about the medicinal properties of the plants we walked past or over every day. I didn't like to ask him straight out: it wasn't the way he did things. But he seemed to have understood it was something I was interested in, and a few gems had appeared during our conversations: artichokes – of which we had one growing wild near the beehives – were helpful for diabetics and people with liver complaints; bitter chamomile, or *botja*, was an antiseptic and could be used to ease sore feet; rock tea, which grew near the spring, was good for almost anything – an anti-inflammatory and detoxifier, as well as being helpful for stomach problems. Meanwhile the savin juniper, which dotted the mountainside, light-green little cones bursting out of the rocks, had been used to rid farm animals of parasites, leaving branches from the tree to soak in water and then giving the water to the animals to drink. Woman had also been known to take it to abort unwanted children. Sometimes the mountains felt like a drugstore where all the prescriptions had been lost and the pharmacists had died or gone into hiding.

Some herbs in particular seemed to have a special importance. Thyme, picked in April or May, when it was in flower, was a stimulant, and good for the circulation. Lying close to the ground and with dull green leaves, you often only became aware of it as your foot crushed it during a walk over the hillsides, releasing a rich scent pregnant with memories of roasted meats and grilled fish. It had strong medicinal properties, being good both for reducing bloating as well as soothing the nerves. The hunters drank thyme tea as a stimulant after a night out on the mountains. Arcadio recommended it to ease period pains, adding that its antiseptic qualities made it a common cure for coughs. Drinking it after a heavy meal also eased digestion.

Rosemary, meanwhile, was the Queen of the Countryside, its pale blue flowers like droplets from the sky. *Romero, para amor verdadero*, people said, as they plucked a twig or two on a country walk to take back home with them: rosemary, for true love. No Spanish woman considered a walk out of her village or town complete without picking up some rosemary along the way – either for cooking (it is used especially in a paella, thrown in just before the rice is done to impart aroma to the dish), or to ward off the evil eye: Gypsy women make a habit of thrusting it in your hands in the hope of opening your purse, while the men can often be seen walking with a sprig of the herb poking from their mouths, almost like a cigarette, to bring luck.

Rosemary, Arcadio informed me, had many medicinal uses. The flowers of the herb are soaked in alcohol for nine days; the resulting liquid was useful for all kinds of skin complaints, from rashes to cuts and bruises, while infusions of rosemary increased circulation and stimulated appetite. The smoke from the plant, placed on a hot plate or stove, was meant to ease the symptoms of asthma.

Rosemary was often used to light a fire, and was highly valued as a firewood. A local Christmas carol, sung after midnight mass as everyone comes out into the cold night air, goes:

Pastorets i pastoretes
fue-me llenya, que tinc fred
no me la feu d'angilaga
feu-me-la de romeret.

O shepherds and shepherdesses,
Bring me some firewood
Not just twigs from the gorsebush
But nice branches of rosemary.

We took the olives down to the press in a nearby village on the feast day of the *Inmaculada* – the Immaculate Conception. At the agricultural co-op, according to what I'd heard, you took your freshly picked crop, they weighed it and then you got a certain amount of oil based on how many olives you'd taken in; everyone's olives were mixed together.

We filled about three large rubber buckets – *capazos* – and drove them down. The co-op was in a warehouse on the edge of the village. Lights were buzzing against the dark winter air and a crowd of people and cars were huddled around. A tall, bald man in grey overalls showed us the ropes – we took a ticket and waited our turn. At the entrance to the warehouse was a large hole in the ground covered by a thick lattice grid. People drove their cars up to it, unloaded their crop, then tipped the contents down the hole, olives, leaves and everything. A conveyor belt picked it all up from the bottom of the hole and carried it towards a machine that separated the olives from the rest. Then another conveyor belt took the clean olives to a big metal container where they were weighed. From here a third conveyor belt took it up to a massive metal trench where all the olives were stored before being pressed. It looked like something Heath Robinson would have been proud of; the whole series of machines made a tremendous racket, while a sour, fruity, not altogether pleasant smell filled the place.

There was great honking of horns and general chaos as cars reversed in and then drove away again with their loads: no one wanted to wait in the cold, so anyone holding things up was sharply reprimanded. One woman with short mousy hair and thick glasses tried to speed things up by helping the people ahead of her in the queue; she was almost pole-axed when the long steel pole she was using to prod olives at the bottom of the hole got stuck in the conveyor belt and snapped back at her viciously. She let go of it just in time, but quickly retreated: no more helping other people.

Most of the others' olives were black or deep purple, with only a handful of green ones. I wondered about those still sitting in the back of our car, waiting their turn to be cast down into this mechanical pit – they were almost all green, some quite hard and small. Perhaps we hadn't given them enough time to ripen.

After a long cold wait, in which we saw the locals pour bucket after bucket of fresh, ripe olives down the hole, it was our turn. In the harsh fluorescent light of the warehouse our crop looked even greener than it had back up on the mountain. Everyone around looked on with disapproval as we very quickly sent our paltry specimens down into the gaping mouth of the olive machine. They simply weren't completely ripe, and our best efforts to clean the fruit of any encumbering leaves and twigs were a waste of time – there was a machine for that. Only a fool would waste hours on such a task. I walked over to the man in the grey overalls, who was standing at a grubby computer taking the measure of how much fruit we'd fed into his great machine.

'Very unripe,' he said with a look of resignation. He'd probably taken a measure of us as soon as we'd walked in – despite wearing dirty, country clothes, we were obviously city types at heart, as green as the olives we'd just brought in.

'How much?' I asked eagerly. After two full days threshing trees, our hands scratched and sore, I wanted to hear a big round number, something that would make me proud of this, our first harvest.

He looked up at the screen. It said 49 kilos. He gave another resigned smile. Then it flashed 50 and stopped.

'That's all right then,' he said. 'You might at least get a litre or two out of that.' He ripped off a piece of paper from the printer and handed it to us. 'Come back in a week or so to collect.' Then he turned to the waiting crowd behind us.

'Next!'

A litre or two. All that work for a litre or two of oil. Despite my disappointment, though, I smiled: it would be *our* oil, from *our* olive trees, doubtless it would be the best olive oil I had ever tasted. That was worth all the effort.

Salud poured us both a glass of wine when we got back. 'To our first olive crop,' she said. We clinked glasses and settled down in front of the fire. Outside an owl was hooting away, while cold draughts did their best to push through the cracks in the doors and windows. A gale was blowing in again from the north-west, blustering bursts of air hurtling over the house. Starting, making mistakes, learning, amending, carrying on. There was a mountain to climb.

★

The thirteenth of December – *Sta Llúcia* – St Lucy's Day. Like thousands of women across the country, Salud takes down last year's mistletoe from where it was hanging over the back door, burns it in a pan outside by squirting lighter fuel on to it and striking a match, then places a new sprig up above the window in its place. I've found some pine trees further up the valley with mistletoe growing on them and cut a bunch down for her. She says it's traditional to do it on this day – it absorbs 'negativity', which is then dissipated at the end of the year when you burn it. Marina would be proud. I am about to ask whether it will work for keeping away the ghost girl, but think better of it.

★

A week or so after dropping off our olives at the co-operative, I went round to see if our oil was ready. Where previously the place had been packed with people delivering their crop, now there was no one and the place seemed deserted. I poked my head round the door and was met by the familiar smell of slightly acidic, fermenting olives.

A girl was sitting at the desk, smoking and listening to the radio. I handed her my receipt.

'Filtered or unfiltered?' she asked.

'What's the difference?' I said.

'Unfiltered's cloudy and you get more of it,' she said.

Half an hour later I was back at the farm clutching two five-litre plastic bottles of thick, green, opaque liquid, a loaf of fresh bread under my arm. Salud was waiting for me.

'Time for an *almuerzo* – a mid-morning snack,' she said.

She decanted some of the oil into a little bottle, broke the bread and placed two plates on the table. We poured drops of oil on to the plates and then simultaneously reached down to dip bread into it before bringing it up to our mouths.

'To our first crop,' she said.

'Cheers.'

Perhaps only once or twice in my life had I tried such a richly flavoured oil. The smell alone was worth every effort we had put into harvesting, a strong, deep, earthy scent that connected directly with some pleasure centre in the brain. It tasted magnificent, too, with just a hint of a spicy kick at the back of the throat.

'How come you can never buy this kind of stuff in the shops?' I asked. Even the best 'named' olive oils I'd tried – usually from Jaén province in northern Andalusia – weren't up to this standard. There was something raw, pure and genuine about this oil.

'Would *you* sell this?' Salud said.

She laughed as we both bent down to dip our bread for a second helping.

⋆

Out on the mountainside planting the oak saplings, I heard a loud cracking sound coming from the top of the cliff-face above. I thought for a moment that the hunters had returned, but there was something different about the noise – less of an explosion and more as if something had been struck. I turned to look up and caught sight of two male ibexes on the very edge of the precipice, great ribbed horns rising proudly from their heads. They were facing each other at close quarters, their bodies seemingly relaxed, but with a tension that was perceptible even from where I was standing. I dropped my tools and fished out my binoculars: before I'd managed to find them and focus there came another crack, echoing across the gorge from hillface to hillface. I scanned the clifftop and found them a few metres on, one standing strong and in his place, the other circling, pacing around him, perhaps the younger of the two. The rutting season must be about to begin: this was a fight over who controlled the harem.

We often saw the ibex trotting around the mountainside. I had caught sight of them about a month before, a whole group of about thirty animals – mostly females. The males, of which there were about three, perhaps four, seemed to be cohabiting peacefully back then – before the females went on heat.

There was a pause in the fight as the two drew breath. I wondered how much of this was show, or if they were really serious. Could they do actual harm to each other?

My question was soon answered as they came together again, raised themselves simultaneously on to their hind legs, then in unison fell crashing down, horns against horns, forehead against forehead. Involuntarily, I took a breath: it was shocking to see the ferocity of the combat. But this time they carried on, and within seconds were back on their hind legs, heads smashing down against one another, the whole weight of each animal bearing down on the other. The pain and pressure where their two skulls met would be immense. How on earth did they not dash each other's brains out?

They lifted again, ready for another clash. This was no mere locking of horns; in fact the horns didn't seem to play too big a role in it: the cranium took the brunt of the blow.

Again they smashed into each other, neither seeming to gain the upper hand. The one I assumed to be older had moved away, but the younger one had yet to defeat him. In fact he, too, looked worn out. There was another brief hiatus as they trotted around each other, sometimes appearing not to care what was going on, with a kind of nonchalant arrogance. I kept my eyes fixed firmly on them.

After a minute or so they were back in the fray. There was a curious moment each time just before they banged their heads together: both on hind legs, both slightly uneasy not to have four legs on the ground, both watching each other intensely, with the hint that either one might back down at any moment. But each time they threw themselves at each other with all their might. It seemed neither would accept defeat. The older one had to be removed, otherwise he would remain as head of the group: he was the man to beat.

They cracked against each other, then cracked again, the sound barrelling across the valley. Neither moved from the edge of the cliff, as though this momentous battle had to take place in the most dramatic and dangerous venue possible.

It seemed they couldn't go on, pounding and pounding each other over and over again. Then they stopped. For a second I thought another pause had come, a mutually agreed suspension of hostilities while each one recuperated for the next round. But something caught my eye. The older of the ibexes staggered a little. The younger one stood still, half turning his head as though only wanting to watch with one eye. Then his opponent stumbled away from him, inches from the edge of the cliff. He kicked in vain at the loosening rocks beneath his feet, but it was as if he could no longer carry his own weight. And in a flash he was falling – falling down the face of the mountain, hitting an outcrop of stone as he dropped before landing heavily on the slope below, his head flopping from side to side lifelessly as he slid another ten, twenty metres, and then disappeared into the bushes and trees near the top of the gorge. There was a brief rustle, then silence.

It all occurred so quickly that it took me several moments to realise what had happened. I had only been able to catch his fall by taking the binoculars away from my eyes. Meanwhile, at the top of the mountain, the younger, victorious ibex looked down for a few seconds at where his enemy had fallen, and then turned and trotted calmly away out of sight. His dead foe might even have been his own father, I thought. How long before the same thing happened to him?

It crossed my mind for a moment to go and look for the ibex's body, but it was some distance away, on a section of the mountainside that was difficult to get to. The sun was falling and it would soon be dark.

Within minutes I noticed great shadows moving overhead. Glancing up I saw the long-fingered, rectangular wings of a couple of vultures, circling gracefully over the cliff-face. Seconds later they were joined by another two. Doubtless the glorious, powerful ibex that had been fighting as head of the herd only minutes before now lay dead where he had fallen. All trace of him would soon be erased from the earth.

*

Strong winds came. We battened ourselves down inside the house as best we could, while the land outside was left battered and bruised. The next morning I went out to inspect and see if any damage had been done. Most of the mature trees had survived, but a few smaller branches lay scattered over the road and in the fields. I remembered a comment of Arcadio's. 'Up here where you are,' he said, 'you're actually *in* the weather.' I loved watching the clouds settling in the valley below us on calmer, rainier days: it gave me a bird's sense of space and freedom. But when the winds came I longed to be several hundred metres lower down, less exposed. There were ruins of *masos* even higher up than we were: these small, squat buildings must have been made to withstand almost anything the weather could throw at them.

The situation was less rosy when I checked the truffle plantation. By now I'd managed to plant about a hundred oak trees, each one carefully placed with its own plastic protecting tube. The tubes weren't exactly attractive, but they were supposed to help the young saplings survive the first few years safe from predators: the ibex, I thought, might well be tempted by their fresh shoots, although the holm oak leaves had little thorns, much like holly. But now I realised that using the protectors had been a mistake. Although staked firmly into the ground with a bamboo stick, they had been shuffled about in the winds: half had been uprooted altogether, while the remainder were just hanging on. The worst of it, though, was that in jiggling about they had exposed and damaged the root balls of many saplings, which were now exposed to the cold.

It was clear what I had to do: I rounded up the stray protecting tubes, pulled out the ones that were still in place, before getting down on my hands and knees and carefully trying to replant the saplings. Many would be all right, I thought: with handfuls of fresh soil packed around the base they would probably pull through. Others, though, were in trouble, and some were even lying flat, having been all but ripped out of the ground. These I planted again, but with little hope for their survival. With a bit of luck I might be able to limit my losses to less than twenty trees. Still, it was a blow: I knew how much effort had gone into planting each one of them.

Later that morning I caught sight of El Clossa's blue pickup making its way towards us from further down the valley.

'Grab your coats,' he said, tapping a crutch impatiently on the ground when he finally reached the *mas*. 'We're going out for lunch.'

We followed him in our car as he took off at speed down the hill. Minutes later we had passed the village and were back on dirt tracks leading towards Penyagolosa.

'Where did he say we were heading?' Salud asked.

'He didn't.'

It was hard to keep up with him as he sped along treacherous lanes covered in loose rocks or pitted with great axle-destroying holes. Yet he drove much as he walked.

As we gained altitude, we hit a snow line where a sprinkling of white had been shaken on to the landscape. Just a few metres further down, back at the farm, it was still T-shirt weather in the intense winter sun, yet here we seemed to have entered another world, one that lay almost on our doorstep, where winter was in full flow.

El Clossa sped along, seeming to care little about details such as corners, precipitous drops at the edge of the track, steep inclines. I rammed the car into four-wheel drive as we started skidding around on the ice. If I lost sight of him we would be in trouble: the track divided at regular intervals with no indication of which way to go. Besides, he hadn't given us time to find out where we were heading.

After almost an hour of rally driving, we passed near the peak of Penyagolosa and started to descend. In the near distance we caught sight of a tiny village perched on a curious outcrop of rock in the middle of a wide valley.

'Xodos!' Salud exclaimed. 'It's a lovely little place. I did some gigs up here a few years back.'

'There?' I said. 'There can't be more than fifty people living there.'

'There aren't, you're right,' she said. 'But they know how to throw a fiesta.'

I was intrigued that this picturesque, hidden village, barely a hamlet by the looks of it, should be the party capital of the province. It certainly didn't appear to be rocking on this midweek afternoon in mid-December.

We drove up into the village, circling past oak woods and barren brown fields, passing underneath the rock on which it was perched before doubling back on ourselves and creeping through a tiny entrance between two old stone houses. We parked next to an old iron spring, a drinking water fountain, in a main square the size of a handkerchief. El Clossa was already out of his car and cooling the back of his head in the stream of spring water before we'd taken stock of where we were.

'Come on,' he called to us. 'We're going to be late.' And he vanished through a doorway covered with a curtain of heavy wooden beads.

We shuffled in behind him as quickly as we could, trying to keep up with his relentless pace.

It was a large, dark bar and restaurant, heavy brown beams stretching across the low roof, small windows on the far side casting a minimum of light into the room. Three elderly men were sitting on wooden chairs around a cast-iron stove in the centre of the main area.

'Victor!' El Clossa called boisterously as we stepped inside. 'I've brought a student for you.'

He turned to me.

'This,' he said, 'is *el Rey de las Trufas* – the Truffle King.'

Small and squat, like so many elderly men in the area, the Truffle King, the owner of the restaurant, held out a rough, suspicious hand for me to shake, then nodded towards Salud.

'It's all right,' El Clossa said, '*son del terreno* – they're part of the land; they're locals.'

The Truffle King's weather-worn face looked to be carved of stone – eyes far apart, a small upturned nose – but there was a noticeable change in his expression, if still wary.

'Well,' he said, his tiny, thin mouth barely opening when he spoke, 'if you're friends of El Clossa, you're welcome.'

We sat at a table next to a window set deep into the stone walls. Everything in the room seemed to speak of cold, hard winters, of long evenings spent huddled in here against the dark and the freezing winds outside. The ceiling was low, the walls were a yard thick, the windows were small and protected inside and out by heavy wooden shutters. The black iron stove stood at the centre of the room, while the chimney pipe stretched diagonally halfway across before rising up through the roof, to take advantage of as much heat as possible. To one side, tucked into a small alcove, was the bar, and behind it another fireplace set high in the wall. From the grills and pans hanging to either side it seemed this was used for cooking. I had picked up the scent of meats and smoking fat as we walked in. We were going to eat well here.

The Truffle King brought us small glasses of beer – *cañas* – to whet our appetites, while a short woman about the same age with grey hair, glasses and a pout came to take our order. She was, I thought, probably his wife, which made her – what? The Truffle Queen? Where exactly had El Clossa brought us? It felt like something out of a fairy tale. Was there a Truffle Princess running about the place somewhere as well?

El Clossa ordered so fast we couldn't catch what he was saying.

'He seems to be speaking in some kind of code language,' Salud whispered to me while his attention was momentarily elsewhere.

'Don't worry,' the Truffle King said turning back to us. 'You'll love it.'

For the first few dishes the food was good, if unexceptional – the usual plates of salad, some *esgarraet* – dried cod and roasted red peppers, fresh bread, a bowl of consommé. All this came out of the kitchen, to the far side of the dining room. But in the meantime, out of the corner of my eye I could see the Truffle King was up to something behind the bar at the little fireplace. Eventually he emerged with the main course: the biggest steaks I had ever seen. Salud went almost white at the size of them, while El Clossa rubbed his hands in glee.

'Bet you've never had anything like this before,' he said. 'Not even in the best restaurants in Paris or London could you eat as well as here.'

Blood drenched my plate as I cut into the thick, soft meat, then raised a morsel to my mouth. As the smell reached my nostrils, a shudder of joy coursed through my body. Then the flavour burst into life on my tongue: tender and sensual. It was an experience not unlike one I had had before. The wood smoke alone would have made them the most delicious steaks we had ever tried, but there was something else there, a richer, darker, enhancing flavour. As my mouth watered, I noticed a paste-like substance coating each piece of meat.

'Truffle pâté,' the Truffle King said as he pulled out a chair and sat down beside us, revelling in our enjoyment of his food. 'You spread it on a minute before you take the steaks out from the fire.' And he smiled at us, a rare, genuine smile.

When we were heavy with food and sipping glasses of Pacharán with ice, the Truffle King joined us and started talking about truffles. He'd been planting truffle trees and harvesting them for over twenty years, long before anyone else in the area had caught on to the idea. The biggest black truffle plantation in Europe was in Spain, to the north, in the province of Soria, but round here cultivation was in its infancy, although the land and conditions were perfect.

I told him about the trees I'd planted, and how I'd lost some in the winds.

'You did right,' he said when I mentioned about removing the plastic protector tubes. 'Waste of time. Won't protect them against anything anyway.'

I told him about the truffle conference I'd been to.

'Not interested,' he said, cutting me off.

'Victor likes to be his own man,' El Clossa said.

The Truffle King waved his hand dismissively. 'Amateurs,' he said. 'Lots of talk and lots of reports and working in laboratories. But the only real laboratory is that one out there.' He pointed at the fields outside. 'You only get to learn by actually doing it.'

'*Andando se aprende a andar*,' Salud quoted the Spanish proverb. 'You learn to walk by walking.'

'She understands,' the Truffle King said with a smile.

He looked at El Clossa and winked, then got up and went to talk with his wife. Moments later he was back at our table, putting on his coat, a small black dog sitting obediently by his feet.

'I'll show you something,' he said.

We drove out of the tiny village, past a little hermitage and up into the mountains behind. Cutting along a dirt track leading off the main road, we continued for another five minutes before driving up to the edge of a field. We jumped out, El Clossa the first out of the car. We were surrounded by a forest of old, craggy trees, their leaves turning a heavy brown and littering the sand-coloured earth beneath our feet. To our right the wedge-shaped peak of Penyagolosa was silhouetted against the pale-blue sky of late afternoon: we were nearing the winter solstice and the light had an almost ghostly feel to it. In front of us were three narrow terraces cut into the hillside and there, in neat rows, stood several dozen young saplings. I recognised them at once as holm oaks, like the ones I was planting back on our mountainside. But these were well over five years old – perhaps even ten.

'Six metres between each tree,' the Truffle King said. Another mistake: some of mine were only three metres apart.

'Doesn't matter,' he said when I explained. 'They'll be fine.'

He pointed down at some of the older trees.

'Look how there's nothing growing around those ones,' he said. I noticed a circular barren patch around each one, with no weeds or grass.

'That's what we call the *quemado*,' he said. 'That shows that these trees are already starting to develop truffles on their roots. Wipes everything else out – doesn't allow it to grow.'

Salud was bending down and stroking the dog. '*Hola, tontolín*,' she said affectionately.

'That's how you know if a tree's got truffles, see?' the Truffle King went on. 'Naturally occurring ones and plantation ones alike. Not all the saplings you plant will produce truffles in the end. But it'll be clear depending on whether they've got a *quemado* or not. Have to wait ten years or so first, though.'

He whistled and the dog suddenly pulled himself away from Salud and stood poised on the edge of the field.

'*¡Busca!*' he called. 'Go search!'

The dog was immediately trotting around the field, his nose to the ground.

'It's still early in the season,' the Truffle King said. 'Best time is January and February. But there might be a few around.'

He stepped down into the field while we stayed on the edge, watching as the dog scampered about, going in one direction first, then quickly changing and turning back on himself as he caught then lost the scent. For a moment it seemed he'd lost interest and had decided there was nothing there to be found, but after another call of encouragement from his master he put his nose back down again and resumed the search. Then he stopped, almost pressing his face into the soil. Scraping away with his front paws for a moment, he sat back and looked proudly up at the Truffle King. Victor pulled out a biscuit from his pocket and gave it to him as he bent down with a trowel and started digging. After a couple of seconds he was holding up a medium-sized black truffle, covered in dirt, about the size of a ping-pong ball.

He climbed back up to where we were and handed the truffle to Salud, crumbling the soil off it with his thumb.

'Bad year this year,' he said. 'Not enough rain. Price has gone up – seven hundred euros a kilo.'

We walked back to the car, the dog jumping and skipping between our feet, enjoying himself now that his day's work had been done. It could be quite fun being a truffle farmer, I thought, even if we did have to wait another decade for our first crop. Might have to find a dog with a sharp nose and train it first, though.

I felt a hand on my arm as I was opening the car door. I turned: the Truffle King was looking at me intensely.

'Whatever you do, you must promise me something,' he said. From his expression it was clear he was being deadly serious.

'What?' I said.

His hand gripped tighter around my arm, fingers pressing into my skin.

'Don't ever, ever tell anyone round here you're planting truffles trees,' he said. 'No one must know. This is black gold, I tell you.'

He seemed to be imploring me, his eyes filled with a strange horror.

'It can drive a man mad with greed.'

The Story of the Devil and the Carob Tree

Once upon a time there lived a poor farmer at the bottom of the valley, halfway between the mountains and the sea. Every day he diligently worked the land, ploughing and sowing, tending his crops and then harvesting them when the time came. Along with wheat, for making bread, he grew oranges and lemons, while carob trees provided food for his horses and mules. Yet despite all his hard work and long hours, the farmer was always poor, barely able to make enough for himself and his family. Whenever there was a drought or a flood he always seemed to be worse affected than any of his neighbours.

Finally, after many years like this, he decided he could bear it no longer, and picking up an old hemp rope, he walked out to the biggest and tallest carob tree on his land with the intention of ending his life.

'Oh Saints in Heaven!' he cried out in desperation. 'If you cannot help me then all I can do is ask for aid from the Devil himself.'

Just as he was about to tie the noose around his neck and sling it over a branch, he caught sight of a well-dressed gentleman coming along the road towards him.

'Well,' thought the farmer, 'I might as well wait and see what this fellow has to say for himself. I'm not in a hurry, and I shan't have anything to lose.'

At that point the gentleman strode up towards him. Despite his elegant appearance, the farmer couldn't help but notice there was a curiously unpleasant odour about him.

'Well, you called – and here I am,' said the stranger.

'You mean you're the Devil – *el Dimoni* in person?' asked the farmer.

'The very same,' said the Devil with a yellow-toothed grin.

'But what can you give me to relieve my misery?'

'This purse should do the trick, I should say.' And he held out a leather bag temptingly in his hand. 'No matter how much money you take out of it, you'll always find it full.'

Now the farmer might have been poor and at his wit's end, but he was no fool, and it didn't take him long to see what was going on.

'That's very kind of you, good sir,' he said, laying the rope to one side. 'But people rarely give something for nothing. Am I to expect you would exact a price for such a gift?'

'Why, of course, now you mention it,' said the stranger. 'Shall we say . . . your soul in return? It's what I usually ask. Cheap at the price.'

'I see,' said the farmer, thinking this through. 'But I would want some time to spend my new riches first.'

'Naturally,' said the Devil. 'But really, I can't just wait until you die of natural causes. Might be years. I'll come for you, er . . .'

'When this carob tree no longer has any fruit on it?' said the farmer. And he pointed to the tree by the side of the road from which he had been about to hang himself.

'Yes, fair enough,' said the Devil. 'Agreed.'

And with that he disappeared in a puff of sulphurous smoke, leaving behind him a large leather purse stuffed with gold coins.

Now it was a hot day that afternoon, and the farmer struggled to lift the gold, but eventually he managed to pick it up and took it home. His wife was delighted when she saw the shiny yellow coins spilling out on the dirt floor of the kitchen; and her husband explained that he had found the treasure buried under a tree. His wife didn't care where the money had come from, and within a short time they were enjoying the benefits of their new-found wealth.

The months passed and fairly soon it was harvest time again. The farmer hadn't forgotten his agreement with the Devil, and expected him to appear again any day soon.

Then one day, just as he was taking a well-earned drink after picking the last of the carobs from his biggest carob tree, *el Dimoni* himself came in a flash.

'Right, let's go. Don't keep me waiting,' said the Devil without any preamble.

'Our agreement,' said the farmer without batting an eyelid, 'was that you would take me once this tree no longer bore any fruit. Am I right?'

'Yes I know,' said the Devil. 'And I've just seen you pick the last carob from it. Now off we go. I've got a busy day.'

'But there still are carobs on the tree,' said the farmer. 'Come with me and you'll see.'

'Ridiculous!' said the Devil. 'You've just finished harvesting it.'

'But look,' said the farmer. And he lifted the leaves of the carob tree, and there, clear for anyone to see, were the buds of the next year's fruit, already in place.

'They may not be ripe now, but they will be twelve months from now. Everyone knows that around the feast of St John the carob tree produces its new fruit, before the ripe crop has been picked.'

The Devil was speechless.

'I believe,' continued the farmer, 'our agreement still holds. I'll be yours the day this carob tree no longer bears any fruit. But until then I don't want to see you round here again, understand?

For a moment the Devil didn't move, then, finally realising he had been outwitted by the farmer and that there was nothing he could do, he flew up into the air in a screaming rage like a tornado before disappearing over the horizon.

And because the farmer tended his trees well, and because the carob tree lives for many hundreds of years, the Devil was never able to return and claim his soul. And the farmer and his family lived happily ever after, and were always very generous to anyone who was as poor as they had once been.

JANUARY

The Latin month Januarius *is called* Kanun el-Tsani *in Syriac, and in Persian* Bahmanmah. *It is made up of thirty-one days, and after the twentieth the Dark Nights are at an end. The winds grow still, the humours begin to circulate in the trees and the bees begin to procreate. It is a time for harvesting oranges and lemons. Water freezes over and the weather gets much colder. Now is a good moment for clearing land of weeds and dry grass. This should be done during the time of the waning moon, that is to say from the sixteenth day of the lunar month until the new moon. Birds celebrate their weddings and frogs begin to croak. They say that wood chopped on the twenty-seventh of this month will not suffer from woodworm.*

This is a busy time for those who look after trees: they dig up the soil around the base of the trees and replace it with fertiliser.

Ibn al-Awam, *Kitab al-Falaha*, The Book of Agriculture, 12th century

Early January, and it is still very hot in the sun. Today we cleared around the house, pruning the roses, the vine outside the front door, the apple trees and fig trees. Despite the air being chilly, you can happily strip down to just a shirt, or even less. Once the sun goes over the hill – at just after four at the moment – you notice the change very suddenly, but the heat from the sun itself is intense – more so than down on the coast. People are talking about a record hot year on the way – no snow in the Alps etc. Here we seem to have skipped from autumn into spring, judging by the way the brambles are beginning to take off again. And yet still there is no sign of rain. Record heat and no rain . . . I wonder how the trees are going to cope. They need a proper winter to establish themselves before spring arrives. Now might just be all right, but February? March? There is an ever growing sense of urgency. Miss this opportunity and I'll have to wait till next winter before being able to plant anything else.

Planting the truffle trees seems an endless task. The Truffle King mentioned the best time for planting was now, after the 'change' of the January moon, i.e. after the full moon has passed and it begins to wane. I asked Arcadio what he thought.

'Any time's a good time to plant,' he said, 'because you're planting. And that's good.

'Answer's in the land, in the soil,' he said. 'Listen to the plants, to the land: they'll tell you what they want in the end.'

*

I recognised Sergio as one of the hunters who had been up to the farm, spinning the wheels of his red and white Mitsubishi four-wheel-drive as he sped up and down the mountain track, curly black hair greased to his scalp.

'Glad you could come,' he said in a high, strained voice as he shook my hand. 'Arcadio said he'd bring you along.'

We stood inside an unpainted breeze-block garage with a cement floor, the doors open wide to let in a shaft of light from the afternoon sun. Six or seven men dressed in the usual hunter's garb stood in a circle in the centre; they greeted the ancient Arcadio warmly, then nodded in my direction.

'Thought it might interest him to see this,' I heard Arcadio explaining to them. Their faces relaxed: there was a reason for my being there, and although Arcadio wasn't a hunter himself his age and knowledge of the land meant he was more than enough of a guarantor.

'Got this one at midday,' Sergio said with a lardy smile. 'Ninety kilos.'

From a beam in the centre of the garage hung the body of a wild boar, its hind legs tied to a piece of wood which was hooked up to a chain. Its eyes were partially open, staring down at the floor, but lifeless and dulled, its exposed belly making it look vulnerable, defeated.

'The shot went through here,' Sergio said, pointing at a gash-like wound in the animal's shoulder, barely visible through the thick brown hair. For a moment it felt like a forensic examination of a murder victim.

'Right,' he said rubbing his hands. 'Call Teresa. Let's get started.'

There were shouts from inside the house next door and presently a portly woman wearing an apron, with glasses and a face that looked as though it had been crushed between two rocks, came out from a side door, flanked by two other women. In her hands she brandished a knife.

'Let's get this over with,' she said, expertly slicing the knife up and down a sharpener.

'Sergio's wife,' Arcadio explained as the powerful little woman approached the dead animal in a resigned, businesslike manner. 'She always does the skinning.'

'Get those two a drink,' Sergio called to a young lad hovering in the background, who scampered off, bringing back with him a bottle of wine and some glasses. He had something of the same, vertically challenged face of the woman with the knife.

'Sergio's son?' I asked Arcadio. He nodded.

I noticed that the others had knocked back a few glasses already, their faces pink, splashes of wine on the floor where they'd been less careful when pouring.

'Help yourselves to whatever you want,' Sergio said grandiosely. Outside, in the yard beyond the garage a group of youngsters, perhaps friends of Sergio's son, were lighting a fire on the ground, the scent of wood smoke drifting in on the breeze as crackling flames began to lick the twigs and kindling.

Teresa wasted no time. Stepping up to the boar, she started making deft cuts in its skin, as though slicing through butter. First on the legs, then up the belly and around the head, across the back of the neck.

'We'll keep the head for a trophy,' Sergio said, 'although it's not very big, this one. Got a whole collection inside. I'll show you after. Been hunting all over the world, me. Just got back from South Africa a couple of weeks back. Great hunting there.'

From the speed and efficiency of her movements, it was clear that Teresa had done this many times before. You still heard people speak of the *matanza del cerdo* – the annual ritual killing of a pig in each Spanish household, a ceremony dating back hundreds, perhaps thousands, of years. It had become particularly important during the time of the Reconquest and the terror of the Inquisition in the sixteenth and seventeenth centuries, when proving you were a Christian, and not a Muslim or Jew, by eating copious amounts of pork, could mean the difference between life and death. The tradition was largely dying out now, but Salud had told me how her mother had still followed it until quite recently, giving it up only in the past twenty years or so. Out here, deep in the countryside of Castellón, it was still very much alive. Although today it would be boar's meat going into the sausages and pâtés that would be produced over the course of the rest of the afternoon and evening.

Teresa finished slicing up the boar and reached up to its hind legs. Grabbing hold of tufts of hair, she began to pull, and the skin started to peel away, exposing a white, pinkish underneath. With a couple of tugs it stripped to around halfway down its back with a wrenching sound, before she stepped up, cut away some more between the flesh and the skin as though to loosen it, and then heaved again. Finishing her slicing around the head, the whole skin was soon ripped from the animal's body.

'Here,' she said, passing it to her son. 'Take this out for salting.'

The boy threw the hide over his shoulder, staining his cheek with dark congealing boar's blood as he carried it outside.

The boar was considerably smaller now it had been shorn of its hair and skin. Lean and naked, taut red muscle tissue pushed through odd rare patches of white-yellow fat. There was something pathetic about it, as though it were only half the animal it had been. How had something so powerful and so fearsome once existed in this body? I tried to imagine it running through the mountains – only hours before. But the creature was now little more than food, meat. And soon even that would be taken away from it.

Teresa started slicing quickly down the middle of the boar's abdomen, its innards slopping heavily out of the fresh wound. Grey intestines curled and slid around a heavy wine-coloured liver, pink heart. Sergio stepped forward and caught them as they oozed out of the animal's body, as though being forcibly ejected. The two women who had come out with Teresa then pulled out metal trays and buckets and scooped them up, Teresa cutting at the rectum where the intestines were still attached to the inside of the body.

The men standing watching gave a cheer.

'Look at that.'

'We'll get a nice load out of this.'

Already their minds were casting forward to the salamis and cured meats that would be made from the guts.

An intense, sharp smell of blood and shit filled the garage, almost blotting out the wood smoke as Teresa joined the other two women carrying the innards to a deep, narrow sink at the side to begin washing them. Squeezing the intestines in their hands they started pushing out the remaining faecal matter in preparation for stuffing them again for making sausages.

Sergio now held the knife and approached the remaining carcass. A pool of blood had formed at his feet, below the now ridiculous looking head.

'She always leaves this bit to me,' he said with a grin. One or two of the others laughed. He plunged the knife into the flesh around the neck, struggling for a moment with the vertebrae, gritting his teeth as he stabbed and twisted, trying to loosen the head from the rest of the body.

'*Iéeah*,' came a low call of encouragement from the men.

'*Venga*, Sergio.'

The tone was flat: these men didn't go in for public demonstrations of emotion. It might almost have been be mocking, sarcastic, but from the looks in their eyes there seemed to be no ironical intent. Straight, no-nonsense, almost bovine.

With a final cut the head came free, and with it a last gushing of blood, a few remaining faint drips tapping the pool below with the vestiges of life of a once vital, vigorous beast. Sergio lifted the head up and showed it to us all like a trophy.

'Seen better ones,' he said with false modesty. 'Still going on the wall, though.'

A sharp chill came over me as I stared at this prize weighing heavily in his arms, detached, now mocked and set to be put on display. Deep, animal fear. I sank the last drops of red wine stewing in the bottom of my glass.

A new bottle was passed round along with plates of food, but for me it was time to go. I shook Arcadio's hand: he was staying.

'The vet's got to test the meat first before we can eat any of it,' Sergio said as I said my goodbyes. 'Check for any germs and stuff. Once we get the all clear we'll start dividing it up. Come on round tomorrow and I'll see if there are any sausages spare.'

The boy was already smoking a few bits and pieces over the fire in the yard, poking and turning them on a grill with a blackened fork. The smell was delicious.

I drove back to the farm, hungry and disturbed.

★

I am enjoying the silence up here more and more. Partly because it is not a complete silence. There is the sound of my own heart and breathing, then beyond that come the sounds of the world around: occasional birdsong, breezes blowing through the pine trees, perhaps a stone loosened by an ibex skipping down the cliff-face. Some birds make a sound as they fly – a kind of whooping noise as they speed overhead. I rarely manage to see them: by the time I have heard them they have moved on. They seem to be of a dark-brown colour, as well, so they can easily be lost against the mountain background. Some kind of swift, perhaps? They seem larger; perhaps a *roqueret* – a crag martin? There is a sense of something alive in the silence – a living landscape that whispers to you quietly. Make too much noise and you won't be able to hear it. Many landscapes roar at you – birds twitter incessantly, cows and sheep moan aloud, rivers gurgle past. Here there is little of that. And yet the place does not feel dead for lack of aural stimulation: rather, it invites you to attune your hearing, stretch your capacity, and capture the quieter sounds that it has to offer. Here, at this time of year, birdsong is an event: in other circumstances I would barely have noticed the pair of coal tits which have made the oak tree their home. Nor would the owls hooting in the early hours of the night have made much impression. In the city I may be surrounded at any time by a thousand dogs, all within a hundred yards or even less, yet I am oblivious to them. Here I know there is a dog living in an old house in the next valley – a house I cannot even see – while at least two wild dogs have the run of the hills around the farm. Silence reduces space and distance. In the absence of noise, any noise becomes important, or has some significance, or even a message. I can hear cars coming up the mountain from several miles away. The tinkling of bells means either the cows and bulls near La Caseta de Ramonet on the other side of the riverbed, or else the goatherd somewhere in the vicinity. The distant sound of clanging metal means the old man is working up at the quarry. Very occasionally – perhaps about once a month – he sets off a charge to loosen the rock, and the explosion echoes and rolls down the river valley like boiling water.

The change from the norm takes some getting used to. I still sometimes find myself rushing out to see who might be about to 'invade' our space when I hear what sounds like a car coming up the hill. Some aspects of 'Englishness' are shed quite easily, others less so, and it is only now I realise how deeply entrenched in me is the idea of my home being a castle. I am having to lose some of this, though, and accept that others can and do come up here, and there's not much I can do about it. As time goes by, I slowly adapt: I've got into the habit of leaving the chain at the bottom of our track unlocked – anyone can get through now. Before, I used to pull it across and padlock it religiously: I didn't want to see anyone while I was up here, and if anyone did dare to appear they were immediately classed as an intruder, unwelcome. My assumption was that people only showed up in order to take something away from me – my privacy, my possessions, my freedom, whatever. That still might happen, but I'm trying to learn to be less possessive about this place. I am a visitor, just like any other person. My time will end here one day, then someone else may or may not live here after me, just as many others have done so in the past. The mountain, however, just lives on, with occasional changes to its outer skin – terraces come and go, as do crops, and even trees. Legally it is mine, but I do not own the mountain; it can never belong to us in any real sense at all.

★

I was invited to visit the truffle market at Sarrión, held near the Mora de Rubielos railway station, starting at around eleven o'clock on a Saturday night. I was told it ran through till about four in the morning. All outside and all in the dark. Come alone.

I arrived at the agreed time, wondering at the air of mystery. At first it was hard to spot a 'market' of any sort taking place: there were few people around, and nothing to see except a virtually empty car park. But as an outsider, I was unlikely to see anything anyway, because once they'd caught sight of me the dealers would vanish or made themselves invisible. Or at least that's what I'd been given to expect.

My contact was waiting for me: a builder who owned a house up there – a friend of a friend, who, with the promise of a few drinks and after telling him over the telephone I had my own plantation up and running, opened up gradually and offered to take me down to where the dealers hung out. He was a buyer: possibly a useful contact in a few years' time when I started getting my own crop.

From the comments and looks – the sheer tension – it started to became apparent that the whole thing was run almost like a drug market: huge amounts of money were involved; there was a wary, nervous atmosphere; and the unannounced but very real presence of weapons of some sort – knives almost certainly, but probably a few shotguns as well. The dealers were often the kind who also hunted, so it wasn't unlikely they should have a rifle or a twelve-bore hidden under a blanket in the boot of the car.

A bar stood to one side of the car park, but it was almost empty. We went inside for a drink, knocking back a couple of brandies to keep us warm in the sub-zero temperatures. We were very high up, near the local ski-runs, and snow lay thick on the ground, icicles hanging from the awning of the bar. We seemed to be waiting for some sign or some moment when it might be all right to venture out and see if there was some 'action' taking place, but I was unclear what the sign was, or if we would have to wait there all night. My contact repeated the Truffle King's comments about it being a bad year for truffles, what with the strange weather. The season that year would be very short – perhaps only another couple of weeks or so. It was mid-January – truffles were usually to be had until late February or even later sometimes.

I'd read about the clandestine nature of truffle dealing in other countries, but this seemed even more under the counter and obscure than I had imagined. Perhaps a certain suspiciousness in the local character. Salud's father had been right in general: the mountain people of Castellón were fairly tight-lipped about most things, untrusting and always looking out for a chance themselves, a quality brought on, one imagined, by the harshness of the surroundings. I'd heard an anecdote about an old local man effectively stealing some fields from his neighbour by taking advantage of a loophole in the land registry, even though his neighbour was a doctor and had once saved his life by giving him first aid while he was having a heart attack. That meant nothing to people here: you got what you could by screwing the other guy, even if you owed him your life.

I couldn't help but draw comparisons with drug markets I'd come across in the past. But even scoring dope or cocaine hadn't been quite as difficult as this. In such environments you knew a place to go and before long someone approached you – it was, after all, a market, and they wanted to sell their produce. Here it was as though the sellers would run as soon as they spotted a possible buyer.

After a third drink it was beginning to feel decidedly warmer. I thought about having a bite to eat to soak things up a bit, perhaps crawling over to one of the more comfortable looking chairs away from the bar and having a bit of a snooze until it was time actually to 'see' something. But my contact suddenly slipped from his chair and moved very quickly towards the door. I was slow to react and he was outside and moving out into the car park before I realised what was going on. The moment had mysteriously arrived. I scurried out and crunched through the crusted snow in his footsteps. He stopped and I caught up with him. Without turning his head he said, 'Can you see it?'

I couldn't see a damned thing, but his eyes were clearly focused on something in the middle distance. I blinked and stared, closed my eyes for a few seconds, hoping they would adjust to the darkness, then opened them again to see just the faintest of lights flickering out there among the few parked cars. Around it were several figures, perhaps three or four, huddled together.

'That's it,' my contact said. Some barely perceptible hand movements were taking place, a cough, a low voice, then the light was switched off and everyone moved away in separate directions. It had finished as soon as it had begun.

'That's it?' It was so quick I could scarcely believe it. My contact had already turned away and was walking back towards the bar.

'Move!' he said, catching my hesitation. The tension was there – no one wanted to be taken for the wrong sort round here. What were they worried about, I wondered, as we shuffled back towards the bright lights of the bar. Policemen? Tax officials? Perhaps dodgy truffle dealers selling some of the plain-tasting Chinese variety. Spend a few thousand on some of those and you wouldn't be very happy. Might even be tempted to reach for your shotgun.

My contact gave a low grunt as we reached the bar. One of the men involved in the transaction we had just seen had arrived at the door at the same time. He winked at my contact, then frowned as he saw me coming up close behind.

'With me,' my contact said. The other man nodded, but his suspicion was plain to see. Once inside I offered him a drink but he refused point-blank.

I thought of heading off, but my contact held me back. He wanted to give it time, see if the other man might warm over the course of the evening. He was a seller, and had some plantations near here. It might be useful for me to talk to him. But it was going to take some time.

The truffle dealer talked to the barman and occasionally to my contact. After a few minutes I decided to go to the loo.

When I came back the atmosphere had changed. As soon as I sat down the dealer pulled his stool over and started to speak. 'So you've planted some truffle trees. How many?'

It was a start. I called to the barman. This time the dealer accepted my offer, and we struck up a conversation. And over the course of the next hour he let me in to the secrets of the truffle world.

*

The winds here are given names, and are considered to have unique characteristics. They can be drawn on a dial-figure, called a *rosa dels vents*. Starting from the north and circling clockwise, they are as follows.

The *Tramuntana*, the fierce, cold north wind which comes from behind the Pyrenees – from across the mountains: *transmontanus* in Latin. A Tramuntana can blow for days and days, arriving suddenly in the autumn to bring a swift end to the remains of summer, but the skies it creates are of an intense, sparkling blue, with visibility so clear you can see as far as the Montgó in Denia, or the Columbrete Islands off the

Castellón coast. Traditionally it will only blow for an odd number of days, so if it passes into a second day you know it will still be there the next morning; if it continues for a fourth day, it will carry on into the fifth, and so on. It is said that this wind can drive people mad.

The *Gregal*, a generally cold wind which blows from the north-east. Sailors used to watch out for it as it was ideal for setting sail for Greece, hence the name, the 'Greek wind'. Modern fishermen are less fond of it, however, especially for the storms it can produce. Their attitude is neatly summed up in the proverb: *Vent de gregal, mal* – 'the Gregal is a bad wind'.

The *Llevant*, or *Levante* in Castilian, comes from the east. This is the basic wind from the sea, and the name is commonly used to describe any breeze coming roughly from that direction, in opposition to the *Ponent*, which comes from inland, from the west. If it is not too strong, it can be a soothing, slightly humid wind, warming in winter and cooling in the summer: the wind that blows when all is right with the world and everything is in its place. Yet it is known also for its high waves and occasional stormy weather. It often picks up in the evening, as the local saying goes: *el Llevant s'alça tard i es gita dejorn* – 'the Llevant gets up late and goes to bed in the morning'. The name refers to the movement of the sun in the east 'rising'.

The *Xaloc* comes from across the Sahara from the south-east, and its name comes from the Arabic *sharq*, meaning 'east'. It is a hot, humid wind which leaves a film of dust and sand over everything, especially if it brings rain with it. *Plou fang*, as people say here, meaning 'It's raining mud'. Sailors like it, as long as it doesn't come in too hard: *Vent de xaloc, ni massa ni poc*, goes the cry, almost like a prayer – the Xaloc wind: neither too strong nor too gentle.

The *Migjorn*, the 'midday' wind, blows directly from the south, but because of its rarity is often confused with the Xaloc and Garbí. It is an unloved wind, considered good neither for sailing nor fishing.

The *Garbí*, or *Llebeig*, blows in from the south-west, often bringing heavy rains. It is common at dawn, but as with other winds blowing from inland it has a bad reputation: *Vent de Llebeig, perdut et veig* – 'With a Llebeig you'll get lost', as the sailors say. The name comes from the Arabic *gharb*, meaning 'west'.

The *Ponent*, or *Poniente* in Castilian, blows in directly from the west. It is the archetypal 'ill-wind', to the extent that all anyone has to say is '*Fa Ponent*' and everything from a headache to a bad harvest to a fall on the stock exchange can be explained away. The wind is invariably dry, blowing in over the Spanish plains, causing temperatures to nose-dive in winter and soar in summer. A Ponent during the summer months can turn most places into ghost towns, as people either flee to somewhere cooler or shut themselves inside their homes, drawing the blinds and shutters against the choking oven heat. Reflecting a general dislike of anything that comes their way from the west, another local proverb says, *De ponent, ni vent ni gent* – 'Neither wind nor people from the west'. The name refers to the 'setting' of the sun.

The *Cerç*, or *Mestral*, comes from the north-west. A cold, dry wind, it is particularly disliked by farmers for the crop-destroying frosts it can bring with it. If the cold itself doesn't do damage to new shoots, the ice crystals of the frost intensify the sun's rays, 'burning' the blossom of fruit trees. *Ha fet mes mal que el Mestral*, as they say – 'It's done more harm than the Mestral'.

Of all these, the prevailing winds, thankfully, are the Llevant and Xaloc combined, the most loved of the family, although the Ponent can come a close second. Penyagolosa, whose peak is about six kilometres from the farm, shelters us from the worst of the northerly winds, but the Tramuntana, which blows strongest towards the end of February and into March, can cause great damage, often uprooting trees, Arcadio says. Much of the firewood used for the following winter comes from trees broken into pieces by these winds.

★

A whirling, wailing mass of animal cries filled the little square as we stepped out from an adjacent alleyway to watch the start of the festivities.

'*Mis gatitos*,' Marina purred as she carried a cat in each arm and headed towards the front steps outside the subdued Baroque church. By the large wooden front doors stood the village priest, all heavy glasses and dog collar, a serious expression on his face as an unorderly queue of locals trailed and heaved towards him across the flagstones. Each one was accompanied by at least one – and in several cases four or five –

animal. Dogs on leashes, cats in people's arms or in plastic-grilled boxes, half a dozen parrots and budgerigars in cages draped in cloth, two pigs, also on leashes, a grey horse, four donkeys, two white mules and a rabbit. The word going around the square was that one of the villagers was also going to bring along his python, but was waiting for the others to go first so as not to frighten their pets.

Above this raucous mass of man and beast, the priest was waving his hands and speaking in low tones as each person brought their animals to be blessed. Some lingered for a while, as though asking for special prayers – perhaps for a specific ailment or malady to be healed. Others just looked as though they wanted to gossip. The priest tried to maintain his dignity as best he could, back straight and stiff, a kindly if distant look in his eye. He seemed uncomfortable with the task, and I wondered if he had any animals of his own. He allowed himself to pat the odd dog on the head, but as for the rest he simply made the sign of the cross in their general direction, muttering some incantation under his breath, and then tried to dispatch the owner as quickly as he could. There were several dozen beasts to get through this afternoon: it might go on for a long time.

'Of course,' Concha said over the din and chatter, her breath heavy with wine and cigarettes, 'the traditions of Sant Antoni date way back – long before Christianity arrived. This is an ancient rite of cleansing and to pray for a good year for farmers.'

St Anthony's Day was a big event in this part of Spain: in many villages it was far more important than Christmas and had become the main midwinter festival. I enjoyed this: Christmas, that overworked and overvalued festival, had barely passed with the ringing of a church bell here. Just another fiesta, a minor one, in a string of many that were dotted throughout the year. Sant Antoni was the big one, the one you waited for and looked forward to. No presents, no Santa Claus, no fake snow sprayed on the inside of shop windows. No Brussels sprouts. It was bliss.

Officially Sant Antoni was held on 17 January, but with so many towns competing to hold the biggest and most important fiesta in the area they tended to stagger them so that people from one village could celebrate in the next, and then the next, and so on, thus extending the whole thing over a week or more. For a few days at least, during the season of the Sanantoná, you were unlikely to come across anyone sober, not even the local police.

St Anthony the Great – *el abad*, the abbot, as he was usually referred to here – had been an Egyptian hermit of the third and fourth centuries, and was regarded, much like St Francis of Assisi, as having a special gift with animals. The legend said he had once cured a group of piglets of blindness, and that henceforth the mother sow (or wild boar, in some versions) had protected him during his lonely existence in the desert. For this reason he was also known as Sant Antoni *del porquet* – 'he of the pig'. Often regarded as the founder of Christian monasticism, he was also said to have been serially tempted by the Devil – trials which, needless to say, he was always able to overcome. This part of his story, like his connection with animals, had entered popular imagination, and as well as scores of pets and beasts of burden, characters dressed up in wildly demoniac costumes wandered around the square, beating drums and pulling faces at laughing, frightened children. They wore white tunics painted with black, red and green designs, hoods pulled over their faces and small flaps dangling over their noses, like beaks, almost like fantasy birds. They reminded me in some ways of harlequins; some, I noticed, were carrying short sticks which they used playfully to beat people in the crowd, particularly the girls.

'Those are the *botargues*,' Concha said. 'Look at that one over there.' She pointed and I saw a broad-shouldered man wearing a skirt and blouse, a headscarf tied over his head. 'That's the *filoseta*. Always played by a man, but representing the sexual temptations of San Antoni in the desert.'

He must have been in a pretty bad way, you couldn't help reflecting, to have found anything tempting in what was on offer that evening.

The 'devils' were dragging a couple of other characters around by a rope. These, Concha told us, were St Anthony himself and a St Paul who was also renowned as a hermit: the two seemed to do a kind of double act.

'They get dragged around the village, entering people's houses and fooling around,' she said.

A sound of wind instruments blasted out from one of the side streets and the drums started beating more intensely. A thin, reedy sound circled in the darkening sky as four musicians emerged into the square playing *dolçainers* – an instrument similar to a shortened oboe or clarinet – with bursts of sharp, catchy folk melodies. The crowd parted to let them through, the drummers falling in behind. Shouts and cheers went up as the 'devils' then ran into the square, spreading mayhem as they launched themselves into the crowd, groping at the women, great shrieks of fear and laughter searing the cold night air as people shouted and pushed, slipped and fell over. Soon after they set off in a procession around the village, cameras flashing as the pageant of misrule surged into a higher gear. Puddles of wine and beer formed underfoot as people spilled their drinks.

The central point of the festivities was an enormous conical bonfire sitting proudly in the middle of the square, over twenty feet high, a central pole with subsidiaries radiating out from it, much like a tepee. It had been covered in branches and leaves, while at the bottom a tunnel ran through the middle, just big enough for a person to walk through. There was, I realised, an obvious resemblance to the Christmas trees of northern European tradition: green, conical, built of pine (or spruce). Even the lighting of it later on would bear echoes of the candles – and later, fairy lights – used to adorn Christmas trees. Perhaps both shared a common heritage with ancient tree religions, combined with a celebration of 'light' at this darkest time of the year. I remembered the stories of Percival and the tree of a thousand candles, which the nineteenth-century writer J.H. Philpot mentioned in her classic study of tree lore. 'The Christmas tree may be said to recapitulate the whole story of tree worship,' she wrote in *The Sacred Tree in Religion and Myth*. 'The tree as the symbol and embodiment of deity, and last but not least, the universal-tree, bearing the lights of heaven for its fruit and covering the world with its branches.'

El Clossa, Pau and Africa now joined us. Africa was showing a marked bump and she smiled as Salud and I looked down in surprise at her belly.

'Five months,' she whispered with a smile.

'A few more minutes now,' El Clossa said, 'and they'll light the *barraca*.' He nodded at the bonfire. 'They chop down the biggest pine tree in the forest to make that.'

The main pole, he told me, was called the *maio* – the may – although no one knew exactly why it was given this name. Childhood memories of dancing around maypoles in an English playground came flooding back: coloured ribbons weaving in and out to form a tight-knit pattern. We'd only performed the maypole dance one year – I think I was about six or seven; perhaps for the Queen's Silver Jubilee. It had been lost after that: no need, it was felt, to continue such archaic traditions.

El Clossa explained to us how several days before the fiesta a group of men went out into the forest to find the tallest pine tree, which they cut down, stripped of its branches and then brought to the square.

'The tunnel in the middle represents the *barraca* – the hut – of the hermit saint,' he said. 'Or at least that's the theory. Quite what a pine-branch tunnel's got to do with a bloke living in the Egyptian desert is beyond me. They have to tell everyone it's all Christian, see? But obviously all this stuff's much, much older.'

What exactly were the origins of this curious rite, I wondered, and how had they been morphed under this veneer of Catholic respectability.

'Look!' said Salud, grabbing my arm and pointing. A group of men carrying flaming torches had entered the square and had dispersed around the edge of the bonfire. Bending down, they lit the branches poking out at the bottom, and flickers of light began to dance underneath as tiny plumes of smoke were lifted up into the night air. Explosions shook the ground as the devils pulled out large firecrackers and started letting them off, their bangs and whistles momentarily silencing the crowd as the two saints ran towards the leafy tunnel. As the flames started rising and licking the sides, they dashed through and out the other side before turning round and repeating their run back the other way. More firecrackers went off, the devils jeering at them and dancing manically and menacingly towards them. Members of the crowd began imitating the hermits' daredevil feat, chasing through the fiery hole and out the other side, covering their heads with their arms for protection from the heat as the blaze now started to take hold. Young men cheered victoriously as they came out unharmed, the girls behind them squealing with nervousness and excitement. One lad kept darting in and out, checking the flames each time before risking it again and again. A gasp went up from the crowd as he made to go in for a last time, removing his T-shirt and running as fast as he could, fire almost consuming the entire cone of the bonfire. He made it, just, but seconds later the first small burning branches of the structure began to break away and fall to the ground. Within a minute no one could stand closer than a dozen paces from the tower of fire lighting up the entire square.

El Clossa approached from behind as we stood open-mouthed, captivated by the sight of this dangerous inferno.

'Come and have a drink,' he said, a bottle in his hand.

Pau and Africa were sitting at a table near one of the makeshift bars set up for the fiesta around the edge of the square. Marina, presumably having put her cats back in the van, was with them. Plastic plates of burnt black sausage and chorizo dotted the table, puddles of red and dark brown fat congealing in the cold. El Clossa greedily picked up a basket of bread from a neighbouring stand and started dipping morsels into the gravy.

'The best bit,' he said. 'Want some?'

Africa was staring angrily at Concha. We sat down, forming a loose circle around the table. The fiesta going on around us seemed to fade. It appeared we had caught them in the middle of an argument.

'You can't go through with this,' Africa said. Her eyes were protruding alarmingly.

'They're going to dig this whole area up and turn it into clay quarries for the ceramics factories. It's in the paper. The proposal's with the regional government right now. And you know they've all been bought. It's just a formality. First the wind farms, now this.'

'We need to think things through,' said Concha.

There was a crash as Pau's fist struck the table.

'We need action, direct action.'

He stood up.

'What these people need, Concha,' he said, 'is not more talk, more politics. That's all you're offering. Do you think standing in the elections is going to make the blindest bit of difference?'

'It's the only way!' Concha cried. 'You and I may feel the same about what they're doing to this land of ours, Pau,' she said. 'But it's clear we have very different ideas about how to save it.

'And what's more . . .'

She tailed off, mouth open, her eyes almost popping out of her head.

'What . . . what are you doing?' she said, shocked but at the same time trying to stifle a laugh.

Pau had quickly taken off first his coat, then his jumper and his shoes, and was now pulling his trousers off in front of us.

'Really, Pau,' El Clossa said as the rest of us watched in stunned silence, 'I didn't know you cared.'

Pau ignored him. It was freezing, but for some reason he had got it into his head to strip down to his underpants. Africa, sitting at his side, didn't bat an eyelid.

'No more talking,' Pau said almost under his breath as he stood there virtually naked in front of us. He was skinny and pale, his navel protruding like a raspberry. His head, however, was still covered by a woollen cap that was rarely removed from his balding scalp. Around us, some of the villagers were beginning to notice him and had started to point and laugh.

'These people need to be shocked! They need to be woken up!' Pau said. 'It's the only way we'll ever get them to listen.'

There was a pause as he seemed to expect us all to react in some way, but we were still too bemused to say anything. Not getting any response, he whipped off his underpants in defiance and ran out towards the bonfire, where the rest of the village was watching the slowly dying fire, warming themselves from its heat. I closed my eyes, hardly wanting to watch.

'And he thinks that he'll get people to listen by running around *en bolas* on Sant Antoni?' Concha was laughing incredulously. Shrieks were coming from the direction of the bonfire as some of the local women caught their first sight of the naked Pau.

'He's not the only one!'

Marina had got up as well and was unbuttoning her coat.

'Not you as well, please!' Concha implored. 'If you get those out you'll give half the men in the village a heart attack.'

Shouts of abuse were coming from the area of the bonfire. Almost everyone around us had moved away from the bar and surged over to get a glimpse of the madman dancing and running in circles around the flames. Marina suddenly decided to join him and pulled off her top, launching herself through the crowd and towards the fire, and Pau. I could only think of his feet: they would be cut to shreds out there on the glass from the broken bottles.

The villagers were getting upset: some of the shouts were turning ugly and aggressive. They didn't want this outsider ruining their fiesta. But once Marina appeared, her white flesh bouncing uncontrollably in the light of the fire, the mood changed and the hint of violence dissipated. Now the two of them were just a laughing stock, people smiling, pointing, and shaking their heads.

Sometimes, I thought to myself, life in Spain could be almost unbearably surreal.

Salud had had enough. She leaned over and whispered in my ear, 'Let's get out of here.'

Concha was holding her head in her hands, while Africa just sat there, a knowing smile playing on her lips.

El Clossa caught up with us as we walked back to the car. The streets seemed to be densely dark after the brightness of the bonfire and I wondered if we would be able to find our way.

'Concha's standing in the local elections,' he said, standing in a pale pool of light cast by a bare bulb hanging over a door.

'Pau's taken his clothes off because Concha's standing in the elections?' I said. It seemed odd that someone wanting to become a village councillor could invoke such passions. But this was Spain: they took their politics seriously here.

'Pau has . . . other ideas,' he said. 'For defending the land. Concha thinks she can protect it by working from the inside.'

While Pau, it seemed, favoured 'direct action'.

'What do you think?' Salud asked.

El Clossa looked down at the floor for a moment, and then turned, as if to go, uncomfortable with the question.

'They're both playing with fire,' he mumbled over his shoulder. 'The land looks after itself.' Then he trotted away back into the blackness, his crutches clattering rhythmically against the stone floor.

We felt our way to the car, the cries and shouts from the bonfire and the fiesta behind us muffled by the stone houses and windy streets.

The Story of the Knight Templar and the Moorish Girl

Soon after it was conquered by the Christians from the Moors, the little town of Benassal, which lies at the heart of the Maestrat area north of Penyagolosa, was handed over to be ruled by the Knights Templar. There, these fierce, monastic warriors established themselves, living side by side with the many Moors who had stayed behind and who continued to live as they always had. One of the new knights in the town was called Cristòfol, a brave and handsome young man. Every morning he would ride out on some task or other, and it wasn't long before his eye fell on the loveliest Moorish girl in the village. He noticed she used to break away from the other women and spend time alone at the spring at the bottom of the Montcàtil mountain, where she would fill her water jugs before heading home once more.

Again and again Cristòfol found himself watching out for her. He quickly discovered her name – Oras – and found any excuse he could to ride to the spring when he knew she would be there. Finally, one day, unable to contain himself any longer, he approached her and declared his love for her.

But when she heard his words, Oras covered her face and wept.

'Don't you see?' she said. 'I too love you, and have watched and waited for you all this time. Yet the rules of your order are very strict – you have taken a vow of chastity. While if my father hears of my love for a Christian he will certainly kill me. We are doomed.'

'The truth of my love for you is stronger than any vow,' Cristòfol told her. 'And your love for me stronger than any fear.' And he reached towards her and gently touched her face.

Oras threw herself into his arms and swore that she would love him forever. And from that day onwards they used to meet by the spring every afternoon to spend a few moments together, alone and in secret.

Time passed, though, and Cristòfol was sent away by the master of his order to carry important messages to foreign lands. He would be away for many months, perhaps years.

The two lovers met for a last time at midnight by the spring, barely able to contain their grief. Cristòfol swore that he would never forget her, and would remain faithful throughout his absence.

'Will you promise to wait for me?' he asked Oras.

'I promise,' she said. 'But you need no oaths from me. Let the water of this spring bear witness to my love. May it speak the truth if I lie.'

And so the lovers were parted, and Cristòfol was sent abroad. Years passed, and he was away for far longer than he had expected. But eventually, after many adventures, he found himself once more riding through the Maestrat, past rocky lime-stone cliffs, the scent of crushed thyme underfoot as his horse headed its way up to the little town of Benassal, home of his beloved Oras.

Before telling anyone he had returned, he made his way straight to the little spring he had dreamed of so often while he had been away. There was no one there, but as he dismounted from his horse and bent down to drink from the cool, fresh water, thoughts of the beautiful Moorish girl filling his mind, he caught an image on the surface of the pool. And to his horror, he saw Oras held in the embrace of another man. She had broken her promise, and the water of the spring, bound by the girl's oath, spoke the truth of what had happened.

Unable to contain his sorrow, Cristòfol took out his dagger and stabbed himself in the heart, his body falling like a stone. There he was found motionless by the locals, and soon the Templar master was informed.

When he heard the story of Cristòfol and his love for Oras, the master commanded that a hermitage be built near the site of the spring where the two lovers had met. And there it stands to this day, on top of Mount Montcàtil, a monument to St Christopher and to the poor Templar knight whose heart was broken by the Moorish girl.

Others insist that Oras did remain true to her beloved knight, but that after years of refusal was finally forced by her father to marry another man. Yet her love for Cristòfol never diminished, and she waited patiently for him, visiting the spring every day to look for him. On the day of Cristòfol's return, she was delayed by a messenger appearing at her door; when she finally went down to the spring she found her dear knight already dead from grief, the treacherous image of her in her husband's arms still shimmering on the surface of the water. Consumed by grief, she threw herself into the pool and was lost in the depths, joining him in death that she might finally be reunited with her beloved Cristòfol.

FEBRUARY

Februarius *in the Latin tongue is called* Shabat *in Syriac and* Esfandmah *in Persian. It is made up of twenty-eight and a quarter days. This is the month when the cold begins to grow weaker and the warmth begins to rise in the ground. Wells, springs and rivers are filled once more with water and the humours begin to flow up the trunks of trees.*

Now the bees begin to hatch in their hives and, according to Abu al-Khayr, trees begin to develop their greenery and vines sprout new leaves.

Now is the time for planting roses, lilies and aromatic plants. It is also a good time for planting trees, which will flourish.

Ibn al-Awam, *Kitab al-Falaha*, The Book of Agriculture, 12th century

The almonds are starting to blossom – almost half the trees are now in flower, despite the late arrival of winter. After a very hot January, some more snow has arrived, although mostly higher up and north of Penyagolosa. So the peaks above the house are covered in a powdering of white, while just a couple of hundred metres below the almond blossom gives almost the same effect, as though the one were mirroring the other. It is the most beautiful time of the year, the bright white and pink – soon to emerge from the remaining trees – bringing early life to the land. The winds and then – hopefully – the rains will come before long. But for the time being we walk around the fields, revelling in the low sunshine catching the petals as they burst from the trees.

★

It had been a while since I'd been down to check on the beehives. Tucked away in a corner behind an olive tree, and with so much else going on, it was easy to forget they were even there sometimes.

Besides, I wasn't quite sure what – if anything – I was supposed to be doing with them. Arcadio had mentioned that May was the time for harvesting, and then again in August if there was any rain during the summer. But this was becoming rarer and rarer. In the meantime they got on with whatever bees did, and we just had to wait.

After our bad start together, the bees seemed to have settled down in their new home. There were plenty of rock roses near the hives for nectar, while just a buzz away they had an endless supply of rosemary, thyme and almond blossom, not to mention the gorse, a few apple and peach trees and a host of other wild flowers peppering the hillside. They hadn't stung me again since the first time, which was a relief, and I'd pop down every now and then to crouch at the front of their hives, watching and listening to them for a while. It was a relaxing pastime, once my fears about being stung had been overcome. I listened to the gentle sound of their flying, a small congregation of them gathered around the entrance, some of them beating their wings to ventilate the inside, others waiting for workers coming back from the fields with news. Every few seconds or so one would dive in, his back legs swollen with bright orange pollen, perhaps approaching the other hive before realising his mistake and diverting off to the one next door: his own. Entranced by the whole thing, I felt I could stay there for hours. And it was as if I could almost begin to detect the mood of the hive by the tone and pitch of their buzzing: a low, continuous drone meant everything was all right; a higher note, more manic sounding, meant they were busy and excited about something, perhaps a new discovery of food; if this went a little bit higher, though, with occasional peaks, it was usually time to back off – they were probably getting angry about something, and it didn't do to be around them.

They seemed quiet that day. Approaching from the back, apart from one, maybe two bees flying around it was all very still. It was late afternoon: they tended to be busier in the morning. But in front I noticed that while there was a small group of bees at the entrance to one of the colonies, the other was completely empty. It had never been like this before, and it struck me as strange. I waited for a while, but still no bees appeared. My protective gear was back at the house, nor did I have a smoker and some dried cowshit to hand to calm them, but, my curiosity piqued, I decided to investigate nonetheless. I prised off the lid, stuck with honey and wax to the rest of the box. Still no bees. If I'd done this in any other circumstances I would already have had half a dozen guard bees on my case escorting me from the premises. Instead there was silence and emptiness. I placed the lid on the floor and went to prise away one of the frames. It was bare, dead: nothing. Something writhing at the base of the hive caught my eye, though. Pulling out a couple more frames, I saw a group of worms and grubs pulsating and twisting around one another, piles of larvae already growing up in the corners and at the sides. It was enough to stop myself retching. No bees, though: not one. Not even dead ones. Like the crew of the *Mary Celeste*, they'd simply vanished.

Arcadio was philosophical when I told him.

'Happening more and more,' he said. 'Lost sixteen hives myself this year. Only got five left.'

Reports of bees disappearing without trace were becoming common in the news. 'Colony collapse disorder' seemed to be a growing problem around the world, and a complete mystery. Of course I'd assumed it would never happen to us: up in the mountains, with fresh, unpolluted air and no mass farming methods for miles, what could possibly affect my bees? Perhaps the theories about pesticides being the cause weren't quite on the mark.

'They say it's the mobile phone masts,' Arcadio said. 'Disorients the bees. Makes them lose their way.'

We had mobile coverage – just – up at the farm, and it was an attractive theory – blame it all on modern technology – but I'd recently seen an article ruling the idea out. Besides, were the signals up here really strong enough to cause something like this? Researchers could say what it wasn't, but they still didn't know what it was.

Perhaps, I wondered, there might be some kind of herbal remedy for the problem, but Arcadio just shrugged. This was a new phenomenon. The plants were good for traditional ailments, not modern mysteries.

I looked around at our unspoilt, untainted countryside. What on earth could be affecting the bees up here? It just didn't seem to make sense. But there was something disturbing about it: echoes of a world in disorder, falling apart. Man had been working with bees in this part of the world for thousands of years: the oldest known representations of beekeepers were painted on the walls of a cave in a sierra just a few miles to the south. But now the bees were vanishing – and no one knew why. It was a chilling thought. With no bees to pollinate plants, it was often said life on the planet itself wouldn't have long to go.

'We'll split your remaining hive,' Arcadio said. 'And try to get you two colonies again. Then again the following year, so you have four.'

'What happens if the other colony disappears in the meantime?' I said.

He shook his head. There was no answer.

*

Cooking with truffles. The main difficulty here is that truffles have a relatively short season and are extraordinarily expensive, so you don't have much time or, usually, that much material for culinary experimentation. In addition, there is a lot of mythology about truffles to be taken on board and either absorbed or discarded before you can properly appreciate them. Often this comes in a kind of 'click' moment, when everything you've heard or read about them suddenly makes sense. It's not easy to describe; only personal experience will really do. It came for Salud one mid-week lunchtime when I presented her with a plate of truffle scrambled eggs. Until that moment she hadn't really got truffles, and regarded my enthusiasm for these black, smelly tubers with some bewilderment. On previous days (we were taking advantage of suddenly finding ourselves in possession of one medium-sized truffle and two much smaller ones – a gift from the Truffle King) I had presented her with plates of truffle salad, truffle pasta and roast meat in truffle sauce, all of which, sadly, failed to provoke any excitement in her. For this dish, however, I had left a small truffle inside a jar with half a dozen eggs for a day or two on the understanding that the flavour would be absorbed through the shell and into the eggs themselves. Following a French recipe, I scrambled these trufflised creatures in a heavy pan with a generous amount of fresh butter, adding a few shavings of the precious truffle itself to the foaming liquid seconds before pouring in the loosely beaten eggs. The smell drifting up from the pan was mouth-watering, but I had grown used to disappointments in trying to convert that smell into flavour. So I wasn't holding out too much hope this time.

The look on Salud's face when she placed the first forkful into her mouth, however, told me that my efforts had not been in vain. She smiled, raised her eyebrows and looked at me in astonishment.

'*¡Qué rico!*'

Her 'click' moment had come.

Something – perhaps it was the butter, perhaps the eggs – had proved to be the perfect vehicle for the complex range of flavours that come in a truffle. Hints of apple and asparagus were there alongside the more usual mushroom and earthy tasting notes, while the thick yellow of the eggs perfectly framed each tiny morsel of black truffle at the bottom of our plates. Not a scrap was left, piece after piece of fresh bread broken off to wipe up all residual flavour. And we immediately placed another half a dozen eggs in the jar with the truffle and sealed it for lunch the next day.

Another preparation that has had some success is truffle oil, where you simply place whole truffles, or pieces of the stuff, in a bottle with some oil in it and let it stand for a week or so for the flavour to absorb. One thing, though: the olive oil shouldn't have too strong a flavour. I made the mistake of using unfiltered cold-pressed extra virgin oil – from our first batch of olives from the farm – for the first experiments making truffle oil. Something lighter would have worked better, and have allowed the flavour of the truffles to have come through more strongly.

Elisabeth Luard's book *Truffles* is the best I've found on all of this in English.

★

I've just come back from the truffle-tree plantation and I can still hardly believe what's happened up there. At least half of the saplings – more than a hundred trees – have been ripped from the ground. It's almost certainly the wild boar. I expected they might be a problem in around ten years from now, when the first truffles are supposed to appear, but from telltale hoof prints nearby it seems they're already scouring the area. The large stones I placed around the base of each tree – and which I thought would offer some protection – have simply been tossed aside. I can't think there's anything 'truffly' to attract them about the saplings – they're far too young. They must just be looking for roots and acorns.

The ground is churned up in that area from working the land in preparation for planting. It's easy pickings for them.

It's too late to replace the missing trees – that will have to wait till next year. Half a winter's work gone overnight. The best I can hope for is to save the ones remaining. There are whole terraces up there with only one sapling left. The rest have just been wiped out. Bring on the hunters. Let them kill all the bastards.

★

The photograph showed a valley that seemed familiar: poplars lining the banks of a river, green pastures, a little hermitage tucked in at one side. But it had changed: in the middle of the picture stood a great big electricity station, cables and pylons flashing in and out of it like a broken spider's web. They had come and built, as they said they would, and now the valley where El Clossa had found the sauropod bones had been ruined: a corner of wild, unspoilt and ancient countryside was lost.

'They got the bones out just in time,' El Clossa said. 'They're down in Castellón museum.'

I handed him back the photograph.

'No water this winter,' he said as we set off on our walk along the dirt track that ran along the side of the riverbed. 'This should be full at this time of year.' He nodded down at the dry, moulded rock, empty pools laid bare like cupped hands pleading to receive nourishment and refreshment. 'If it doesn't rain . . .'

He hobbled on. The butt of his crutches made their familiar *TOK, TOK* sound as he propelled himself forward with each step in a complex, whole-body motion, powerful hands pushing against the well-worn handles. The veins stood out against his thickened wrists, a delicate gold chain nestling in the dark hairs of one of his forearms.

There was little more than twilight down at the bottom of the valley: the low, late winter sun couldn't penetrate down here, and we walked in heavy shade while catching odd glimpses above of a crystal-blue sky filtering through the pine trees. The only colour came from the pink sand of the track beneath our feet, while the green of the oleander bushes lining the banks of the riverbed contrasted with the sharp white rocks of the mountains rising up on either side. Every so often I caught sight of yellow gorse blooms pushing through, but the landscape felt as if it were on hold down here, waiting patiently, desperately, for the rains to come and restore things to their natural state; to flood the hillsides and send gushing torrents of clear, healing, life-giving water down this parched channel, scratched, like a wound, into the flesh of the earth.

I had only ever driven up this part of the track – just beyond the turning up to our mountain. After a few miles it ended at a small quarry where a man in a truck came once a day to dig out some chunks of low-grade marble for use in road building. I'd been to have a look once, out of curiosity, but had found little of interest and so had never returned: the village lay in the other direction and this was a dead end; there was nothing else up here. Or so I had thought until El Clossa had informed me otherwise. There was much, he'd said, to be discovered. And so we'd fixed a date to spend the day walking around the area. At least, I walked; what El Clossa did was closer to flying.

El Clossa had insisted on an early start: there was still little daylight at this time of year and we would need every hour available to complete the route he had in mind. After meeting him down at the chain at the bottom of our road, he'd set off as usual like a rocket: the able-bodied just had to keep up: there was no time for loafing about.

Crossing the riverbed for a second time as it curled around the track, I wondered aloud about fossils in this area. I'd come across strange forms and shapes in the rocks I used for building dry-stone walls and during the restoration of the house, things that seemed to hint at ancient life, now petrified, buried inside them, but never anything a layman such as myself could identify as a 'fossil'.

'There are some marine animals around,' he said, 'but not a huge number in this particular valley. Some a bit further up, closer to the peak of Penyagolosa.'

I bent down quickly to pick up a stone at the side of the track that caught my eye – deep red lines running through pale white. It felt good in my hand as I turned it over, rubbing my thumb over the contours, warm and pleasing. Today it lay at the foot of pine trees and gorse bushes, but what else had this rock seen through the millions of years of its life?

'This area is Cretaceous,' El Clossa said. 'As most of the province is, except for the south, which is mostly Jurassic and Triassic. There's some Jurassic rock not far from here, but the Penyagolosa massif – what we're at the edge of and just about to climb – is Cretaceous.'

I tried to remember something from my primary school classes about the dinosaurs, and anything else I'd picked up on the subject since. We were in the Mesozoic era, I seemed to remember, made up of the Triassic, then the Jurassic and finally the Cretaceous periods. But when exactly had all this been?

'About a hundred million years ago,' El Clossa said. 'Roughly. Give or take thirty or forty million years. That's when all these rocks around us would have been formed.'

I tried, but simply couldn't get my head around the figures. He could have pulled any number out and I would have believed him. A hundred million years?

'Not that old if you think the earth is about four billion years old,' he said.

For a moment I felt I could understand the creationists and their simple stories about how all this had begun. It was so much more emotionally appealing to think some bloke had just made the world by snapping his fingers over the course of a few days virtually within human memory, than to take on board timescales that were beyond our ordinary imagination.

'Cretaceous comes from the Latin for "chalk",' El Clossa went on. 'All this rock would originally have been seabed. That's what makes limestone, and sometimes chalk.'

'And that's why you find marine fossils round here,' I said, putting the pieces together.

'There are mussel shells at the top of Penyagolosa,' he said. 'Almost two thousand metres above the current sea level.'

I liked the way he used the word 'current'. El Clossa lived not in the fixed world most of us saw, but one in a state of flux. The earthquakes and shifting plates that had churned those sea creatures up and lifted them into the sky were part of the landscape he inhabited.

He talked more about the geology of the area as we walked on. The Cretaceous period had been when the first bees had appeared, co-evolving towards the end of that time with the first flowering plants. It had also seen the appearance of ants and grasshoppers, as well as leafy trees such as figs and magnolias. Meanwhile, these mountains around us, as most of the mountains in the country, had been formed at the same time as the Alps – the Alpine Orogeny. It was at a time when the Iberian Peninsula, on a minor tectonic plate of its own, semi-detached from the rest of Europe, had crashed into what was now southern France, creating the Pyrenees as it merged with the mainland.

'Geologically,' he said, 'we're not really part of Europe and we're not part of Africa either. We're on our own, almost like an island.'

In an instant so much of the Spanish character seemed to be explained: the controversial 'difference' of Spain, its insularity and strong sense of independence; its wanting to join Europe but never quite being a part of it. It was no mere country: it was a mini-subcontinent. Could the geology of the place, events that had happened a hundred million years before, really have played a part in the formation of a national character?

We reached the end of the track, the quarry just ahead of us, an empty space with piles of dark-grey rock piled up here and there waiting to be picked up and carted away. Occasionally we had heard the explosions from this spot up at the farm as they blasted away at the stone to loosen it. It was a curious place, this tiny vein of black marble surrounded by the white and pink limestone of the rest of the landscape.

'Marble is metamorphosed limestone,' El Clossa explained. 'Lime that's been transformed by heat and pressure of the years. There's not much of it round here, but where there is they get at it and dig it out as best they can.'

'But you haven't just brought me to look at the quarry,' I said.

'There used to be an ancient fortress here,' he said. 'But it was destroyed by them digging all this out. Iberian, probably.'

Now there was just a big hole.

'We,' El Clossa said with a grin, 'are going up here.'

And he was off again, charging off the track, across the riverbed and disappearing into some oleander bushes at the bottom of what looked like a steep slope. I followed as fast as I could: blink and I might lose him altogether. There didn't seem to be any path in sight, though. Perhaps he liked engaging in a bit of off-road hobbling. Did they make four-wheel-drive crutches?

I pushed through the oleander leaves trying to figure out where he had gone. I could hear him further along, cracking at the ground as he flung himself upwards. Just which track was he walking on? Then, as I scanned the land ahead, peering through the thick foliage, I caught sight of what looked like steps, built into the rock. For a moment I felt like an explorer in the Amazon suddenly discovering a trail in the jungle to a long-lost city. I must be seeing things, though. We were in the middle of nowhere. Why would there be steps here? I moved closer in and poked at the ground with my foot, clearing away some of the undergrowth. Smooth, worn stone steps glared back at me. With a deep, sudden longing I knew nothing but the urgent desire to find out where they led.

'Come on!' El Clossa called from higher up. 'We have to keep moving.'

Five breathless minutes later I caught up with him, fighting my way through the bushes and trees as I attempted to follow the almost invisible path. The steps seemed to vanish and then reappear at times, while broken twigs and flattened plants showed me where my companion had passed only moments before. The climb was steep, but I found him standing by an ancient juniper tree, waiting. We had climbed high enough now to feel the first rays of sun on our faces. Behind, the bare mountain rose up in a kind of bulge, black smoky stains on the overhang underneath. There was a flat area here, with signs of it having once been used as a shelter by humans.

'That's an *abrigo*,' El Clossa said pointing to the area with a crutch. 'Open caves in the rock. Farmers used to shelter in them during rainstorms.'

'And light fires to keep warm, by the looks of things,' I said.

'This used to be an important route we're walking on,' he said. 'They'd bring their produce down from the mountains, then meet up with the river we've just left and follow it down all the way to the coast. It was a main road linking the sea and the mountains.'

And now it was a lost path winding up an overgrown, abandoned mountainside. For a moment I saw trains of donkeys and mules trekking up and down past where we were standing, wicker baskets thrown over their backs filled with wheat, figs, grapes, almonds. What did the *masovers* bring back with them from the towns and villages where they sold their produce?

'Ironware – knives, tools,' El Clossa said. 'Material for making clothes. They were strongly independent folk. It was a hard life for them: they had to be tough. Most of them just dreamed of earning enough money to buy a little flat in the village to live out their last days. You couldn't survive up here with arthritis or a dodgy hip. If you weren't fit to be out working and climbing mountains all day you had to jack it in. No comforts back then. Effectively they didn't even have the wheel until about a hundred years ago.'

I knew the wheel hadn't reached the New World until the Spanish invasions, but we were definitely in the Old World here, despite my earlier Amazonian fantasies.

'The first proper road to the village from the coast wasn't built until the end of the nineteenth century,' he said. 'Before then you could only travel up here on horseback. No roads, no wheels. And up here where we are now the wheel probably never made it at all.'

Once again I had the sense of time-travelling, of having been transported, unwittingly, to an ancient land, one that existed on my very doorstep.

'Okay, they probably *knew* about the wheel here,' he said, 'but it was something other people had, not them. They had animals, and their own legs to carry them.'

There was a pause: no bitterness in his voice or expression. He picked up his crutches and launched himself back on to the path.

'Let's go,' he said.

We continued upwards, past a few burnt out stumps left from the forest fire years before, where the greenery had for some reason failed to re-establish itself. Exposed limestone pushed through the earth; strange, wave-like erosion patterns formed on the surface. From a few metres higher up we were able to look down at the overhang where we had just been. Black and orange streaks cascaded down the rockface above it where water filtering from above had left mineral deposits. In some places weird rounded shapes had formed over the years, faces and dragons staring out like gargoyles.

Slowly, the climb began to ease as the path reached flatter land. We were high up above the valley here, and the surrounding mountains felt more like friends now, less imposing, as the sky opened up over our heads. Stumpy holm oaks lined the path, dense and prickly, the ground beneath them covered in a very similar looking oak bush – *coscoll*. There would be plenty of wild boar up here, I felt sure, and I started looking for telltale signs of their burrowing in the soil for acorns and roots, bitter memories of the damage they had done to my own small attempt to plant a forest bubbling angrily inside me.

There were no more carved steps now, but I noticed a low stone wall running along the side of us as we walked on. Rather than marking a field division, it actually seemed to be there to show the route we should follow. Was this one of the ancient transhumance trails El Clossa had mentioned to me before, the day we saw the dinosaur bones?

Just then I heard him call out. I looked up and saw him pointing forwards. Up ahead of us was a white abandoned *mas* standing proudly on a flat area of land.

'The Mas Roig,' he said. 'Your neighbours.'

We walked closer, over open fields of thick, short grass. The *mas* was like a little village or hamlet, a group of four or five houses grouped around in one corner, while another house was set apart, perhaps three hundred yards away. They were built on a horizontal tongue of land jutting out from the slope of the mountainside, the land cascading away steeply on three sides. Behind the farmhouses, cut into the earth, terraced fields curled away following the contours, almost completing a semi-circle so that it looked not unlike a gigantic Greek theatre. Above, a bulbous, red-faced mountain loomed large.

'That's the Cabeço Roig,' El Clossa said. 'Right behind that is the peak of the Penyagolosa. Can't see it from here – this one's standing in the way.'

The weather was clearly much harsher up here. To one side stood an oak tree leaning with every branch towards the south, as though it had been frozen during a northerly gale. There was nothing on that side to protect it, no shelter from the harshest wind round here – the

Tramuntana. The views were spectacular, but winter nights must have been long and hard. Today it was sunny and the air was still. You wouldn't want to be stuck up here during a storm.

In fact we were only a short distance from our own farm, but looking at the land and vegetation around us I realised there was quite a difference in the plant life. It had a windswept look about it, with fewer trees, grass hugging the ground as though for protection. The odd pine tree up here was also of a darker hue to our Aleppo pines. Probably Scots pine, I guessed: I'd look it up when I got home.

After poking around the empty shell-like farmhouses for a few moments, bending under broken beams and rubbing my fingers on the blue-and-white lime-washed inside walls, I found El Clossa standing by a small walled enclosure – perhaps an old pigpen or shelter for sheep.

'The *masovers* didn't have much time for churchgoing,' El Clossa said. 'When you're looking after animals you can't just take a day off to celebrate mass all the time. They need constant attention. So you never saw them at the fiestas or anything. The only religious feast the priests insisted they attend was Corpus Christi – they had to be there, once a year. All the others – Christmas, Easter – they were exempt from.

'Here, I want to show you something.'

I followed him round to the back of the farmhouses and up a short incline. At the top was a low, white, domed structure made out of stone and mud. A small, dark hole in one side like a mouth led out to a stone channel, where water trickled down, leading to a small pool. I stepped up and looked inside the dome and found a spring of fresh water, the surface rippling ever so slightly. It felt cool in there, with a dank, cellar-like smell.

'The dome is probably only a few hundred years old,' El Clossa said. 'But some people think the springs themselves have been around since Iberian times – before the Romans.'

I remembered that on the far side of the village there were the remains of an old Iberian tower, a small but important local clue to what was still a mysterious ancient people. They had clearly populated this area back then. Had our own spring back at the farm also originally been dug out by them? Tempting though the idea was, I doubted it. But there was a problem trying to date any of the buildings and structures scattered and abandoned over the local countryside. Building techniques had changed so little over the centuries that a terraced field could date from the Bronze Age or from just a hundred years ago. There was little way of telling.

The Iberians are fascinating if only because so little is known about them. Their writing system resembled runes in appearance, but has yet to be deciphered, while very few physical remains from their times have been found. The problem is that they appeared to have absorbed much from the other Mediterranean peoples setting up trading centres and towns on the Spanish coast – Greeks, Phoenicians and Carthaginians, later Romans. So historians have had difficulty differentiating the truly 'Iberian' from what might – or might not – have been influences from Eastern Mediterranean culture. They cremated their dead, and gave religious importance to a Mother Goddess figure, while the fourth-century Roman writer Avienus admired them for their writing and artwork. Many Iberian settlements give the impression of an unsophisticated people. Houses were usually only one storey high and made up of one small room. There was rarely any street plan, no monuments or temples. The largest and strongest building was generally reserved for defence, while there was very little sign of social hierarchies or meeting places. In fact, they were not unlike the *masos* around us here in the mountains – crudely built, simple, geared more to a life in the open. But then you came across Iberian artworks such as the *Dama de Elche* or the *Dama de Baza* – both statues of rather regal-looking women housed in the Archaeological Museum in Madrid – and you wondered how the same civilisation could have produced such masterpieces. There is something heavier about them than classical Greek or Roman artwork – more gravitas, perhaps – but there is a high degree of realism and, in the case of the *Dama de Baza*, a kind of presence you normally don't find in European art until the Renaissance. It was all part of the Iberian 'enigma', something that went to the heart of the permanent question mark that is part of the essence of Spain.

'There was an old man in the village years back who mentioned some caves round here,' El Clossa said. 'Said they had schematic cave paintings in them. I've tried to find them a few times, but never discovered anything.'

'Let's go now,' I said.

'Not today,' he said. 'Today I want to show you something else.'

We walked back down to the houses and then along a path that led south-west, passing below the theatre-like terraced fields. A few wild flowers were growing up here, delicate splashes of yellows and blues on the ochre background of the dry grass. A pine wood blanketed the path, and we found ourselves cast once again into the shade as we passed our way through. The sepulchral silence was broken only by the sound of our feet, El Clossa's crutches and the very occasional burst of birdsong. It was coming up to midday now, the heat at its strongest, and the animals and birds, as ever at this hour, were resting or hiding somewhere.

We stopped by some rocks to eat the sandwiches I'd brought. El Clossa was impressed by the taste of the HP Sauce I'd spread on the ham.

'English food's terrible,' he said. 'My cousin went there once and came back five kilos lighter – couldn't stomach it. This, though, isn't bad.'

I asked him whether the path we were on had been one of the ancient transhumance routes.

'Not this one,' he said. 'But there are plenty round here. Up there, for example.'

He pointed at the side of the mountain rising up behind us. Scouring the landscape I caught sight of two low walls running parallel, going straight up the slope before reaching the top and then curling round to the right.

'Surely that's too steep for anyone to climb,' I said.

He explained that the routes had usually gone straight over the countryside as they also marked boundaries between one pastoral area and another. The farmers just had to get up cliff-faces and other difficult terrain as best they could. The walls were there to stop the sheep from wandering all over other people's land and eating everything in sight.

But so much money was being made from wool that fights used to break out between the owners of one piece of land and the next. So they had to set up controls, with the transhumance routes marking the boundaries in many cases.

The herdsmen used to be charged for moving their sheep around, having to pay a certain amount per head. Places where the path narrowed down so that they had to trot in single file were used as toll areas – *comptadors* – where the sheep could easily be counted. There was one close to where we were, up at the top of the Cabeço Roig.

'There aren't many transhumance farmers left round here these days. Some near Morella. But they're mostly moving cows around.'

We walked on for another hour before striking off the path and heading away to the right. In the far distance, at the end of the valley, we could see the village nestling in the hillside, while up and beyond it the mountain tops of the Sierra de Espadán to the south. Ahead of us, at the top of a small hill we were climbing, another *mas* was appearing, as abandoned and ghost-like as the one we had just visited.

The Mas de les Roques was perhaps even more eerie than the Mas Roig: the houses huddled together like an ancient fortress, with even fewer signs, if that were possible, of men having trodden the paths and 'streets' in some years. An old blue enamelled pot, half-rusted, sat shining in the sunlight where it had been dropped by the entrance of a large wooden barn door. Shutters in the windows – most of them still intact, were shut firm against the wind and rain, with small cracks developing down them and signs of woodworm. A chestnut tree, less common in these parts, had established itself by the corner of one of the houses, casting a cool, delicious shade over a patch of grass where children might have played decades before. The whitewash was peeling from the walls, some of the roofs were falling in where tiles had come loose and the beams underneath had been exposed to the wet. A group of partridges, undisturbed for God knows how long, took fright, wobbling as fast as they could away from us from their hideaway in a nearby bush before eventually, and reluctantly, taking flight for a few yards to seek new sanctuary.

This, El Clossa explained, had been where the local goatherd – a man I had come across often as he traipsed up and down the valley, sometimes passing with his animals by our *mas* – had been born. Probably the last person to start his life up here before the houses had all been abandoned.

'What I really want to show you, though, is something else,' he said. 'Up there by those rocks.'

Twenty minutes later, after a stiff climb through the fields, we came across a towering cliff-face cutting across our path – an outcrop of rock at the foot of the Cabeço Roig. Jutting almost straight up from the ground, and a darker, browner colour than most of the stone around, I imagined the cliff to be some geological anomaly: a chunk of former seabed from some other period thrown up by a freak earthquake tens of millions of years before. El Clossa put me straight, though – it was Cretaceous, just like everything else round here.

'The curious thing about this place,' he said, 'apart from some of the fossils I've found round here, is that over there.'

Where he pointed I noticed an odd, smooth feature in the rock, something that didn't seem to fit. Stepping forwards to get a closer look I realised a stone wall had been built here, closing off a cave inside, with an old door opening through to it.

'This,' El Clossa said with a triumphant grin, 'is an old hideout of the *maquis*.'

After Franco crushed the Republicans in the Spanish Civil War, many left-wingers fled the country for France. There, they barely had time to find their feet before the Nazis invaded in 1940 at the start of the Second World War. Many Spanish fighters, with their previous experience of warfare, joined the French Resistance, which adopted the name 'maquis' from the low shrub-like woodland of Corsica and other areas of the Mediterranean – an ecosystem not unlike the one where we were now. Once the Nazis had been defeated, many of these veterans tried to take the fight back to Spain and reignite a civil conflict to overthrow Franco. Right-wing regimes had become unfashionable, they reasoned, and so the Allies would help them rid Europe of the last remaining fascist leader. Many, therefore, crept over the border back into Spain to set up or join guerrilla groups, bringing the French name 'maquis' with them. What they hadn't grasped, though, was the change in the political landscape after the defeat of Hitler, and the new threat of a conflict with the Soviet Union. Britain and America were in no mood after 1944 to help aid a group of communists bolster Moscow's influence in Western Europe. So the *maquis* fought alone, unaided and often divided, shooting policemen, blowing up buildings and creating fear among the populace, tapping into a long-held Spanish tradition of bandoleros and outcasts swarming over an untamed countryside. They created pockets of mayhem, but were rarely more than a nuisance. After five or six years most had either been killed or imprisoned by the Guardia Civil, a police force set up especially in the nineteenth century to deal with rural crime. One of the areas where they had been operating, I now learned, was right were we were standing.

I scampered up the rockface to the cave door and it opened on rusty, grating hinges. Inside it was black, the daylight barely making it through. It was just about possible to make out the sides of what looked like a cave stretching back some way, although how far was difficult to tell.

'There's nothing left here,' El Clossa said stepping in behind me. 'Been emptied by curio-seekers ages ago. But this was one of their dens, to hide from the Guardia Civil.' He flicked on a cigarette lighter and a grey gloom brought some of the cave into focus. There was a stone floor, while the ceiling, just about head height, sloped towards the back before curling down and touching the ground. At a guess it seemed no more than about fifteen or twenty square yards in size, although it was hard to say from its irregular, almost triangular shape. Above, what looked like black smoke stains marked some of the walls. It reminded me of the *abrigo* we had seen near the start of our walk, where the *masovers* had sought shelter during storms.

'That's what this would have been, originally,' El Clossa said. 'Then the *maquis* would have taken it over. They probably built the wall, although no one's certain.'

I tried to imagine what it would have been like living up here, perhaps half a dozen men and women huddled together for warmth, planning raids on the nearby villages and towns, fearful that their hideout might be discovered at any moment and at the prospect of a shootout to the death with the police. The threat, the danger and the sense of simply being alive must have been a heady mixture.

'Look at this.' El Clossa brought me in close to one of the walls and bent down. There, scratched into the rock, as he traced his finger over it, a crude hammer and sickle came into view.

'I've scoured this place. That's all there is – all to show they were once here. But you talk to some of the locals and they remember it – lived through all that as kids. The *maquis* would trek down to the Mas de les Roques at night to steal food, beating up the *masovers* and sometimes raping their women, while the Guardia Civil would come up during the daytime and do exactly the same. The *masovers* were always at the bottom of the pile, being shat on from both sides. You won't find them too often reminiscing fondly about "freedom fighters".'

The group that operated up here was eventually flushed out in an ambush in the late 1940s – two of their members were killed over in the next valley and the others caught. Few people round here had mourned their demise, even if they hadn't been particularly fond of the Guardia Civil either.

I had come across other local tales of the *maquis*. Juana la Pastora had been one of the more colourful characters leading the movement in this part of Spain. El Clossa now told me she had been operating a few miles further north, in the Maestrat, but people still remembered her name. Born in Vallibona, Juana was a hermaphrodite. The local doctor had advised her parents to bring her up as a girl, it being easier for a girl to hide her modesty while avoiding such potentially embarrassing situations as military service. But Juana was a tough mountain type, and over the years became more 'male' than 'female'. With strong left-wing beliefs, she joined the *maquis* in the 1940s and became one of their leaders. Eventually, however, she was betrayed by someone who owed her money, and was captured. At first the authorities placed her in a women's jail, but after a more thorough medical examination, they decided she was actually a man and packed her off to the harsher male prison where she lived out her lengthy sentence. It was said that when she finally got out, she changed her name to Florencio, married a local woman and spent the rest of her years in obscurity as a man. Only recently had it emerged that she – now a he – had died a few years back, in 2004, aged eighty-seven. Mystery still surrounded much of her life but a local historian was said to be writing a definitive biography, soon to be published.

We walked back down towards the Mas de les Roques, retracing our steps before heading home. We would have to hurry: there were only a few hours' daylight left and the air was already beginning to cool on our faces. I looked around at the mountains and valleys, forests and gorges surrounding us. To the south I could just make out the crest of land that marked the top of our mountain and the cliff-face that fell down to the farm. So many new hues and colours seemed to come to life in front of me, a landscape now peopled by Iberians, *masovers*, anti-Franco guerrillas and merino sheep farmers. It was a land of fossils, of Cretaceous seabeds – the fig trees at the farm, the magnolia I had bought and was going to plant in the garden, and the bees soon, I hoped, to give us our first crop of honey, directly descended from plants and insects that had emerged at that time. Slowly, first through the plants, now through glimpses of the history, I had a sense of discovery, of burying my hands in the earth and uncovering wonders and secrets. There was more – far more – to learn, I felt sure. But for now, as the falling sun cast a more golden, richer light over us, I marvelled at the vibrating, living earth.

⋆

Fierce blustering gales came from the north-west. The mountain rising behind the farm gave us some shelter from the worst of it, and we would sit in the kitchen watching through the window as the trees and bushes on either side of the valley above were beaten mercilessly by the growing storm. At night, the winds keeping the sky cloud-free, we'd glance up, half-expecting the stars themselves to be tossed around as we were. But they'd sit there, high above it all, maintaining their own cycles to a slower and more lasting rhythm.

Having an appointment to keep in the city, we packed a few things, jumped in the car and drove off, feeling concerned but confident that things would be all right. The houses had stood here for centuries. No harm could come to them now.

We were right – up to a point. When we returned, two days later, the older buildings were still the same – untouched and in place. What had changed was the new, still unfinished section of the house we had been building and working on.

Despite being such a large and important part of any structure, it took some time for me to register that the roof was missing. At first all

I could see was one of the windows, still in its frame, lying on the ground outside with its glass smashed. The doors and windows we'd installed had a sentimental value, having been handmade by my father, rediscovering his carpentry skills in his retirement. Confused, I leaned down to pick it up. The hinges were twisted into strange, torn shapes, while the five-inch bolts that were meant to keep it in place, keying it into the structure of the building, were bent like the necks of swans. Nothing of what I was seeing made any sense. No force I was aware of could have done such a thing.

It was then that the warning signals inside me began to make themselves heard. The light was wrong as I peered at the hole in the wall where once this window had been. I stood up and walked over. Looking up, I saw that the sky was visible from the inside of the house. Even at that point, though, understanding that the roof was no longer there was slow in coming. Finally I heard myself say, 'The roof's gone', as though some other, more conscious part of me had temporarily managed to wrest control of my voice. Seconds later, Salud was standing beside me looking up, open mouthed. 'Oh,' she said.

Trying to pull myself out of the stunned, hypnotised state I seemed to have fallen into, I started walking around the house, looking for any signs of the mysterious roof. Where the hell had it gone? But there was nothing, no scraps of wood or beams anywhere. Surely a roof couldn't go very far. I knew how heavy the thing was, having put it up there myself. Had someone come and stolen it while we were away? The idea was too incredible. But if not, where was it?

I slumped down the hillside falling away to the east of the house, down through fields of untended olive trees belonging to some absent neighbour, now long since abandoned. If there was to be any sign of the roof, it would be down here, I reasoned. I jumped down from terrace to terrace, but still there was nothing in sight, just the usual peaceful scenery now that the winds had died down: a loving blue sky smiling down on a harmonious, bucolic world.

It was only after I had made it as far as the track leading to Arcadio's fields that the first signs of debris began to appear: it looked like the scene of a plane crash: pieces of splintered wood and nails, scraps of roofing felt and insulation, chipboard panels smashed into pieces all lying along a trail where it must have hit the ground.

Incredible as it seemed, the gale had blown the roof 200 yards eastwards down this mountainside. Beams that were so heavy they had needed three men to lift, had been tossed away like so many matchsticks. Now they lay broken on a distant terrace amid the long grass and rock roses. Realisation of what had happened eventually sank in: the wind must have dipped down into the hollow in front of the farm on the other side before circling and whipping upwards at an almost unimaginable speed, catching the roof like a sail, ripping it away from the house before letting it drop further on down here. The roof had been waterproofed and was virtually finished, but had yet to be tiled, so it was lighter than it should have been, while a few tiny gaps in the walls still waiting to be filled must have been enough for the wind to get inside and pick the whole thing up from underneath. It would have been a spectacular sight, but I was deeply, deeply grateful that we hadn't been there when it happened.

I inspected the scattered remains down on the lower terrace, trying to work out if anything could be salvaged, wondering how on earth I was going to haul it all back up. The farm was beginning to feel less like a house and more like a ship. The weather here didn't come in halves. Whatever we did here – to the houses, the garden, the land – would have to take anything the elements could throw at it, like a boat battling through treacherous currents and storms.

Salud was back up at the house, looking slightly pale and shocked but composed.

'Did you find it?' she said as I dragged myself back up the slope towards the house. I wondered if anyone had ever been asked that question of a roof before, and told her where I'd found the remains.

'Any other damage?' I asked.

'It's as though nothing had happened,' she said. 'Except for the window and the roof – the ex-roof – you wouldn't have known there'd been a gale.' She put her hand on my arm. 'Drink?'

We sat for a while in our new alfresco kitchen, staring up at the sky, nursing glasses of warming, soothing brown liquor. I felt overwhelmed, beaten. First the bees disappearing, then the wild boar digging up the truffle trees, now this. What was the point of it all if anything we did just turned into nothing? The age-old question.

It didn't matter: what mattered was momentum, moving forwards somehow: that in itself was reason and motive enough. Screw the wild boar digging up the oak trees and screw the wind blowing off our roof. We'd just have to press on: set up a new makeshift kitchen in another part of the house and then start thinking about remaking what had been lost. And better this time: in my mind I imagined great iron bolts tying and holding the thing down. The bigger the better. With big heavy terracotta tiles pressing it all down so that it would never escape again. Why had none of the older buildings suffered? It was obvious. They hadn't been skilled masons or artisans, the men who'd built these farmhouses, but they knew what they had to do to make something weatherproof: small windows, thick walls, bloody heavy roofs.

You made mistakes, you learned and you moved on: wasn't that what this was all about? How else had we imagined life out here would be like?

'If you go in for big projects you'll get big problems,' Salud said, still looking up at the now darkening sky.

'What do you mean?' I said.

'You know the proverb: *Burro grande, ande o no ande*,' she said. 'It's got to be a big donkey, whether it can walk or not.'

I laughed: she knew me better than I knew myself.

Part III

Water

The Story of the Parrot

Once there were two friends who lived in the mountains. One day one of them decided to go and make his fortune abroad, and he asked the other if he wanted him to bring anything back for him.

Now his friend had heard people talk about parrots.

'That's what you can bring me,' he said. 'Bring me back a parrot.'

So the first man went off abroad and was away for many years. When he sailed back home he realised he'd forgotten his promise to his friend in the mountains. So he went to the city and searched and searched for a parrot. But he couldn't find one.

'I know,' he said to himself. 'My friend's never seen a parrot in his life. I'll just buy him an owl instead.'

So he went to the bird market, bought an owl and had it sent up to the mountains to his friend's *mas*.

Some time later he travelled up to the mountains himself and he went to visit his friend.

'Did you get the parrot?' he asked.

'Oh, yes,' said his friend.

'And does it talk?' he said.

'Well, not exactly,' said his friend. 'But when he hears you talking, he listens and stares at you intensely as though he was really trying to understand.'

MARCH

There now follows the season of spring, which is made up of three months, the first of which is known by the Latins as Martius *and is the first month of their year. In Syriac the month is called* Adar *and in Persian,* Farvardinmah. *It is made up of thirty-one days. During this time the days are of the same length as the nights, it being the time of the vernal equinox. Now is the time for working the soil around the base of trees, to clean them of weeds. It is also good for planting and pruning vines. According to Azib in his* Book of Astronomy, *this is the month for planting beans, as well as wheat and barley if the rains are late in coming.*

Ibn al-Awam, *Kitab al-Falaha*, The Book of Agriculture, 12th century

A final experiment with a remaining scrap of truffle – truffle gratin, from another Elisabeth Luard recipe. We had about half a truffle left, already slightly mildewy from having sat in the fridge for some time. Potatoes are sliced thinly and then placed in a flat dish which has previously been rubbed with a split-open garlic. Laced with butter and salt, the sliced truffles are then placed on top before a final layer of potato is laid over them. An hour and a half in the oven at 150 degrees covered in foil and with a tight lid. Flavour? Elisabeth Luard talks about the smell of truffle as you remove the lid after cooking. Our lid probably wasn't tight enough . . . Some flavour was detectable, but not much. A subtle one, not quite up there with the scrambled egg, but good nonetheless. The quality of the truffle might have had something to do with it, although I noticed as I was preparing it that the smell was even stronger than when it was fresh, as if there was a slight whiff of rot in there. Going over Luard's recipes again, I noticed that almost all of the ones for *black* truffles involved eggs in one form or another. *White* truffles might be suitable for pastas and salads, but for the best results with black ones, I don't think anything beats an egg.

★

The loss of the roof had effectively pushed us back into an older part of the house. It was cramped, but we could just manage to live there, if without some of the modern comforts – such as windows – that we had grown accustomed to in the newer section: it had been built more as a shelter from the elements than as a 'living' space. When word began to get out about what had happened, though, we quickly received offers to come and help us rebuild what had been lost. The response took me by surprise. Within a matter of days we were astonished to find a small group of friends and family from England had travelled out to Spain and were up on the mountain with us, eagerly helping to put the whole thing back together.

By tying ropes around the back of a tow bar we were able to salvage almost all the beams that had been sent flying down the mountainside – in the end only two had been smashed beyond repair. The roofing boards all had to be replaced, but apart from that our losses could have been much, much worse. Once we had got it all back up to the house we launched ourselves into it in earnest, wiser, more experienced, and determined we should never have to do this again. This time we double-bolted and keyed everything in as best we could, strapping down the beams and bedding them properly into the walls where before we had assumed their own considerable weight would be enough. And once they were in place, and the boards screwed in, we immediately tiled the roof with traditional, old, trough-shaped 'Moorish tiles' that felt like they weighed half a tonne each. There were plenty around on the farm, faded and moss-eaten, for us to salvage and use.

After only five days, working ten to twelve hours a day in the intense mountain sun, drinking ourselves to sleep at night to help kill the pain of aching muscles, we had finished, our new pale pink and orange terracotta roof like a smile beaming on the mountainside. It looked heavy and solid, I thought. After working on the house for so long, I had begun to develop an intuition about buildings: which walls were in danger of falling down, which ones could be pulled down without endangering the structure, how secure a floor or ceiling might be. This new roof was a vast improvement on the previous one: the errors of before had been corrected, while the tiles – something we should have got round to putting on long before – had an air of semi-permanence, at least. I'd noticed the local farmers in the valley had a habit of placing large stones around the edge of the roof, to hold the tiles on. It didn't look particularly pretty, but I decided to follow their example none the less: aesthetic considerations became secondary when you simply had to concentrate on making the house weatherproof. After a while they didn't even bother me: it was, I reflected, a nice way of tapping into the local culture. Besides, the stones and the tiles were almost the same colour, and it seemed to make the house blend in more with the landscape – something I was happy for it to do. Nature, here, was in command. We were visitors, scratching away as best we could at the surface, allowed a small space in which to live our life, battered, sometimes, by the elements, but still hanging on. I didn't want to leave a mark on the landscape, rather blend with it and understand it. It was as though I had been thrown into a cage with a lion, struggling to survive by observing and slowly learning the ways of a dangerous, majestic beast.

Arcadio came up when the work was finished to help toast the new roof.

'It looks happier now,' he said, drinking a cup of wine and fixing me with a look. 'The house looks happier than before.'

A few days later, once the toasting was over and our saviours from England had returned home, we came in late one night having been out for the day, stumbling in the dark into our newly recovered kitchen laden with shopping. Something caught my eye as I fumbled for the light switch. Two small golden lights, about the size of bees, appeared to be hovering by the window. I turned my head to get a better look, unsure what I was seeing. They sped away in unison, crossing the kitchen away from us, darting around one another playfully for a split second before seeming to go through the window and disappear outside.

My fingers found the light switch and the kitchen was illuminated. Salud was already putting the shopping bags on the table. I picked up my own and did likewise. Had something odd just happened, or was I imagining things?

'Did you see that?' I asked after a pause, unsure whether to say anything at all.

'What?' Salud said.

'Those golden lights by the window just now as we came in.'

'I saw *something*,' she said. We looked at each other for a moment, both wondering, it seemed, if it were best to leave it unsaid.

'You don't think –'

'Probably just a reflection from something,' I said, interrupting.

Salud started opening the shopping bags and putting things away in the cupboard.

'Yes,' she said, 'probably.' Then she turned and grinned, a playful flash in her eyes.

'Or perhaps they were . . . fairies,' she said.

She held my gaze for a moment, then with a skip went back to sorting out the shopping. I felt a curious flutter in my stomach and walked over to the chimney to start preparing a fire.

'I'm glad you said it,' I mumbled to myself as I lit a match and stared hard at the flame, trying to make sure it was really there, 'and not me.'

⋆

Lunch with the Truffle King in Xodos. He's got some horse manure for me, for which I'm going to end up driving a hundred-kilometre round trip. What a man won't do for good quality shite . . . It is mid-March and now that the almond blossom has gone the landscape is changing – the pink and whites fading as the strong yellow of the gorse streaks over the abandoned terraces. I drive up on a road I've never used before linking Atzeneta with Xodos – winding and curling its way up the side of the valley through olive and carob-tree groves. New vistas burst into view ahead, great green pastures. The stones here are as white as clouds, as though burnt by the sun, a sharp, bright Mediterranean light glaring back into your eyes as they rush past. Xodos is perched on its outcrop of rock, peacefully hidden and largely undamaged by the ravages occurring nearby. A few pig barns are all that blot the landscape up here, the whitewashed walls of the hermitage on the rock above the village gleaming like a lighthouse.

The Truffle King is there when I arrive, small and compact, soaking up the sunlight in the little square outside the restaurant. The sun is intense and hot up here, despite the time of year, and the altitude: Xodos must be up at something like 900 metres. I tell the Truffle King about my problems with the boar. He suggests I hang up some strips of plastic around the area to frighten them off. They are sensitive to sound, it seems, and the plastic will rustle in the breeze.

'If that doesn't work you can always try pissing round there,' he says. 'Smell of humans frightens them.'

I'll give it a try and see what happens. At least if I can prevent them digging up any more trees . . .

After lunch, with the manure in the back of the car, and some onions the Truffle King has given me to plant, I drive back along the track leading to Penyagolosa: the Camino Real de Aragon, the ancient thoroughfare that runs north–south through this region. More abandoned *masos* dot the hillsides. Despite the general sense that things are getting warmer, it is still too harsh a life to be living all the way up here. Our farm, set further down, hidden from view in the valley below, is just at the edge of possibility for this region. Things may change, more people may come in, set up hotels and countryside bed and breakfasts. But the recent winds are a reminder that things up here are still tough, despite the beauty. A family living up here years ago would have been self-sufficient in virtually everything – not just food and water, but clothes, entertainment, healthcare, everything. They would only have gone into the village to sell their produce or for emergencies. The skills they learned over centuries that enabled them to survive in such conditions have been lost in all but a generation. How long, I wonder, would it take to recover them if the need ever arose?

*

Far more time than I had expected was taken up with the truffle plantation and the best season for planting trees, winter, was already coming to an end. The cold and the wet allowed them time to get bedded in and their roots established before the long months of summer arrived. Ibn al-Awam insisted that autumn was the best time of all: *The wise prefer to plant trees in autumn over spring, as trees planted in the autumn will grow stronger roots, while those planted in the spring will only grow more above ground.* He did say, however, that there was still time before spring arrived: *Planting is often carried out once the harshest of the cold has passed, and the branches are about to start budding new leaves.* We were still all right – just – but planting now meant I'd have to take more care of the trees over July and August to ensure they didn't dry out. I'd finished with oaks for now – I could get some more the following winter perhaps – so I turned my attention to other species in the time available.

At first I worked on an oval shaped group of three terraces above the house. The land was relatively clear here, and within a day I had cut down a couple of forlorn almond trees and a dying fig tree and eradicated the weeds using the brush-cutter in preparation for planting. My red-headed nephew had got hold of some strawberry-tree saplings for us – *arbutus unedo* – and this seemed to be a good place for them, with a certain amount of shade from some mature pines standing close by. From my reading it appeared that the strawberry tree would be able to cope with our long, dry summers. I hadn't seen any in the rest of the valley – and Arcadio later confirmed this for me – but I'd come across them in some of the other valleys heading further inland towards the Millars River. Ibn al-Awam said they were ideal for mountain conditions, and recommended planting them at least six cubits away from each other. I had half a dozen, and spaced them out following the same routine from my oak-planting, placing heavy stones around the base of each sapling to help retain the moisture in the soil. I liked the idea of having a small grove of them up there. The fruit was alcoholic, hence the Portuguese liqueur Medrohno, while you could also make jam out of them. Birds were said to love them. Salud quickly christened the area 'Strawberry Field'.

I then turned to a small patch of land sitting at the top of the path that led down to our olive grove. Here I planted a couple of yew trees and a cypress. As with the strawberry trees, I had seen neither species in the valley itself, but had spotted them in the surrounding area on occasion. I associated cypresses more with tame, well-kept palatial gardens in Tuscany and elsewhere rather than our more rough-edged, peasant environment, but still, with time, its needle-point stretching into the sky would add a new, welcome aesthetic to our mountainside.

And the conditions were right for it, once it had established itself well enough. Ibn al-Awam suggested fertilising them with shredded human excrement during the first year.

Yews, I had heard, were locally considered an endangered species, although I had seen a handful at higher altitudes. I had a lasting childhood memory of running around yew-filled churchyards; there was a strength about them I had always loved, while in vain I tried to fashion longbows out of their branches in imitation of the weapons of Robin Hood, and the archers of Agincourt. In Spain the symbol of everlasting life – and hence the common churchyard tree – was the cypress, so it seemed fitting to put the two species together: a marriage of Celtic, Northern European and Mediterranean cultures.

In addition to these trees of eternity, I decided to plant a cedar of Lebanon. I began to realise that my choice of trees – while being governed largely by the conditions and climate – also owed something to fond childhood memories of certain species. Cedars had always fascinated me, with their gigantic, horizontal branches, hands stretching out as though deliberately trying to cast shade for the people below sheltering from the sun. In my imagination they were like gods, or giants, friendly creatures protecting and defending the little folk below. It would take some time for my own sapling to reach such proportions – it was barely three feet high. But even Capability Brown, I assured myself, must have been through moments like this at some point.

Magnolia was another tree that had its inspiration in some childhood corner of my mind: great goblet-like flowers brightening a spring morning; thick, leathery leaves. I wanted something that might add some colour when all the rest of the blossom had gone. An apricot tree planted years before stood nearby, and was flashing bright pink against the whitewashed walls of the house. Yet soon the stiff breezes would erase this. The magnolia went close to the front door of the house, on the western side: I wanted to be able to see it from my bedroom window when I got up in the morning.

Over the course of the following days, my planting spree continued – mostly around the farmhouses themselves as by now I'd run out of time to clear any more terraces on the mountainside. An araucaria, a 'monkey puzzle', went in further down the slope from the cedar; no self-respecting arboretum, I reasoned, would be complete without one. Nearby I also planted a thuya – the tree of life – which would be well suited to the dry conditions. Although I dearly wanted to plant them as well, I had to rule out mimosas and jacarandas, as they would almost certainly perish with the winter frosts. They grew in abundance further down the valley, but we were just a little too exposed for them. Perhaps at a future date, with a little more tree-nurturing experience under my belt, I might try nursing a couple of specimens through the colder months.

To the east and south of the house, I also planted two nettle trees – *llidoners* in Valencian. Similar in appearance to elms, they were a common local tree. The idea was that they would eventually offer some welcome summer shade for the kitchen terrace. Ibn al-Awam warned about planting them in dry areas, but said they could do well in most places: with regular watering during the first couple of years I reckoned they would flourish.

In all of this it was always something of a struggle to imagine these tiny creatures one day soaring high above. The temptation was to plant them too close together – a little sapling standing in a large space of its own could be a melancholy sight. It took a certain leap of faith to realise it would often need more than we could give it on our rocky, sloping ground.

I did my best to follow Ibn al-Awam's advice about tree-planting, digging a big hole, placing manure at the bottom, and then more around the top to protect the roots afterwards. All simple stuff to an experienced gardener, but it was invaluable advice to a novice like me. He also warned against planting trees on rainy days – except olive trees – although cloudy days were preferable to sunny ones. Fridays and Sundays were also advised against, being the holy days of Muslims and Christians respectively; interestingly, no mention was made of the Jewish holy day, Saturday, despite the sizeable Iberian Jewish population in his day.

Slowly, I began to get the hang of planting in general, and started to develop a sense for what kind of trees might survive. I still had doubts, and only with time would I see if I was getting it right, but our land was clearly suited to hardy species and varieties. I could have said that at the start, having read it somewhere, but now these words actually began to mean something. Experience was beginning to fill in where books and comments from other people only gave a sketch.

Apart from the trees, I also planted a few herbs and climbers at this time. One of the last things Agustí, the previous owner, had done before leaving the farm, was to put in a septic tank. He'd managed to half-bury it in one of the stone animal shelters that stood near the house, but frankly it was an eyesore, with its square cement roof plonked right in the middle of the garden. Perhaps at a later date, I thought, we might build a new one in a less conspicuous spot, but for the time being I decided to disguise it as best I could by cultivating a herb garden around it. Laurel, sage, lemon thyme and rosemary were tucked around the edge, while I planted some thornless blackberries on the south side in the hope that they might grow over the structure and mask some of its ugliness. A box plant and some holly joined them.

Meanwhile, I turned my attention to some of the ruins standing near our own houses. These were crumbling down in most cases, the roof having caved in years before and the walls slowly dissolving as the rain seeped in and washed away the simple mud mixture that held the stones together. The owners never came up here, but, even so, I couldn't really pull them down, despite the temptation: word would get out and I would almost certainly end up with a feud on my hands. The best bet, as with the septic tank, was to try to beautify them in some way. And so I planted some ivy and jasmine against the walls, with Virginia creeper for autumn colour. Agustí had already planted a couple of roses beside them. Now, after heavy pruning, it seemed they might come back to life: new buds were quickly appearing. Near the ruins stood a pomegranate tree that had sprouted over two dozen shoots and was looking more like a bush than a tree. I pruned it back as harshly as I dared, hoping that a proper tree – and with it some fruit – might appear in time.

Finally, I planted the onions the Truffle King had given me, placing them on a little terrace below the kitchen where some of the water from the sink ran out. That way, I reasoned, watering them would take care of itself, even if the soap suds and other elements washed down on to them might give them an interesting flavour when it came round to harvesting. Half a dozen lettuces went in next to them, to give us something cool and watery to eat in the heat of the summer.

*

A westerly Ponent had been blowing since the night before: that ill-wind that brought dry, dusty air in from the central plains, charged with a curiously negative energy almost guaranteed to put everyone in an odd mood. We are usually blessed with fresher winds coming in off the Mediterranean, but the Ponent seemed to bring with it dirt and anger picked up during its overland flight and dumped it down on the coastal mountains.

I stepped out of Concha's *mas*, pulling my coat tighter around me as I leaned in against the force of the breeze, tears peeling down the side of my face as my eyes squinted, struggling not to dry out in this desiccating air. El Clossa came out after me and we headed towards a four-wheel-drive where Pau was already sitting inside.

'We're on red alert,' he said for the third time that day. 'This kind of wind is the worst for forest fires.'

'And what with the lack of rain this winter,' El Clossa chipped in.

We'd come over for lunch, Concha tempting me with a trip to a nearby abandoned village – a magical, mysterious place hidden in a secret valley. La Estrella, she said, was one of the most 'powerful' places in the whole Penyagolosa area. We could drive there in the afternoon.

'Where the fuck are they?' Pau was getting impatient as we waited in silence for Concha and Marina to appear. Africa was now seven months pregnant, and Salud had wisely decided to stay behind and keep her company while we went for our jaunt.

'Switch on the engine,' El Clossa said. 'They'll think we're leaving without them.'

'I'm not emitting any more carbons than is absolutely necessary,' Pau said.

At that moment the rounded figures of Concha and Marina came bundling through the tiny door. Marina wrapped a large green boa round her neck, smiling.

Pau didn't speak as he turned the ignition and clunked the car into gear. It had that peculiar leather-and-damp-socks smell of an old car, and it came as a relief when El Clossa wound down his window as we set off.

We headed down from the *mas* to the village to hook up with the main road. There was little traffic about. An old man with a straw hat and a holey, thin jumper ambled past as we drove along, his wife in her apron a few feet in front of him picking herbs by the roadside and placing them in a plastic bag to take home.

After a while we pulled off the road and down a dirt track near the crest of a hill. It was almost hidden by the low bushes and undergrowth surrounding it and I had probably driven past it dozens of times without even noticing. It was not one of the better-kept forest tracks, and we bumped and crashed around inside the car as Pau manoeuvred around holes in the road and abnormally sized rocks that had fallen in our way. Scots and Austrian pines lined some of the route, while a rare handful of yew trees huddled in a dark corner beneath a cliff as we started heading down into a deep, narrow valley. The gorse was no longer in bloom, but patches of broom plant gave flashes of yellow in their place. After a while the trees and plants simply disappeared, and we carried on past naked rock as the track fell down and down, hugging one side of the valley as it cascaded away in front of us before turning away out of view.

The drop beside the track was steep and very long. I was thankful that Pau, for all his faults, appeared to be a good driver. All eyes were on the road, looking for a sign of our intended destination: La Estrella, the mysterious abandoned village.

We turned a corner into another branch of the valley and continued our descent. It was dark down here, pale, fading sunlight just catching the tops of the valley from where we had come. The land felt bare, unloved. Other areas nearby were similar in many ways – no trees, bare rock – but there was something different about this, as though the spark and energy that seemed to light up the earth was missing. I felt trapped.

'There it is.' El Clossa broke the silence, pointing ahead towards a small group of houses nestling down at the bottom of the valley, by the banks of an empty, dry riverbed. In the middle a church tower rose up above the tiled roofs.

'La Estrella,' Concha announced. 'The valley of the curse.'

We parked the car a few yards outside the village, by an ancient, decrepit cemetery, its walls crumbling slowly into the ground. Through a gap you could see the small patch of land inside had been taken over by weeds.

The path took us through almond groves before we came to the first house at the edge of the village. There, on the wall, was a sign carved into the stone, the letters painted black. Concha read aloud: 'RIP. The Estrella flood. Ninth of October 1883. Seventeen houses destroyed. Twenty-six people dead.'

The place was deserted. Rough cobbled streets led from where we stood into the village proper. The stone houses looked well built: it appeared once to have been a wealthy village. Beautifully carved stones formed fan-like arches over the doors; carefully carved gables were still visible; the doors were tall and solid, the first floor windows had delicate little iron balconies. This was far superior to the quality of building of most *masos*. And yet there was no one around. All this had been left and abandoned. Some of the houses looked the worse for it: roofs were beginning to bend where soon they would fall in, while the walls of others were already beginning to fall, exposing the interiors. Many of the houses, though, probably the majority, were in fine condition, even now, over a hundred years after they had been abandoned.

'The flood virtually wiped the place out,' Concha said. I looked over towards the parched riverbed running next to us: it was hard to imagine such a destructive amount of water pouring down here. 'The survivors stuck around for a while but then just left. They said the place was cursed and ill luck would come to anyone who chose to live here again.'

It felt colder down here; the wind was less strong than higher up, but there was a dampness in the air.

'There's another version of the story, a local legend,' El Clossa said, stepping closer. The others started walking away, towards the centre of the village; they didn't want to hear.

'Locals say there used to be a special convent down here,' El Clossa said. 'It was meant for lovers of the king and the nobles at the royal court. Whenever a woman became pregnant by them she was sent here, to La Estrella, miles from anywhere, so no one could find her.'

He paused for a moment and checked where the others were. Concha and Marina were some way ahead; Pau seemed to be lingering within earshot.

'One day,' El Clossa went on, 'a woman at court got pregnant by an important man of state. She was expelled from the court and sent here. When she gave birth to a healthy baby boy it was snatched away from her and its brains dashed out.'

A few paces away Pau gave a shiver.

'The woman was mad with grief, so she called on the stars for justice. One night, in September, they say, a star in human form came down to her. The mother asked for vengeance, but the star refused, saying it could only help her if in her heart she could truly forgive. So the next night the woman climbed the mountain and called out to the Devil. He appeared before her and agreed to grant her wish in return for her soul. A storm broke out and that's when the floodwaters came down and washed the village away. But the convent and the church still survive, and there you can see the Virgin and child, protected by the star.'

We strolled on towards the church and what had been the centre of the village. There, in the middle of the tiny square, stood a proud mulberry tree. It was still bare of leaves and its spindly branches shot out like needles from the thick, heavy trunk. On one side was a high wall behind which lay the riverbed. To the other side stood a large stone building. Its walls were painted with heavy Baroque designs in pinks and browns: columns and amphorae, a coat of arms and pretend facing stones. It was as though this abandoned structure sitting at the bottom of a forgotten valley in the middle of the empty Spanish countryside were meant to look like a palazzo in the centre of Florence. It was incongruously kitsch, and the effect was to heighten the slightly unreal feeling. It was softened, in part, by the sight of the church in front of us, far more plain and classical and easier on the eye. I walked towards it to have a closer look.

'That's where the real power is, *cariño*,' Concha said enigmatically, pointing to the church and looking at me.

'My pendulum's going all over the place,' Marina said. She was standing by the mulberry tree, her head bent down as she stared at the ball and string circling energetically from her hand. Images of her deciding the place needed 'cleansing' and pulling her pants down again to piss everywhere sprang to mind and I determined to make myself scarce. The door of the church was firmly locked, though: there was no way of escape.

A yowling came from the side of the square and for the first time I became aware of a group of cats dozing on a stone bench built against the side of one of the houses. They looked clean and well fed, with that satisfied, smiling, feline siesta look on their faces. There seemed nothing extraordinary about it at first, but then I wondered: someone must be feeding them. Cats wouldn't otherwise be lounging around looking so pleased with themselves. And they seemed more than comfortable with our presence in the square, as though it wasn't unusual for them to see people there.

We were, I felt certain, not entirely alone down here. This was supposed to be an abandoned village – a cursed abandoned village what's more. But there were signs of life.

'I've never come across anything as strong as this,' Marina was saying, still fixed on her pendulum. 'This is the perfect place for it.'

'For what?' I asked, slightly warily.

'From here,' Marina said, 'I can place a hex on all that evil development and building they're doing down on the coast. Marina d'Or,' she cried, raising her hands high above her head, 'shall be no more!'

I'd had enough of Marina's crazy magic, and turned my back on her, preferring not to see what her 'curse' would entail. As long as it didn't involve her stripping off: dear God, please not that again.

I walked away as she began mumbling something, and began to study the church. The façade was fairly simple, with a white, heavy statue of the Virgin Mary above the door, the baby Jesus in one arm and in her other, outstretched hand a star. On the pedestal beneath her a pentacle was clearly engraved – the *estrella* – or star – that gave the place its name.

Me-eh. A curious sound came from the side of the church. I looked up: on top of the wall, where it met the façade, was a black goat, staring down at us with wide, curious eyes. *Me-eh*, it bleated again, its mouth like a red gash against its coat. For a second it seemed to be holding its ground, perhaps even trying to frighten us away, but it suddenly became startled by something, jumped down behind the wall and vanished. I tried to climb up the wall to see where it had gone, but it was too high and there were no footholds.

I was beginning to get the feeling I'd walked on to the set of a B-grade horror film.

There was a cry. El Clossa was pointing back up the mountain.

'Smoke!' he said. 'Up there.'

We all followed the line of his pointed finger and looked up at the top of the valley. A plume of black smoke was rising and blowing out almost horizontally as it was caught by the powerful winds.

No one said anything for a moment as we stared, transfixed. Up above, a forest fire was catching hold.

'Quick!' El Clossa cried, as though breaking everyone out of a trance.

No one stirred. Concha and Pau looked at one another.

'Come on!' El Clossa called. He was already scuttling back to the car at lightning speed. I started after him, the others eventually rousing themselves and following.

By the time we managed to get back up the side of the valley, smoke was pouring out across the sky, a grey and black shoot curling and twisting as it headed out to the east. At its base, almost smothered by the fumes, small licks of angry orange and red flame could be seen, greedily consuming bushes and small trees. It lay about a kilometre from the track, and was blowing in the opposite direction, but even so I felt a primitive fear grow inside me. Pau was on the phone to the local foresters, but already we could see the blue and yellow flashing lights of the fire brigade in the distance making their way over. Within minutes they would be on the scene.

'We'll have to go,' El Clossa said. 'Can't stay around here.'

We remained in the car as Pau talked to some of the arriving foresters. The firemen raced past, slinging their heavy jackets on as they jumped out of the engines. A sickness grew in my stomach as I tried not to look out of the window at the blaze, praying that they would be able to bring it under control. It was a good job Salud wasn't seeing this. The very thought of it would be enough to make her weep.

The firemen eventually waved us out of the way and we headed back. Pau had wanted to stay, to help, but they didn't want him around. Dusk was falling and they would have to act quickly in the remaining hours of daylight. We watched the plume of smoke as it fell away into the distance, growing smaller and smaller, our fears growing. I couldn't help wondering if, in making her curse, Marina had got her bearings mixed up and sent it in the wrong direction.

By the time we had reached Concha's *mas*, Pau had received a phone call saying the blaze was under control. It would burn out that night, but would quickly be extinguished in the morning. As long as the winds didn't change.

'Not much chance of that, I should think,' I said, looking up at the Ponent still blowing in stiffly from the west.

'Can't rule it out,' Pau said, getting out of the car. 'Knowing our luck . . .'

año

The Story of the Three Lemons of Love

Once there was a prince who one night dreamed of the most beautiful girl in the world. When he woke up, he went to the King and said, 'Father, I must leave, for I have dreamed of the woman I would marry and must go out and find her.'

And with that he packed his things and set out on his search.

After he had been travelling for some time he came across an old woman along the way.

'Where are you going, fine prince?' asked the old hag.

'I'm off to find my bride, for I have dreamed of her,' said the prince.

'Well,' said the old woman, 'take these three lemons. When you find a spring, cut them in half and the woman you seek will appear before you. But make sure to give her some water to drink if she asks for it!'

The prince thanked her for the three lemons and they both went their separate ways.

Not long afterwards, the prince came across a spring underneath a carob tree.

'Here I shall find my princess,' he said to himself, and he cut one of the lemons in half as the old woman had told him to. No sooner had he done so than the girl who had appeared in his dreams suddenly stood before him. And she was even more beautiful than he had remembered. The prince was overwhelmed by her beauty, and when the girl asked him for some water to drink, he was so dumbstruck he couldn't say anything. And so at the striking of the church bell the girl vanished as quickly as she had appeared.

The prince carried on his way until he came across another spring, not unlike the first. There he cut open the second lemon, and again the beautiful girl stood before him. But once again he was so struck by her that when she asked for something to drink he couldn't move, and so she vanished once again.

The prince decided that he wouldn't let this happen the next time, and so when he came across a third spring he pulled out a goblet and filled it with water first before cutting open the lemon. And when the girl appeared before him again, her beauty lighting up the whole world around him, he was just able to give her the goblet when she asked for something to drink. And so she drank, and this time she stayed.

Now the couple fell quickly in love, but the girl had nothing to wear.

'Climb up into the tree there,' said the prince, 'and wait for me here. I'll go to the palace and tell them what's happened and I'll bring back the finest robes for you to put on. Then we'll go back and get married straightaway.'

So the girl climbed the tree and the prince ran off as fast as he could.

While he was gone, though, another young girl came to fetch water from the spring. But this girl was not as pretty as the first. In fact she was so ugly everyone knew her as 'Pig-Face'. Now as she was bending down to fill her water jugs, she caught sight of the face of the beautiful girl up in the tree reflected on the surface of the water. Pig-Face had never seen her own reflection before, and she started to wonder.

'Why do they all call me names?' she said, 'when in fact I am as beautiful as this?'

And she was so angry that she lifted her water jug and smashed it on the ground. But as she looked up she caught sight of the girl in the tree.

'Who are you and what are you doing there?' asked Pig-Face.

And the girl told her all about the prince.

Now Pig-Face became jealous on hearing her story, and so she said to her: 'Your hair needs combing if you are to marry a prince. Let me come up there and do it for you.'

And so she climbed the tree and started combing and combing the girl's hair. As she did so, she pulled out a pin and stuck it into the girl's head. The beautiful girl suddenly turned into a dove and flew out of the tree and high up into the air.

When the prince returned he looked up into the tree at his bride and was amazed. How had he thought the girl was so beautiful before, he thought. But he had given his word that they would be married and so he dressed Pig-Face in the fine robes he had brought – still thinking she was the girl of his dreams – and took her back to the palace, where they were married.

Some time after the wedding, when the prince had now become King, some of the servants in the palace kitchen saw a white dove flying around the open window, and it sang to them: *The King has married Pig-Face, the King has married Pig-Face.*

The servants laughed, but didn't pay it much attention. The next day, though, the dove came back, and the next, and always singing the same song. So the servants went and told the King. When he heard about the dove, the King ordered them to capture it and kill it. And this they did. But where they killed it, three drops of blood fell to the earth.

A few days later a lemon tree had grown where the drops of blood had fallen, and the servants went and told the King. The King told them to look after and nurture the tree, and so after a few more days they brought him three large ripe lemons that they had picked from it, and placed them in front of him as he was eating.

The King cut into one of the lemons, and in a flash there was the girl he had dreamed of all those years earlier. As before, the girl asked him for something to drink, and, reaching for his goblet, which was always filled with water, the King handed it to her and she drank. And so she stayed.

Now the King was very perplexed by all this, and so he asked the girl to tell her story. The girl told of how she had appeared out of a lemon, and how she had climbed a tree to wait for the prince to bring her fine robes so that they might go to the palace and be married. But that a girl had climbed into the tree with her to comb her hair, and had stuck a pin into her head and turned her into a dove.

The King turned to his wife, who hung her head in shame. And she confessed the truth of what the girl had said.

And so the King declared that from that moment on the girl who had appeared from the lemon would be his wife, as it was she he had intended to marry all along. And Pig-Face was condemned for having tricked him, and was put to death.

And the King and the girl who came out of a lemon lived happily ever after.

APRIL

The month known as Aprilis *in the Latin tongue is called* Nisan *in Syriac and* Ordibeheshtmah *in Persian, and is made up of thirty days. It is the month of roses: for making rosewater, as well as rose sherbets, sweetmeats and oils. Azib says this is the month that horses are set to mate with mares, having to spend seventy days with them until the day of* Ansarat, *or 24 June. On the sixth of this month the star* al-simak [Spica] *begins to dip below the horizon, it being the third of the constellations known for their beneficial influence on harvests. During the last five days it usually starts to rain – by 5 May at the very latest. In Spain this is the end of the sowing and planting season. During the last ten days of the month and the first ten days of May, olive and fig trees begin to bud. Bees begin to swarm and the water in springs and wells rises.*

Ibn al-Awam, *Kitab al-Falaha*, The Book of Agriculture, 12th century

Farmers down in the valley are starting to prune their olive trees, so I've decided to try doing the same. Ours look like they haven't had much attention in a good many years. Whereas theirs are neat, small affairs, never more than about eight feet high and branching out parallel to the earth like vast umbrellas, ours reach proudly up to the sky with shoots like arrows stretching high, high out of reach. We didn't have that many olives at the last harvest: pruning may hold the key to a larger crop.

It is, needless to say, more complicated than it looks. The general idea, from what I've gathered, is to get rid of anything that's growing vertically, leaving only the horizontal branches, from which the olives are then easier to pick. In addition, some amount of general weeding out of branches is required, just enough, so the folk wisdom goes, to let a bird fly through unhindered. So far, so good. The problem is, of course, that not all branches fall easily into the 'vertical' and 'horizontal' categories. Some are diagonal, others start off being vertical, then become horizontal, and end up with an attempt at a vertical flourish at the end. So which to cut off? Which ones to get rid of? Arcadio said you had to learn to be ruthless with plants. It sounds like good advice – but only if you have some kind of an idea about what you're doing.

So, armed with some long-handled pruning shears and a saw I have now given half a dozen of the trees a short back and sides. They look terrible, with stumpy branches sticking out in all the wrong places, not at all like the perfectly manicured specimens you see elsewhere. I have to keep telling myself they'll recover, and that we'll enjoy the benefits come the next harvest. The proof will be in the pudding – or rather the olive oil – that we get next winter. Or not.

In the meantime we made a new culinary discovery while I was out pruning. Salud popped down to see how I was getting on and spotted some long green sprouts pushing out of the ground at the side of the terrace. I had barely registered them before, lost as they were in the rest of the undergrowth, but she suddenly got very excited: this was wild asparagus. I was doubtful at first – they looked too thin, not enough like the thick stalks I was used to buying in supermarkets, but over lunch I was persuaded: fried with a little oil, some salt and a squeeze of lemon juice they were absolutely delicious. Afterwards, we spent the rest of the afternoon scouring the hillside for more: it looks like they will be appearing regularly on the menu for the next few days or so.

⋆

'There they are!'

El Clossa lifted a crutch and pointed up towards the top of the hill. Far in the distance, wending their way through bushes standing shoulder high, a group of men emerged. They walked in a steadily growing line, more and more of them pouring over the crest of the hill and snaking their way down towards us. Silence fell over the small huddle of people resting in the shade of a carob tree nearby. Our ears strained to listen. I caught the clatter of horses' hooves beating the stones along the path. The procession was almost a mile away, but even from here the sounds seemed concentrated, as though hearing them through a stethoscope. Peering through binoculars, I could see the horses come into view, stepping carefully, heads down, eyes fixed on the way forward, men walking in front of them and leading them gently and patiently by the reins.

'They're carrying the supplies,' El Clossa said. 'It's a two-day walk, remember.'

The procession advanced, the vanguard disappearing into a small wood further down the slope of the hill as they came closer towards us.

'They're always at the front, leading the way. The pilgrims come after them.'

We could hear voices now, the odd word spoken by the horsemen and the other figures accompanying them on the walk. Ramblers, with brightly coloured waterproofs tied around their waists and heavy staffs in their hands, appeared just before them. Locals, in many cases, or people from the coast, performing the same rite alongside the official event. The landscape, always empty, almost barren, was becoming alive with people.

The murmur among the crowd that had slowly built up was suddenly hushed as someone called for silence. We listened: still the sound of the horses, and the occasional word from the men leading them, but there was something new. It seemed almost like a goat or a sheep calling, but was too strong a voice and was carrying too far. Up towards the top of the hill a man was singing; it was faint at first, barely audible, but then as he reached the top and started coming down the path behind the horsemen, his strange, unmelodious Latin chant filled the valley below where we stood. It was unlike anything I had ever heard: a curious, strangled sound, sliding between notes and wailing. There was no tempo, and the intervals were unusual: cascading down and then reaching a higher, inharmonious note again. I knew something about Spanish music, but this was not like anything I had ever heard in flamenco, or even the *saetas* sung in honour of Jesus and the Virgin Mary at Easter time down in Andalusia, with their strong Middle Eastern influence. What we were hearing now, if anything, reminded me more of Eastern European chants: I had never thought I would find anything like it in Spain, let alone in the next valley to our farm.

'The singer usually comes just ahead of the pilgrims themselves,' El Clossa said, moving a step or two closer. 'There, look, you can see them now.'

Through the binoculars I could make out a line of figures emerging over the hill wearing dark-blue cloaks, heavy, black, bell-shaped hats pulled down over their heads. As they had done for centuries, the thirteen pilgrims of the village of Les Useres were crossing the Filador Pass and making their way to the first important stop on their annual journey to Penyagolosa: the sanctuary of Sant Miquel de les Torrocelles.

It is common in Spain for villages to perform a mini-pilgrimage of some sort on one of their holy days, usually around springtime. These *romerías*, as they are called, usually involve a group walk out into the countryside to some nearby sacred site – perhaps a monastery on top of a hill where a monk once lived, or a spring where centuries before a peasant discovered a hidden statue of the Virgin Mary. The name hints at the importance of the *romero*, or rosemary, that women usually pick on these occasions. It is often an excuse for a bit of a drunken picnic in the countryside, a way for the 'urban' world of the town or village to pay symbolic homage to the natural world around as it awakes from the sleep of winter. And they often don't go very far – perhaps a mile or two at most. Usually a 'pilgrimage' suggests going elsewhere. Here it felt more about reminding yourself of what lay on our own doorstep.

Some of these walks had become rather big affairs, the best known of them being the *romería del Rocío* in western Andalusia, where up to a million people walked and rode on horseback through the countryside towards a small town north of Cadiz, the women dressed up in their finest polka dot *Sevillana* dresses, the men often looking like members of a matador's entourage. The most important one in our area, however, was the rite of Els Pelegríns de Les Useres, a village just over in the next valley from us. Every year, on the last weekend in April, thirteen hand-picked men set off for a punishing twenty-two-mile walk over the mountains to the sanctuary of St John – Sant Joan – at the foot of Penyagolosa where they spend the night in prayer before walking all the way back again the next day. It has become one of the biggest events in the local calendar, and people from all over come to watch, or even to follow the trail themselves alongside the pilgrims. El

Clossa had agreed to bring Salud and me along to show us sections of the route.

The first of the horsemen – *els càrregues* – started appearing where the path emerged through a gap in the bushes near where we were waiting for the procession to pass. They walked in silence, occasionally glancing up at the sky as the clear light of morning gave way to heavy clouds blowing in from the north. The only sound came from the horses themselves, and the clopping of their hooves on the stones, the odd word or click of the tongue from their masters if their concentration broke. They were heavily laden with leather saddle bags thrown over their haunches. The *càrregues* offered almost no recognition to the few people huddled beside the path watching them come through: there was a look of calm seriousness on their faces, as though in spirit they were already reaching out to Penyagolosa and their final, distant destination.

The singing from behind became louder as the horses walked through and the pilgrims behind them approached. The odd, lilting chant carried along the breeze had the sense of turning the landscape into a vast open-air cathedral. But although the church was officially involved and organising the event, there was already a feeling of this being something outside the normal confines of Catholic rituals; the song on its own had a heightening, disturbing effect unlike any choir or Western religious chant. As we waited for the pilgrims themselves to appear, El Clossa told us something of the history of the event.

The earliest written records dated the pilgrimage back to the eighteenth century, but it was generally believed to be much older than that, probably originating some time in the fourteenth, not long after the conquest of these territories from the Moors. No one knew what the impulse for the procession had been, but they were usually to give thanks for the passing of the plague, or as an appeal for rain, or in response to some other natural catastrophe. That was the theory at least, but the pilgrimage of Les Useres was far more like an ancient initiation rite than anything else. The men from the village who were to act as pilgrims were specially picked every year. On the last Sunday of March anyone wanting to participate put their name on a list and then the church officials would decide which men from each particular street would be allowed to put on the distinctive blue cloak that signalled them out as a *pelegrí* for that year. The current cloaks were almost twenty years old; the previous ones had been worn for over four decades. On their heads they wore black hats, while rope belts were tied around their waists and rosaries draped around their necks. Everything started before dawn, when special masses were celebrated, first for the *càrregues* and then for the pilgrims. They left the village around seven or eight in the morning, walking the first section of the route to the edge of the village barefoot. Some pilgrims had been known to do the whole pilgrimage this way, but it was more common now for them to wear ordinary shoes to cross the mountains. It was also customary for the men chosen to let their beards grow from the moment they were picked, refusing to shave until the pilgrimage had been completed. Twelve of them represented the apostles, while the thirteenth, officially know as the *guía* – the guide – was supposed to represent Christ. When they reached the sanctuary of Sant Joan they were taken to a special room and told a secret – one that had remained a mystery down the centuries.

'This has long been a land of heretics and strange beliefs,' El Clossa said. 'Templars, Cathars; they've all been here at one time or another.'

A quote from Umberto Eco was dislodged from some corner of my memory: 'A lunatic is easily recognised,' he'd once said. 'Sooner or later he brings up the Knights Templar.' There was so much drivel written about these warrior monks it was probably impossible ever to know the truth about them. They had been in control of this part of the country for just over half a century before they were disbanded. Time enough for some influence of theirs to be felt? The problem was, how would you recognise it even if you saw it?

'This area where we are now,' El Clossa went on, 'used to be the boundary between the Maestrat – the land of the Templars and Hospitallers – and the Alcalatén, the ancient "land of the two castles". This pilgrimage route basically traces the line that separated the religious orders who controlled on one side and the secular aristocrats who governed on the other.'

I tried to imagine knights with white cloaks daubed with a red cross riding through this land. It wasn't difficult: the procession passing in front of us had already done half the job of taking us back in time.

'Cathars,' said Salud. 'You said there were Cathars *here*?'

'Usually think of them being up in southern France, right?' El Clossa said with a grin. 'This was actually the last place they found refuge from the Church. Crossed the Pyrenees and came to the Maestrat. There's something in the land round here, I'm telling you. It just seems to suit oddballs. They've been coming here and settling in these mountains for centuries. Why do you think we've got this pilgrimage? Definite links with all that lot.'

I'd come to rely on him to tell me something of the history of the area. When it came to the geology, or the secular history, he seemed fine, but get him on to anything religious, and, just like Concha, it all seemed to get a bit hazy. After doing some research myself into the local Cathars I'd learned they had mostly been hiding out not far from where we were now, around the hill town of Morella, a stunning, walled medieval fortress that Salud and I had visited a couple of times while exploring the area.

Morella would have been an ideal place in the early fourteenth century for southern French heretics to seek refuge. Away from the busy traffic of the main coastal road running back to France, where there was a greater risk of being recognised, it was a former base of El Cid, nestling in the north of the Kingdom of Valencia – a relatively tolerant place in those times. Someone from just across the Pyrenees, although obviously not a local, could pass virtually unnoticed by virtue of speaking Occitan, barely distinguishable from the Romance dialect – today called Valencian – of his neighbours. In addition, Morella was linked to the French Pyrenees by the transhumance routes across the mountains used by farmers and shepherds: routes by which heretics could escape their persecutors – and also be returned to them.

Heresies were nothing new in Europe, but the small number of Cathars who found themselves in the Morella area were something special, the last of their kind. After over a century of massacres and persecution they were grouped around their last remaining 'Perfect', or spiritual guide: Guilhem Belibaste.

By 1320, when Belibaste and his *credentes* – believers – were living a quiet, if eventually doomed, life in Morella and nearby Sant Mateu, the Cathars were all but extinct. A series of campaigns during the thirteenth century had seen them reduced from masters of southern France and a real threat to the Catholic Church, to a dissipated handful of survivors, scattered over a few villages in France and Aragon. Where military might had crushed their political powerbase, religious persecution had continued in its wake, weeding the Cathars out to the last man and woman. The Church had good reason to fear them. Preaching a gentler, subtler form of Christianity which rejected the priesthood and regarded the world as the Devil's, not God's, creation, and believing in something approaching equal rights for women, Catharism had quickly found mass appeal, not least for its rejection of all forms of killing, including capital punishment.

It was in response to the Cathar threat that the first Inquisition was created in 1184, designed expressly to root out and exterminate the remaining heretics left after the military campaign. Thanks to its efforts, by the late 1200s it had all but extinguished Catharism.

A tiny group of adherents had managed to survive, however, and pursued by the inquisitor Jacques Fournier had crossed the Pyrenees looking for a new home in exile where they might continue their faith undisturbed. They had settled in the Maestrat, and their leader, Belibaste, was working as a card-maker for the wool trade in Morella under the pseudonym of Pere Pentiner.

Belibaste was a curious type to be a Cathar 'priest'. 'Perfect' was a name the inquisitors gave these men and women, for they considered their heresy to be 'complete' – *perfectus* in Latin – with no chance for salvation or return to the Church. A Cathar of his rank was called a 'Good Man', 'Good Woman', or 'Good Christian' within the Cathar community itself. Supposedly free from the corrupting influence of the Devil's world around them, they were meant to preach, fast and be celibate. Failure to do so would mean an immediate fall from their pure state. Belibaste, though, sometimes found toeing this strict line somewhat problematical.

To begin with, he was a convicted murderer. Born into a wealthy family in Cubières in 1280, he had killed a Catholic man named Bartolomé Garnier during a fight at the Archbishop of Narbonne's residence in the town of Villerouge-Termenès. He was tried and found guilty and his property was confiscated as punishment. At this point he joined the Cathars, although whether he was drawn in an act of penitence by their ideas of non-violence, or in desperation to find a way out of his predicament, is unclear. He changed his name to Pere and learned the ways of his new faith.

In 1308 a new campaign to eradicate the last remaining Cathars began, and Belibaste was arrested and imprisoned at Carcassonne in a jail known as 'the wall'. The following year, however, he managed to escape and crossed the Pyrenees into Catalonia. Having worked for a while as a shepherd, he eventually made it down to the Maestrat, where he settled with a small group of followers.

In order not to raise suspicions, he took a 'pretend' wife – Raimonda, a fellow Cathar – to disguise his sexual abstinence. But the two soon ended up sleeping together, and not long after Raimonda became pregnant. Belibaste was in trouble: as the last Cathar 'Perfect' there was no one else to 'absolve' him and return him to a state of spiritual purity. So he persuaded one of his flock, Pere Mauri, to marry Raimonda instead, and act as father of the child. A few days after the wedding, though, racked with jealousy, he repented, and freed the new couple of their vows: Raimonda would have to be his, and he came up with some new theological tenets to defend his decision.

The community lived on in this curious state of affairs, quietly carrying out their religious beliefs in secret, but without too much of a threat from the local authorities. Back over the Pyrenees, however, the inquisitors were still determined to root out the heretics once and for all. Jacques Fournier hatched a plan to lure this elusive band back into his own territory. And he had at hand the ideal double agent to carry out his scheme.

Arnau Sicre was a cobbler from the Montaillou area who had lost his inheritance after his mother was exposed as a Cathar and burnt at the stake. Far from blaming the Church for murdering his mother, Sicre was more upset at losing his anticipated wealth and blamed his mother and her beliefs for his penury. Fournier promised Sicre that if he handed over the remaining band of Cathars hiding out in the Maestrat, he could have his inheritance back.

Sicre crossed the Pyrenees in the autumn of 1318 and spent some time sniffing out his prey until one day, after arriving in Sant Mateu, near Morella, in October of that year, he bumped into a woman from Montaillou. Guillemeta Mauri was glad to see someone from home, and soon introduced Sicre to her friends. Hardly believing his luck, Sicre had fallen in with the very people he was hunting down.

The group had heard of what had happened to his Cathar mother, and how she had died without betraying any of her fellow believers. Sicre came with good credentials; they could trust him. Nonetheless, Belibaste was surprised, when they first met, that Sicre didn't know the ritual *melhorament* greeting a believer was supposed to offer a Perfect. But he didn't attach any importance to the matter, and Sicre was welcomed into their little community.

Over the next two and a half years, Sicre wheedled his way into their lives, offering them money and buying them presents. Belibaste was a tight-fisted man, and Sicre's wealth, with promises of more to come, seems to have blinded him to any doubts he might have had about the young man. Sicre talked of other Cathar members of his family back in the Pyrenees, including a rich elderly aunt called Alazais who was being tended by his sister. Alazais, Sicre said, wanted to be given *consolamentum*, the blessing that only a Perfect could bestow. Belibaste should, he suggested, travel up to see her. The community was reluctant to make this move, however, for the inherent dangers it posed. Then Belibaste suggested that Sicre's sister should marry the son of Guillemeta Mauri, that way joining the two fledgling Cathar communities. His sister couldn't travel to the Maestrat, however, Sicre said, as she couldn't leave her ailing Aunt Alazais – Belibaste himself would have to make the journey to her.

It seemed there was no choice, and so, in March 1321, Belibaste left the Maestrat to walk back towards the Pyrenees, travelling along the transhumance routes through the mountains for safety. With him went Sicre, along with the supposed bridegroom-to-be and another member of the Mauri family, Pere. At this point suspicions of Sicre's motives began to appear. Stopping off for the night en route, Pere decided to get Sicre drunk to see if he might betray his true motives. Realising what was happening, Sicre pretended to lose control very quickly, and when Pere took him outside and suggested handing in Belibaste to the authorities in return for a large reward, Sicre refused. He was, it seemed, trustworthy after all.

Still, as they approached the Pyrenees and the jurisdiction of Jacques Fournier, Belibaste's fears grew. A chattering magpie crossed the path in front of them three times before flying away – a bad omen. Heading towards the town of Tirvia, in the Pallars district, he called out to Sicre, 'Beware of false prophets, Arnau. God grant that you take me to a good place.'

The following morning, at dawn, Belibaste was arrested by the French Inquisition. He was taken to Castellbo, then back to Carcassonne, and the prison he had escaped from years before. He offered no resistance, and even gave Sicre the chance to redeem himself before it was too late. 'If you could return with better sentiments and repent for what you have done to me,' he said at their last interview at Castellbo, 'I would give you the *consolamentum* and the two of us would throw ourselves from the top of this tower and our souls would rise to God in Heaven. I do not fear for my body, because it means nothing to me; it belongs to the worms. Neither does the celestial father care for my body; he does not want it in his Kingdom, for the body of man belongs to the lord of this world, who made it. The heavenly Father wants nothing to do with what has been made by the god and prince of this world.'

Sicre, needless to say, refused his offer of joint suicide.

Guilhem Belibaste, the last-known Cathar Perfect, was burnt alive at Villerouge-Termenès on 24 August 1321. With his death the last man able to pass on the message of Catharism was lost, and the religion quickly withered and died. A few remaining Cathars were executed some years after, but Belibaste's death is commonly regarded as the final chapter in the history of the sect.

On completion of his task, Sicre received his mother's confiscated wealth from Fournier, as promised, along with more money and special privileges. Nothing is known about what happened to him afterwards.

⋆

The curious Latin chant that had so transformed the landscape intensified as the singer emerged from the bushes and out along the path in front of us. He was a middle-aged man, dressed in a white tunic and holding a large cross. Behind him walked two other men in similar robes, occasionally punctuating the chant with an *amen*. They passed in single file as the horsemen had done before, a look of fixed concentration on their faces, as though nothing else existed for them at that moment save the song and path they were traversing.

Moments later, the pilgrims themselves appeared, at the rear of the great procession. Dark-skinned, and with heavy black beards, they pounded the earth as they passed by with long sturdy staffs. Rosaries with wooden beads the size of golf balls hung like chains around their neck, while a dozen or more smaller, brightly coloured ones were slipped through their belts – carried, you suspected, at the behest of relatives and friends hoping they might thereby be bestowed with a special blessing incurred during the performance of the pilgrimage. All twelve of them strode along with their heads slightly bent, as though in penitence, or prayer. If it was rain they were asking for, they couldn't pray enough: the land was still bearing the signs of our waterless winter, the plants seeming to scream out for something to relieve the drought. I looked carefully as each one passed: none went barefoot: all wore shoes. Only the last of them – the thirteenth, the guide – walked with his head held high, eyes scanning the path ahead: it was his job to see the pilgrims to their destination and then back the following day.

At a respectful distance, a crowd of ramblers came along in the pilgrims' wake.

'Right,' said El Clossa, jumping to his feet. 'We've got to go.'

We joined the throng and set off along the path with them, El Clossa pushing his way through where people weren't going fast enough for him. Some were amused to see this Speedy Gonzalez on crutches racing past, but most were concentrating too hard on negotiating the difficult terrain to take too much notice. Along with the young and relatively fit, there were plenty of the infirm and elderly, bravely taking to the hills on this holy day.

Further along, near a spring nestling beneath a *mas*, the pilgrims were making their first stop along the route, standing in a circle while the singers chanted a new song – this time more harmonious, more like 'church' music.

'We'll pass them there,' El Clossa said.

They were eating a snack of hard-boiled eggs and olives washed down with some wine when we sped past them. I paused for a second to catch a glimpse of them. Already, only a few hours into their two-day travail, there was an air of fatigue about them, but also something else, something unusual. They sat in a line along the edge of the spring, their faces shaded by the fringes of their black hats, barely paying attention to the crowds passing them by, many of whom were snapping photographs of the scene. There was nothing arrogant or haughty about them; rather, they were simultaneously present and somewhere else, as though a combination of the intense concentration on the task at hand, the landscape and the curious chant that had accompanied them since dawn was already inducing an altered state in them. It was an expression I had occasionally come across in other religious people: meditative, present, but also absent at the same time. It was said the participants were never quite able to describe what they felt carrying out this pilgrimage. Looking at them now, I could almost understand why.

We raced on and within a few minutes had entered a new valley where a stone building with Gothic arches crowned a small hill lying at the bend in a stream.

'Sant Miquel de les Torrocelles,' El Clossa said. 'Our next stop.'

Lombardy poplars giving off a sweet-sap smell lined the gorge as we walked down the path before fording the stream and then climbing back up towards the sanctuary. The place was packed, people crowding into this small, castle-like structure waiting for the pilgrims to arrive. Journalists from the local TV station were there and several stalls had been set up serving coffee and snacks.

Sant Miquel had a walled courtyard with a large, ancient olive tree growing in the middle, while beside it, to one side, stood a chapel, and at the other a tiny lodging where once monks had lived. It was whitewashed, a handful of geraniums placed in pots on one of the windowsills. It had started life as a Moorish castle, and was later used to secure this area during the land disputes of the fourteenth and fifteenth centuries. Later, it had become a prison, then a religious sanctuary.

'There are two theories about the name, though,' El Clossa said.

'Torrecelles, meaning a prison tower – *torre-celles*. Or the other, local spelling, Torrocelles, which some say comes from the poppies that grow in abundance round here – *tot roselles* – "all poppies".'

I immediately liked the place: there was a good feeling about it, and I could tell why a different etymology had been sought for it: there was none of the heaviness and deadness that former prisons often retained. It felt light, positive, a place you would choose to be rather than be sent by force. The fact that the pilgrimage passed through here paid testament to its special character, you sensed.

We stood in the shade of a tree and waited for the pilgrims to arrive. There was more of a carnival feeling about the event here, young teenagers climbing on to the sanctuary walls in excitement to watch out for the procession. People pushed and shoved to get a good view in a constant, wave-like scramble for positions. Cries from the older spectators for quiet were consistently ignored as the tension mounted: only a few of us had already seen the pilgrims; for the rest this was going to be their first glimpse of the day.

The *càrregues* arrived first, as earlier, passing by with their horses and mules laden with supplies. The buzzing of the crowd continued regardless, barely parting to let them through: they wanted to see the pilgrims, and were leaning in so as to get the best view. Only when one of the horses circled frantically in response to the press of the people around it did a pathway emerge through which they could make their way. All at once a silence descended and order of some sort was established when the first notes of the chant from the singers accompanying the pilgrims reached our ears. As though a spell had been cast, the crowd stood still and quiet, captured by the song. They waited patiently at the crest of the hill for the first members of the procession to appear along the track. The singers arrived first, three abreast, the two at the sides carrying long poles with what looked like metal lanterns perched on the top; the singer in the middle was holding the cross. Afterwards came a priest, long purple robes flowing over his white tunic, a relic of St John the Baptist encased in a silver reliquary clasped in his hands. The singers were chanting in unison now, but more softly. The only other sound was the metallic clang of the chapel bell ringing every few seconds or so. After the priest, three figures who hadn't been present before emerged dressed in seventeenth-century-style long, black capes with broad brimmed hats. Each one held a long candle in his hand. A few moments later the pilgrims appeared. A low murmur of emotion circled through the crowd, as though witnessing a minor miracle at the sight of these blue-clad men, with their staffs and beards and heavy wooden crosses hung from their necks. Ahead of them the singers had reached the chapel and their chant had become something more like a song, the same one that they had sung on reaching this point every year for the past three or four centuries. The pilgrims, in single file and with several paces separating each one, halted, heads bent down, their eyes covered by the brims of their hats. Then slowly, one by one, they marched forwards. Moments later they were inside the chapel and the special mass that was held at the Sant Miquel stage of their route could begin.

El Clossa had wanted us to do the whole day's walk with the pilgrims, but we'd had to rein him in. Now, as we drove away from the crowds and headed up towards Penyagolosa and our next rendezvous with the procession, I was glad we had done so: the clouds that had been blowing in most of the morning were turning a threatening shade of grey. If the pilgrims didn't stop praying for rain soon they were going to get drenched during the second half of the day.

We drove up deep into the Maestrat towards Vistabella, a village lying to the north of Penyagolosa. There was a shift in the landscape as we rose higher and higher: at first greener and more wooded before bare, high plains began to appear, stretching away to the north. The weather on this northern side of the mountain was harsher than on the southern and eastern slopes where our *mas* was, and the thick, dark clouds were clinging to the summit, smothering it from view.

We sat at a crude wooden table in a bar outside the village on the edge of a wide, flat expanse of land. At over 3000 feet it was curious to see something so open and level here, ringed by mountains on almost all sides.

'The Condor Legion – the German troops Hitler sent to help Franco – used this as an airstrip during the civil war,' El Clossa told us as we waited for plates of lamb and snail stew – *tombet* – to be placed in front of us. 'There's still a swastika visible up where they had their base.'

We slurped the hot, thick food down greedily, a buffer against the increasingly cold and wet world outside. The clouds had suddenly descended and it had started to rain. One bottle of wine was quickly dispatched: El Clossa ordered another.

'The pilgrims will be getting soaked,' Salud said, looking out of the window. By now they would be passing by Xodos and the land of the Truffle King, and heading up the slopes of the Marinet mountain towards the Pla de la Creu – the Plain of the Cross. Yet they still had a few hours ahead of them.

'Some years it's blisteringly hot,' said El Clossa, 'others it rains. They're prepared for all kinds of weather. Have to be, walking at this time of year – have to expect snow, even. Snowed on them a few years back, I remember.'

His face was reddening with the wine. Perhaps it came from being so fit, I wondered: the booze went straight to his head.

'You've never,' he said, raising a finger, 'had a *carajillo* if you haven't had the ones they make here.'

And before we knew it he'd ordered a round for our table.

Carajillo is a great Spanish institution, a gloriously alcoholic coffee typically taken after a particularly indulgent meal, although some drink it on a regular basis, hence the term 'a *carajillero* voice' for the gravelly, cement-mixer type voices of so many Spanish men – and women, too, in some cases. The proper way to make it is by dissolving sugar in rum or brandy which is warmed with a coffee bean and a tiny slice of lemon peel floating in it, the coffee then mixed in before being served. Pieces of cinnamon stick are also a common ingredient. The problem is that this is a rather elaborate process, with the result that in many, if not most, bars in Spain, what is called a *carajillo* is simply an espresso with a splash of liquor. What we were going to get here, El Clossa assured us, was 'even better than the real thing'.

It arrived in terracotta cups, rough-edged and rounded so they sat comfortably in your hands, slowly warming you through before a drop had been drunk. A light foam sat on the top, almost like a cappuccino, quickly dissipating as I blew down to cool it. Aromas of sweet black coffee, lemon and sharp spirits rose up to greet me. Already I was being seduced by the claims that this was the best *carajillo* you could get. It is normal for the Spanish to claim that anything that comes from their local area is 'the best in the world': the best wine, olive oil, food, bread, weather, water, whatever, always comes from within no more than a five-mile radius of where they live or were born. It was a natural prejudice I had grown used to over the years. This time, though, it seemed it might be justified. Raising the *carajillo* to my mouth for a first sip I was met by a velvety, rich, hot liquid that seemed to slip effortlessly over my tongue. Immediately there was a sense of being wrapped in a warm, comforting eiderdown, sinking, relaxing: a feeling that you would never want to cast off the protective veil it had magically cast over you. Outside, the rain was intensifying, and the poor pilgrims up on the mountain, whose path we were meant to be following, would be getting drenched. Yet here inside, with hot, thick *carajillo* sliding down our throats, it was an easy and happy business to forget all about them for a few moments. It had more than just the usual flavours: the tiny piece of cinnamon stick floating on top next to the lemon peel showed they took the preparation seriously, but there was something else.

'Vanilla essence,' El Clossa said with a belch when I asked him. 'And whisky – they add that to the brandy. But don't tell anyone. Shhh. It's the barman's secret.'

He'd said it so loudly everyone there had heard anyway. Up near the kitchen I saw the barman rolling his eyes. It looked as though this wasn't the first time he'd seen El Clossa in this state.

It was getting dark by the time we came to Sant Joan de Penyagolosa. The small sanctuary lay near the foot of the mountain, tucked in on its north side on the edge of a great Scots pine forest that stretched up towards the summit. Great column-like trees rose into the sky forming a dark, protecting canopy high above our heads. Where the road ended a group of stone buildings was visible, forming a three-sided courtyard. There were already hundreds of people there, and a similar carnival atmosphere to the one we had left at Sant Miquel de les Torrocelles, despite the inclement weather. In a pause in the rain a group of stalls had been set up, while inside an open covered area people huddled around a blaze in an inglenook fireplace. El Clossa looked at his watch.

'They'll be here soon.'

Children were running around a dead tree near the centre of the courtyard, singing and shouting.

'An ancient sacred elm,' El Clossa said. 'Died some years back.'

He seemed to have sobered up quite quickly, filling us in on the history of the place. Personally I felt the *carajillos* were only just beginning to kick in.

Sant Joan seemed very small and humble for such a holy place. People had mentioned it to me many times before, Concha and Marina in particular stressing its ancient origins. Was it actually a pre-Christian site? 'Probably,' murmured El Clossa when I asked. The present-day building, however, dated from the fourteenth century.

We pushed through the crowds to get a better look. Inside was another, tiny courtyard, with a small chapel on one side. Seventeenth-century frescoes painted in dark tones and showing religious scenes decorated the outside walls under an overhang from a balcony running overhead. On the other side, a bar seemingly twice the size of the chapel was placed underneath guest rooms where walkers performing the pilgrimage alongside the official procession would be staying. Crude and basic, often they were booked up years in advance.

We could barely move for the crowds, and decided to head out again in the direction from which the pilgrims would be arriving. From out in the depths of the forest, once again we heard the strange chant accompanying the silent walkers as they approached. First the horsemen, as before, then the singers, and finally, behind them, the drenched, exhausted-looking pilgrims and their guide. Salud pulled on my arm and pointed: this time they came barefoot.

A priest in a golden robe from Vistabella came out to greet them, and the chant changed from the melancholy call of earlier to a song of celebration. Then the procession circled around the sanctuary before entering the tiny courtyard and the chapel, to pray. We edged forward to get a glimpse of what was going on inside, but it was almost impossible to squeeze through. Mass was being celebrated, by the sounds of it, and we withdrew to the bar opposite. El Clossa filled us in on what happened next.

'This is where the mystery and secret at the heart of the pilgrimage lies,' he said ominously as – thankfully – he poured himself some fizzy water out of a bottle. He paused for a moment as he swallowed, put his hand on his stomach, closed his eyes in concentration, belched, then resumed.

'After mass has finished, in about half an hour, the pilgrims will be taken into a small side-room off the chapel known as the *Cova*, the "Cave". There they will spend most of the night engaged in secret spiritual exercises. Branches of green pine trees and other herbs and plants from the mountain are burned in a corner to produce a heavy smoke that will induce special states of consciousness in them as they spend the entire night without sleeping, in prayer.'

He opened his eyes wide for dramatic effect as he told us this. Bloodshot and dimmed from the hangover that seemed already to be creeping over him, there was something quite demoniacal about his appearance, while the smoke and high-volume chat coming from the patrons of the bar around us were in danger of producing unusual states of consciousness of their own. I felt certain someone somewhere in there was smoking some powerful weed, although I could scarcely credit it given the official, churchy nature of the event.

El Clossa continued.

'The details of what goes on are sketchy. They say that firstly the guide, who represents Jesus, asks forgiveness of the twelve pilgrims, or apostles. Then he washes and kisses their feet. The pilgrims then do likewise to one another. Afterwards each one is told his sins, so that they might be absolved, and then, and only then, are they told the secret – the reason for the whole pilgrimage. They are given some dinner – beans and cod, the same dish always – and then they spend the rest of the night in prayer, although no one's really sure what happens in there. Then at dawn tomorrow, after mass, they're given breakfast – fig bread and strong liquor – and they set off back over the mountains to Les Useres. But now they're no longer 'pilgrims' but *els sants* – the saints. People line the streets with flowers and put leaves on the ground for them to walk over, while they hand out pieces of *pa beneit* – blessed bread. They finally make it back to their own village tomorrow night, but aren't allowed to get there, according to the rule, till it's impossible to tell a white thread from a black one. So it's got to be completely dark, in other words.'

I had come across this custom before: it was part of Islamic tradition, particularly during Ramadan when it signalled the end of the day's fast.

'What happens then?' I asked.

'There's a big fiesta to celebrate their return.'

'They must be tired by that point,' Salud said.

'Pilgrims have been known to stay up all night dancing,' he said. 'It's a spring festival – fertility and all that.'

'This secret they get told inside there,' I said. 'Does anyone outside know what it is? Hasn't anyone ever spilled the beans over the centuries?'

'Never,' he said firmly. 'They are forbidden from telling anyone, and no one has ever disobeyed. The pilgrimage has continued through wars and famine and natural disaster, and yet still they come back every spring and men in the village wait years for their chance to take part in it. And they cross the mountains come what may, exhausted, silent, stuck in a tiny room full of smoke all night, praying, not allowed to sleep, then have to do it all over again the next day. I think that's the secret, right there – the power this has over the local people. It has carried on for years and it will carry on for years to come, and no one can explain why, or what is really happening here, or why it is such an important event. The people outside don't want to know what the secret of the *Cova* is. They don't need to know, or, rather, they need not to know. They just want to think something special and holy is taking place. That's all it is.'

Outside the rain had returned and was hammering the stone floor of the little courtyard between the bar and the chapel. A flock of walkers, now wearing their brightly coloured waterproofs, surged in through the door looking for shelter. Many were carrying sleeping bags and were clearly concerned about finding a dry patch of floor, somewhere to spend the night. We picked up our things, paid and headed out into the downpour. After the hot, dry winter months it couldn't rain enough, I thought, and I imagined my trees back at the farm soaking up every drop of the precious liquid now falling finally from the sky. Whatever the pilgrims did to make this happen had worked. It seemed a shame they limited themselves to only once a year: we could do with more miracles like this.

El Clossa had fallen asleep when we dropped him off in the village. He grunted a goodbye and scuttled off into the darkness, pulling his jacket up over his head to stay dry. Outside, the land was quietly coming to life.

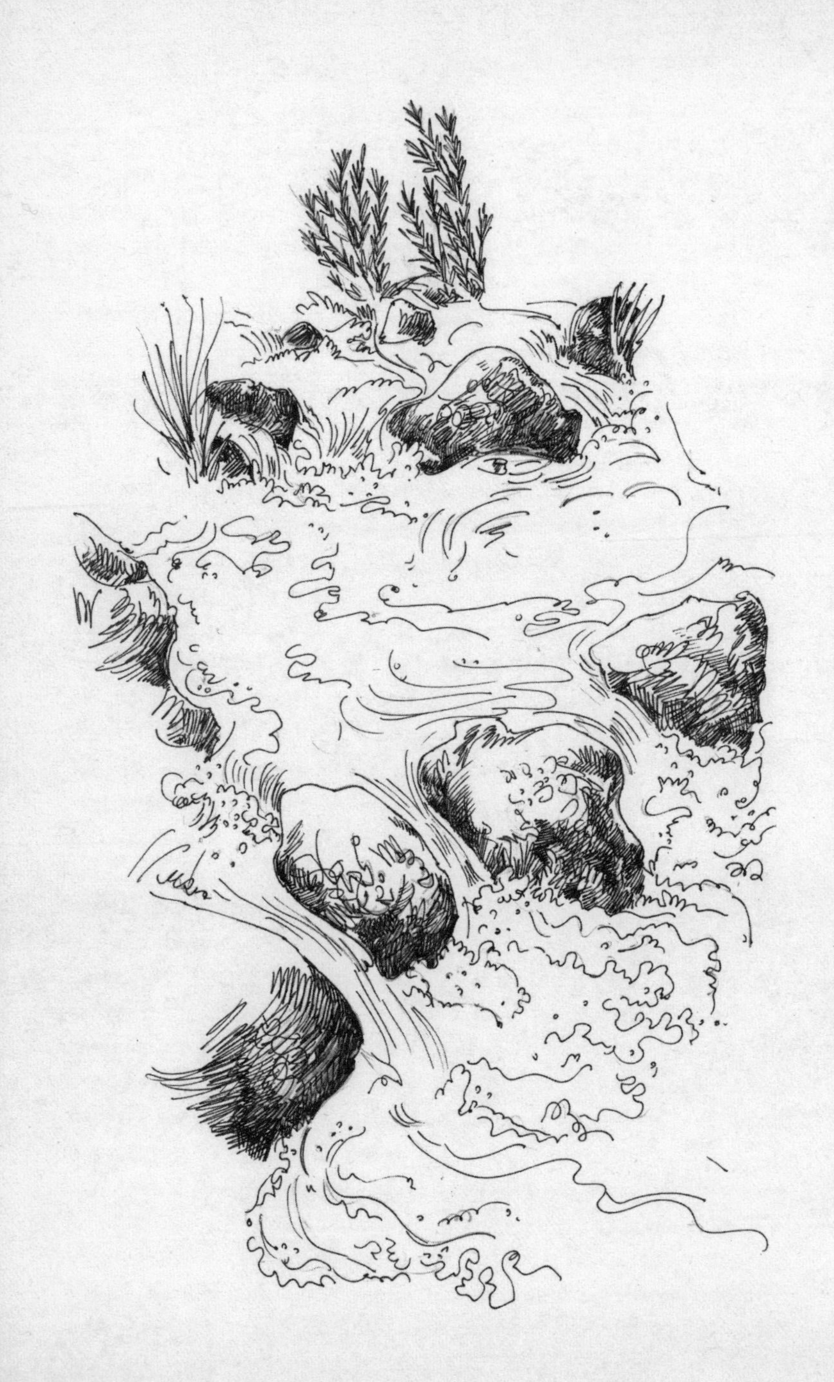

The Story of the Golden Bull

When the Moors were chased from these lands, abandoning their kingdoms in the face of the Christian advance, they decided to hide all the treasure they had accumulated over the centuries until their eventual return. And so in the village of Xodos, they placed a hoard of gold in a secret corner of a cave on the slopes of the Eagle's Rock, near the Marinet mountain. To make the treasure as safe as possible, an enchantment was placed on one of the King's sons and he was left to guard the gold in the form of a giant bull.

When the Christians eventually conquered the village, they heard the story of incredible wealth that had been spirited away to the nearby mountains, and they searched and searched for it. But no matter how hard they tried, they never found anything. Eventually, as they scoured the land, they came across an old Moor who had stayed behind after his companions had fled, and they tortured him to tell them where the treasure was hidden. With his last breath, the old Moor gave the secret away. But, he added, there was only one way to break the enchantment that protected the gold. The Christian soldiers listened eagerly.

'You must take a very sharp sack needle,' the Moor said, the life ebbing away from him, 'and enter the cave at midnight on Midsummer's Eve. A ferocious bull is waiting there, standing guard. When it charges at you, you must stand firm and plunge the needle into the bull's back, right between his shoulder blades. Then, and only then, will the spell be broken and the bull will turn into a statue of gold. You must leave the cave without ever looking back, for if you do the golden bull will turn into dust before your very eyes. A moment's bravery, and patience, will be rewarded with a lifetime of wealth.'

And with that the Moor fell to the floor and died.

Midsummer's Eve was the following day, and at midnight the Christian soldiers lined up outside the cave on the slopes of the Eagle's Rock to have their chance at winning the gold. First went the captain, with dreams of unimaginable wealth. Perhaps, he thought, with all that gold he might even become a king. So wielding a sack needle between his fingers, he stormed into the cave at the stroke of midnight and disappeared into the darkness.

The soldiers outside waited and waited, but the captain didn't reappear. Eventually the second in command decided to go in after him. Where his commander had failed, he thought, he would succeed. Perhaps he might become a lord with all that gold. And so, too, he vanished into the blackness of the cave.

The soldiers outside waited and waited . . . and waited. But still no one came out. Some of them were beginning to grow afraid. But the sergeant stepped forward. He would go in and find the treasure. Perhaps, he thought, with all that gold, he could buy a big house and become a landowner. So with sack needle in hand he rushed into the cave . . . and disappeared.

And they say there are still some men out at the entrance to the cave, waiting for their chance to challenge the bull. But to this day no one has succeeded. The story has lived on, though, and the cave can still be visited, on the slopes of the Eagle's Rock. Perhaps one day its secrets will be revealed.

MAY

The Latin month Maius *is called* Ayar *in Syriac and* Khordadmah *in Persian. It is made up of thirty-one days and is the last month of spring. All trees except for the fig will now need regular watering. On the first day of this month bulls are let loose to mate with cows; in the Babylonia area they leave them together like this for forty days, the first calves being born eleven months later. According to Azib, during this month people on the coast in places such as Malaga and Medina Sidonia start harvesting, while in the countryside around Cordoba, towards the end of the month, the first onions are picked. From my observations, in Seville this is the time for sowing late fennel, for eating a month later.*

Ibn al-Awam, *Kitab al-Falaha*, The Book of Agriculture, 12th century

The bells from the cows on the other side of the valley tinkle away in a seemingly random fashion, coming and going on the easterly breeze. I pick up my binoculars and stare out towards the animals – a cow as white as snow is meandering towards an abandoned farmhouse on the opposite hillside, jumping over stone walls in search of fresh grass and herbs. It is an amazing sight – her whiteness contrasting with the dark-green vegetation surrounding her. Then, just above, I notice a black shadow: it is half hidden among the bushes, but then moves out towards the white cow. I see a huge creature with gigantic, pale horns jutting out from its forehead – a bull, the kind that tries to kill people at village fiestas, is roaming freely on the other side of the valley. The cow seems unperturbed, but I can't help myself uttering a quiet, pensive 'Holy shit' as I catch sight of the beast. It doesn't seem such a long way away.

We've harvested the artichokes down near the beehives – catching them just before they got too dry. Salud prepared them in the Spanish way, stripping the outer leaves, then cutting the heart into slices and cooking them *a la plancha* with a little oil and salt and a few squirts of lemon juice. They were already a little too tough, but still delicious.

I've been popping up every now and then to check up on the truffle trees. It seems one or two more have been wiped out since the wild boar destroyed so much of my work earlier in the year. Just the sight of it is enough to bring on sharp stomach pains. God damn those stupid animals. But I remember some of the herbal lore Arcadio has passed on and bend down to pick up some sprigs of *mançanilla vera* – cotton lavender. A small, greyish, unassuming plant, it pops up everywhere, and is perhaps even more common than either rosemary or thyme. Back at the house, I steep it in hot water for a few minutes; it is very soothing, and in minutes my indigestion – or whatever it is – has gone. Not that it can bring back my truffle trees . . .

⋆

Arcadio came up to help me harvest our first batch of honey. It seemed a miracle we could get any at all, what with having lost one colony already, and the general lack of rain limiting the amount of blossom available for the bees. But May was the traditional month for gathering honey.

He found me lime-rendering the walls of our bedroom: a sticky, tiring business, so I was happy to be distracted for a while working on something else. I had some lumps of cow dung left over from the last time, so we grabbed them, put on our gear, and headed down to the hives. I still wasn't entirely convinced the smoking cow dung did very much to calm the bees down: they got pretty excited – and aggressive – no matter how much I blew on them. In fact, Arcadio just gave them a couple of puffs of the stuff and then got down to opening the hive up and hauling out the frames, all gummed up with wax. At least, I thought, we could give them a proper shot of it before antagonising them, so I picked up the smoker can and blasted away, but to no visible effect. Perhaps we could try burning something a bit stronger the next time . . .

Ibn al-Awam talked quite a bit about beekeeping, but I was disappointed to find he didn't seem to have any tips on tranquillising them. Quite the reverse: he revelled in the story of how a whole army of Kurds was wiped out when the people of a town they were attacking – possibly Al-Qaria – set their bees on them. The Kurds ran away so quickly the defenders were able to raid their baggage train. Apart from that, it was interesting to note how, quoting Aristotle, he referred to the queen of a colony as a 'king'.

'Mestral blowing today,' Arcadio said. 'North-east wind. That's good. They don't like the Llevant coming in from the sea. Humidity puts them in a bad mood.'

We pulled out three or four of the frames, leaving the remaining ones so as not to deprive the bees too much of their own stocks. As long as I had this one colony we'd be all right, although I'd heard queen bees could be sent to you through the post. Arcadio turned up his nose when I mentioned it.

'You'll be fine. I'll find you another colony if it comes to that.' He sniffed. 'Bees through the post . . .'

We carried the frames back up to the *era* to extract the honey. Arcadio had brought a big green metal tub in the back of the car – an extractor, where the frames were dropped and then spun round quickly inside like a merry-go-round, the centrifugal force pushing the honey out of the comb and down into the tub, from where it could be tapped off. He'd mentioned it before, but said that for the small quantities we were going to get it wasn't worth lifting it out of the car.

'Bring me a bowl, and some pieces of linen or material,' he said.

We didn't have any spare sheets, so I took him a piece of mosquito netting instead.

'Will this do?'

'Perfect,' he said.

Kneeling down, he placed the netting over the bowl, fixing it in place with some stones lying around. Then, breaking handfuls of sticky honeycomb from off the frame, he started squeezing it, the honey oozing out between his fingers and down on top of the netting. This acted as a filter, clearer, purer honey then dripping down into the bowl below.

'Your turn,' he said.

Cautiously, I tried to copy him, grabbing pieces of the dark, strongly smelling wax from the frame, peeling it away from the wires that keyed it in, then pulping it between my hands, watching in fascination as a multi-coloured goo poured thickly down into the bowl. Apart from the light tones of the honey, there were dead bees, lumps of bright, orange pollen, and a whole host of other elements in there which I struggled to identify: royal jelly, perhaps? Propolis? What was that brown streaky stuff that seemed to be mixed in with it all?

After a few minutes, we finished, and an enormous great lump of squashed beeswax was sitting on top of the netting at the mouth of the bowl, the last drops of the honey slowly filtering down.

'Leave it like that in a safe place overnight,' Arcadio said. 'By morning it'll all be through. Got a fairly good amount there – almost a couple of kilos.'

A few bees had already found us and were buzzing around energetically as we walked over to the house to wash our hands. We should leave the tools and the frames outside, Arcadio said. The bees themselves would clean them up for us as they tried to recuperate tiny lost amounts of the food supplies we had so arrogantly stolen from them.

I poured him some wine and we sat down for a moment. The honey bowl was inside a cupboard where we hoped neither the bees – nor anything else – would be able to find it.

'They want me to have an operation,' Arcadio said with a funny smile. I had no idea there was anything wrong with him.

'My eye,' he said. 'Got a cataract in my left eye.'

'Can you see anything with it?' I asked.

'No,' he said. 'I'm totally blind on this side.' And he raised a finger to his affected eye. It was so difficult even to see his eyes sometimes, with all the folds of skin, it was no wonder I hadn't noticed anything wrong before.

'And your right eye?' I said.

'Oh, that's not too bad,' he said. 'Need that one for driving.' He laughed. He knew the tracks round here as though they were an extension of himself, so he could probably drive round with no vision at all if need be. Up here in the mountains it still seemed perfectly reasonable for a half-blind eightysomething-year-old to be put-putting around in an ancient Land Rover. Perhaps the authorities simply didn't know, but down in the city his licence would have been revoked before you could blink. Come to think of it, for a second I wondered if Arcadio even had a licence to revoke in the first place.

'When's the operation, then?' I said.

'Might be next week. Say they're going to let me know,' he said.

I could tell he was frightened.

'I've heard it's very quick and simple for removing cataracts,' I said. 'I'm sure you'll be fine.'

His herbs had kept him going all these years. Unfortunately, I doubted there was a herbal cure for cataracts.

'Don't like doctors,' he said. 'Never been to one in my life.'

He stopped for a moment as I walked him back to his car. He looked out over the valley. It didn't matter how much of it he could see, I thought. This landscape was so much a part of him.

'My daughter wants me to move into the village with her,' he said. 'Says I'm getting too old to live in the *mas*.'

He put a finger into his right eye and rubbed it hard.

'But there's too much hustle and bustle in the town.'

The 'town' had barely a thousand people living in it.

'I like the silence here.'

★

Salud came back from a walk with her pockets stuffed with *caracoles* – snails.

'They've all come out with the rain,' she said. 'Hundreds of them.'

She tossed her catch into a bucket with some water in the bottom and put a lid on tightly.

'Right,' she said. 'Coming to get some more?'

We picked up a couple of baskets and headed out into the damp afternoon air. Snails with spiral stripes on their shells were easy to find – many were simply sliding slowly across the paths in front of us, while turning up leaves and poking around bushes produced dozens more.

'Don't pick them if they're near ivy or cypress trees,' Salud said. 'Snails love them but it makes them poisonous for humans.'

I'd seen bigger ones, what locals sometimes referred to as *Moros* – Moorish snails. But these were large enough and would do for a couple of meals at least. I just hoped Salud remembered all the steps of the complicated process of preparing them for eating. Get it wrong, I seemed to remember, and you might regret it for some time. Some of the snails were eyeing me somewhat suspiciously as I popped them in the basket. What if they'd been tucking into some venomous toadstools just moments before? There was no way of telling.

Thankfully, Salud had done this dozens of times as a girl back home, so it came as second nature to go through the steps of cleaning them.

Firstly, we had to purge them on the inside. This was done by leaving them for about three days in the bucket with a plate of water, some flour and a few twigs of rosemary. On this forced diet, they eventually crapped out anything they might have eaten over the previous few days that could interfere with a human digestive system. Also, the rosemary imparted a subtle flavour when eventually you got round to eating them.

Once they had been purified in this way, you had to wash them on the outside. This involved rinsing them in water mixed with a bit of salt and vinegar. Not surprisingly, the snails didn't take too kindly to this, and quickly vanished into their shells at the first whiff of the acidic, salty water. So that led to the next technique – *engañarles* – 'tricking them' to come out into the open again, so that when you ate them there was actually something sticking out of the shells to grab hold of. To do this we took a large pan of fresh water and placed them inside. The contrast to the vinegar solution of earlier made them pop their heads out again, not without some degree of relief. What they didn't realise, though, is that the pan was on a low flame to heat the water. Just when they'd all come back to normal and were slithering all over each other, we turned the heat up to full, and they were very quickly boiled to death. After five minutes or so, the snails were now fully purged and edible and ready to be added to a dish.

There are hundreds of different ways of cooking with snails at this stage, mostly involving preparing special sauces for them. Anything but the dreaded French method of cooking them with garlic butter, an idea repugnant to most self-respecting Spaniards. The most common recipe is usually a variant of the following.

For a largeish dish with enough for about four or five people, depending on appetite, you need about half a kilo of snails, a handful of *jamón serrano*, cut up into little cubes, three good-sized ripe tomatoes, two onions, a handful of almonds, three or four cloves of garlic, a chilli pepper, paprika, a bay leaf, saffron, salt and parsley.

Put some olive oil in a large pan and turn the heat to medium-high. Add the chopped onion and tomatoes (these can be skinned, but it really doesn't matter). Once the onion has sweated a little, add the sliced garlic, bay leaf and the chilli pepper – chopped if you like the dish quite spicy; leave it whole if not. Add a pinch or two of salt, then simmer for about twenty minutes, stirring regularly. Once the sauce has thickened and the onions have properly softened, add the *jamón serrano* pieces, a pinch of saffron and about half a teaspoon of paprika, depending on taste. Stir in well and then add the snails. Crush the almonds in a mortar and pestle and add to the sauce, then cook for another ten minutes over a low heat. When done, pour the snails and their sauce into a terracotta dish, placing the bay leaf and the chilli in the middle as decoration. Eat with bread and a good Rioja or Ribera del Duero.

Some like to add mint to the above recipe, which gives an unusual, almost Moorish flavour to the dish.

⋆

Over a month had gone by since I'd seen Concha. She'd been busy with preparations for the local elections, while life on the farm had kept me tied down for a few weeks. When I found I had an afternoon free I drove over to her *mas* to pay a visit.

I didn't follow local politics: it seemed too much part of a world I was keen to move away from. But word reached me nonetheless that her party hadn't done very well on election night. Words like 'disaster' were being bandied about. Meanwhile, the politicians associated with the worst kind of exploitation of the land appeared to be rubbing their hands with glee.

I found her alone, sitting on the front step of her house, staring out at the horizon. The last of the irises were beginning to wilt and fade, while the late orange light cast a glow over the front of the house. She pulled hard on her cigarette as I walked over.

'*Bueno*,' she said. '*¿Has venido a ver lo que queda?* – Come to see what's left?'

She didn't get up. I sat down gently on the doorstep beside her.

'I heard the election didn't go too well.'

'That's the least of it,' she said.

She bent her head down and seemed about to say something, then checked herself. The cigarette smoke curled around her face, sifting through her hair before lifting up and being carried away by the breeze.

'We'd never done so bad in an election,' she said after a pause. 'Got fewer votes than last time.'

She flicked the ash to the floor by her feet.

'But that's just the bloody election. There'll be another one. This Concha doesn't believe in defeat.'

Above the trees in front of us martins were circling frantically, hunting down their evening meals, screaming like tiny jet planes as they raced past.

'How about your job at the town hall?' I asked.

'They can't sack me,' she said. 'But they can make life very difficult for me if they want.'

A weighty, dark cloud seemed to hang over her as she sank into her depression. I had often sensed an insecurity in her about her life in the mountains: she dealt with it by keeping herself busy and by surrounding herself with other people – the commune acted as a kind of buffer.

'Africa had a baby,' she said at last, opening her packet of cigarettes and lighting another. 'A boy.'

'Oh, fantastic,' I said. 'Where are they? Are they here?' The house seemed curiously quiet for the home of a new-born child.

'They've gone,' she said, looking blankly out towards the hills.

'They're no longer living here?' I asked.

'Pau's brother turned up,' she said. 'He's a Jehovah's Witness, down on the coast. Came up here, told Pau he was a sinner, then carted him and Africa off back to his place. Said they'd help look after the baby, and this was no kind of place to bring him up.'

Pau had seemed so rooted in the mountains; I could hardly believe it.

'Pau needs a structure, something to tell him what's right and what's wrong,' Concha said. 'That was the problem: he needs order, otherwise he starts going off the rails. The Jehovahs will give them everything they need. We'll probably see him up here in a couple of years' time selling bibles.'

Pau the radical, from eco-warrior to Bible-basher in one quick move. It was odd, but somehow, as I thought about it, it seemed to fit a pattern. Here he had had a community and a cause, and now down with his brother on the coast it looked like he'd found something very similar. Same beast, just a different saddle.

'I'm sorry,' I said. Not only had she been wiped out in the polls, the commune which formed such a large part of her life was breaking up around her as well.

'Oh, I don't care about them,' she said gruffly. 'Better off without them anyway.'

'How does Marina feel about it?' I said.

She turned and looked at me with surprise. 'Marina?' she said. '*Ay, cariño*, I can see you really don't know anything that's been going on.'

She got up wearily from the doorstep, knees cracking loudly. Outside it was starting to get chilly as the sun dipped over the tops of the hills.

I lit a fire as she pulled out a bottle and started pouring herself a large measure of *orujo* in a grimy glass. Taking a sip, she closed her eyes, breathed out, then leaned back against the sofa and smiled broadly.

'Ah,' she cried. The inside of the house was a mess, and the smell of cat's piss seemed stronger than ever. The colourful blankets and rugs usually covering the sofas were falling on the floor; empty wine bottles rolled about in a corner; ashtrays were piled high and overflowed with butts and torn packets of Rizlas. A scene of long, indulgent nights.

'I'm afraid,' she said at last, 'that my beloved Marina decided this was the best time for her to move on as well.'

'You've split up?' I said.

'In a manner of speaking.'

I looked around again at the debris of the living room: there was meaning now behind the chaos. 'This was after Pau and Africa had gone?' I asked.

'After the election; after Pau's flight to Egypt with the baby Jesus.'

'Where's she gone?' I said.

'Somewhere near Barcelona,' she answered. 'Reckons she's going to open a car saleroom up there.'

I almost choked. Marina, the witch, was going to sell cars?

'Said she saw it in a dream. She was going to go to Barcelona and make her fortune selling second-hand Seats. It was a message from the angels, and she couldn't ignore it.'

'Even if it meant leaving you.'

'It was in order to leave me,' she said. Her glass was empty. She picked up the bottle from the floor near her feet and filled it again.

'Oh, look, it's too complicated to go into now. Marina's complicated. It's all complicated.'

'What about El Clossa?' I said.

'Oh, he's a love. He still comes round. Helped me drink those bottles last night.' She waved with her hand at the empties in the corner.

'He hasn't threatened to disappear, then.'

'El Clossa? Nah.' She put her glass down amid the piles of cigarette ends in the ashtray, looked in vain for a cigarette in an empty packet, then threw it on the fire.

'Perhaps I'll seduce him,' she said. 'Sex with Marina was getting boring anyway.'

⋆

One of the most common sights around the *masos* of the area, as you walk over the mountains after the April rains, are the banks of deep violet irises tucked under windowsills or along the edges of ancient footpaths, long abandoned and now barely visible. So much of the life of the *masovers* was channelled into simply surviving in a difficult environment that there was little time and energy left over for the beautification of their surroundings. Yet they did manage to plant irises, and there is a local folktale about the flower which may explain why it was so popular in rural areas.

Once upon a time there was a king who was very ill, and he sent his three sons out to find an iris for him, as that was the only thing in the world that could cure him. Whoever found the flower, he told them, would be named Crown Prince.

The eldest one set off first, and after a short while he came across an old hag along the path.

'Could you give alms to a poor old woman?' she called out as he approached.

'A fine mess we'd be in if we gave alms to people every time they asked for them,' said the prince.

And he stepped past the old woman without giving her anything.

'Are there any irises down this way,' he asked behind his back as he was walking away.

'That depends on you,' said the old woman. But the prince took no notice and carried on his way.

The next day the second prince set off to find the precious flower, and not long afterwards he came across the old hag.

'Could you give alms to a poor old woman?' she called out as he approached.

'I haven't got any money on me,' said the second prince, and he went on his way.

The next day the third prince set off, and like his brothers, he soon came across the old woman.

'Could you give alms?' she called out as he approached. The young prince looked into his empty bag and then handed it over to her. 'Here,' he said. 'It's all I've got.'

'Thank you,' she said. 'Where are you going?'

'I'm off to find an iris,' said the prince. 'My father needs it, for he is very ill, but I don't know where to look for it.'

'I can help you,' said the old woman. 'It's up there, on the top of that far, steep mountain.' And she pointed the way he needed to take.

So the young prince took the route she had said, and there, at the top of the mountain, he found the iris.

Back home, the three brothers were gathered again. The young prince said nothing about finding the iris, but his elder brother suspected him and so he searched his things, and there he discovered the iris, carefully stashed away. Furious, the eldest prince decided to kill his little brother on the spot. Ignoring the pleas of the second brother to spare him, he dug a hole in a sandbank nearby and threw him in, and raced off with the iris to give it to the King. Soon afterwards he was declared Crown Prince and heir to the throne.

But in his rush to get rid of his little brother, he didn't realise that he'd left one of his fingers still poking up out of the ground.

Now a few days later a shepherd was walking in the area where the young prince had been buried, and he spotted a white reed growing out of a sandbank that would make for a perfect flute. So he picked the reed and started to play. But instead of the musical notes he'd expected, out came a mysterious voice singing:

Toca, toca, bon pastor
toca, toca i no m'anomenes,
per la flor del lliri blau
m'han mort en riu d'arenes.

Play on, play on good shepherd,
Play, but do not mention my name,
For the sake of the iris flower
My death in this sandbank is to blame.

Now the shepherd thought this was the strangest thing, but he carried on playing, and the same mysterious voice kept sounding out, until soon he found himself outside the walls of the palace, where the King, now cured, was looking out for his youngest son, who appeared to have vanished. The King heard the strange song coming from the shepherd's flute, and he began to realise what had happened.

'Where did you find that flute?' he called out to the shepherd.

'Down by the sandbanks,' came the reply.

So the King gathered his courtiers and the two eldest princes, and ordered them to ride with him to the sandbanks, the shepherd beside them playing his flute all the while. And when they came to where the young prince was buried, and the second brother rode his horse over the spot, the song of the shepherd's flute suddenly changed:

Passa, passa, bon germá
Passa, passa i no m'anomenes
per la flor del lliri blau
m'han mort en riu d'arenes.

Carry on, my good brother
But do not mention my name
For the sake of the iris flower
My death in this sandbank is to blame.

The eldest prince was filled with fear when he heard this, but the King ordered him to ride over the same spot, and as soon as his horse stepped over where the young prince was buried, the flute's song changed again.

Passa, passa, mal germá
passa, passa, i no m'anomes
per la flor del lliri blau
m'has mort en riu d'arenes.

Carry on, oh evil brother,
But do not mention my name.
For the sake of the iris flower
My death in this sandbank you are to blame.

So the King ordered that the young prince be dug up from out of the sandbank, and, miraculously, he was still alive. But he was missing a finger, for that was the reed that the shepherd had picked and turned into a flute.

So the young prince told the King everything that had happened, and the King named him heir to the throne. The second brother was pardoned, but the eldest was sent into exile and was never seen again.

*

I went down to the village to collect the mail.

'Bad news about Concha.' Jordi the postman was scurrying around his office, reading glasses perched on the end of his nose as he sorted out that morning's deliveries, but he still had time for gossip, and greeted me with a clenched fist.

'Yes,' I said.

'They'll try and get rid of her, I reckon,' he said.

'I thought her job was for life.'

'Yeah, but . . .'

He made a face, then jerked his head to the side in the direction of the mayor's office. The powers that be, he seemed to suggest, were going to get the knives out.

'Surely you'd do something about it,' I said. 'You wouldn't just stand by and watch while they did that. What about all this talk of activism and workers' rights?'

He looked shocked at the very thought.

'We're not going to start a bloody revolution over one lost job!' he said. He muttered under his breath as he searched through the letters addressed to us, wrapped them up with an elastic band and then handed them over with a grimace. In the tiny world of the village and surrounding area, Jordi was a useful person to know: it didn't do to start making enemies.

'Concha'll be all right,' he said. 'She's a fighter. Known her a long time. She'll get back on her feet. Sink close to the bottom first. But she'll be fine in a few months, trying to take over the world, as usual.'

He smiled and I walked out.

By the fountain in the square I flicked through the official looking envelopes, but something squeezed in the middle of them caught my eye: a postcard from a relative in England. I lifted it out and found myself staring at an image I hadn't seen for a long time. I flicked it over: it was a brief message, just a greeting from someone living up in Lancashire, where my family originated. But it was the photograph on the front that most caught my imagination: a simple shape of a long, green hill, unmistakeable and wholly evocative to anyone who has ever known it. I stood still, gazing at it, lost for a few moments, then went to look for a place to sit in the bar across the square. I needed to savour the memories suddenly filling my brain.

⋆

Pendle Hill was just a few feet short of officially being a mountain, but it rose large above the undulating green-grey landscape: a focal point, a reference, a place to glance up to from the cobbled streets and rows of matchbox houses of the towns that sat at its feet. For years the grime and the smog had blotted it out of sight completely, factories and mills coughing out dense black coal smoke, but it stayed fixed in the collective imagination, like a memory of a blissful childhood. Pendle, where they had all come from, and where they all wished to return.

Physically, it was an unremarkable hill, for all the importance people gave it – a long, gently rising slope running east to west that eventually came to a stop and fell down more steeply just in time to prevent it from crossing into Yorkshire. It looked something like a giant, sleeping creature. There were no trees covering its sides, no sharp edges, or cliff-faces. From a distance it seemed complete, smooth and had a gentleness about it that was reflected in the eyes of local people whenever they mentioned its name. Pendle was more than just a hill.

Anywhere else it might have gone unnoticed altogether, and might not even have had a name – just another ridge overshadowed by taller, more magnificent presences towering over it and jostling for our attention. Yet here, amid the low slopes and rust-coloured riverbeds, it stood in full view, a temple to a different world.

There was magic in the land around there – a magic you could sense very strongly, as though you might touch it, or see it, or feel it with your fingertips. It ran in the ground itself, like a current, charging the rocks and trees with a spark and energy that set the place apart. Down south, where we lived, because of my father's work, an activity like hanging a rope from a branch to make a swing was all about finding a tree strong enough and securing the knots properly. Here, where we came to visit my grandmother, you felt the trees were living beings: choose the wrong one – perhaps one that was known for its ill temper or for not liking children – and the consequences could be severe. I knew all this without being told – the land was alive, vital, different, and to be respected.

The local topography gave clues to this: a group of trees in the middle of a field on the other side of the village was known as the Seven Sisters, while the Nine Brothers sat below them just a few yards away. Bee, as we called my grandmother, puffing away on her Embassy No. 1 cigarettes, always said there were fairies living there. I went as often as I could, hoping to see one. Then, when the sun came out – a rare event in the wettest part of the country – she would hurry us all out of the door to go for a walk down to the Sandbanks – a secluded spot in the fields below the village where a brook flattened out as it passed through some trees, a brief stretch of sandy shore – the nearest equivalent we had to a beach during our inland summer holidays. We always had to be careful on our way down as we approached the low wooden bridge across the stream: a troll lived underneath and he would get very angry if we woke him up: we always had to make sure Grandma was with us when we crossed over, otherwise he might come out and gobble us up. And then there was the fairy wall – a long stretch of dry-stone wall made up of the local dark slate, permanently damp and covered in ivies and lichens. But here, Bee never failed to tell us, if we left a coin in one of the cracks on our way down, and then were able to find it again on our way back up, the fairies would have imbued it with magic, and it would bring us good luck. And she would open her purse and hand out penny and twopenny pieces that we held excitedly in the palms of our hands, each of us running off to find our own secret hiding place for the fairies to find it. Needless to say, an hour or two later, tired from playing down at the Sandbanks, with aching legs and moaning that it was too far to walk back home, we never found our coins again, no matter how hard we tried to remember the exact spot we'd left them in.

'The fairies have them now,' Bee would say. It was compensation, of a sort.

The fairies and trolls were only part of the story, however. More important for Pendle and the villages and towns surrounding it were the local witches. It was said that at certain times of year, around spring, when people would perform a pilgrimage of sorts on Good Friday to the top of the hill, you could see the form of a witch on the side of Pendle, the diagonal path leading up to the summit marking her broomstick, while the heather in bloom marked the shape of her peaked hat. For years I looked and looked, trying to see the figure supposedly there – a testament of nature to the long history of witches in the area – but without success. Until one day, long after Bee had died, as I was driving along the lanes past the village, I finally saw her there, flying up into the leaden sky. Bee was no witch, but she came from a place where witches formed part of the landscape.

My memories of her were less clear than I would have liked: she died before my ninth birthday, but she was a huge presence – large not just physically, but in spirit. I remembered her with reddish hair, burst capillaries around her cheekbones. She smiled a lot, and her thick rubbery skin would be squeezed upwards towards her eyes as she gave deep belly laughs. She seemed to be busy and active most of the time, wringing clothes dry with a mangle in the living room, chopping potatoes for dinner, feeding Boyo, the cat, with yesterday's leftovers, searching frantically for a match or cigarette lighter, bending down stiffly to embrace and kiss us, her beloved grandchildren, unaware, as we scampered around the tiny space of her council house, that we would have her for so short a time. Whenever there was a pause or lull, in a flash she would ease her enormous behind on to a stool by the piano and start bashing out traditional songs and music-hall numbers, singing as loudly and gaily as she could to drown out the occasional dud note struck on the keyboard by her thick working fingers. A heavy knock would come on the wall from the neighbours, jealous that so much fun was being had next door, but the songs would carry on regardless, children, adults, the whole family joining in.

'Stick it up your jumper,' Bee would cry out at the complaining one-eyed Methodist on the other side of the wall, before crashing away on another number.

'*Dance, dance, wherever you may be . . .*'

A scream, the music would stop, and she'd rush into the kitchen, where the chips – long since forgotten – had either burned or caught fire.

'Right,' she'd say once the crisis had been dealt with, walking back into the living room wiping her hands on her apron, 'Cuppa tea?' It would be salad and bread again for dinner.

Illness struck her lungs and her legs, and in a short time she became less mobile. But unable to bustle around as she once had, she would sit with us and tell stories, placing us on her knee, or else sitting in deckchairs on the tiny patch of communal lawn outside the front door. Atlantic winds soon brought an end to our attempts at sunbathing, but there was always time for some little anecdote or tale. And the Witches of Pendle was one of our favourites.

They had lived, she said, in the next village along, beyond the mill where she used to work – a group of old women with black cats curled under their feet, long noses with warts on the end and big black hats with brims as wide as tables. And they would fly about the midnight sky on broomsticks, causing trouble and mischief wherever they went. But if they liked you, and you paid them in gold, they might help you with one of their magical spells, or a powerful potion, made from frogs' legs, bats' wings and secret herbs and flowers that only the witches knew where to find. Some said they were in league with the fairies, others that they could only marry trolls, but they were special people, to be respected, and sometimes feared.

There had been more of them in the past, she said. Now there were hardly any left. Perhaps none at all. Many years ago, men like the one next door who banged on the walls with his walking stick had come and taken them all away and hanged them in a public square in the city, where their magic, which came from the earth of the countryside, could not help them.

'It was Pendle, you see, the hill which gave it to them. Take them away from Pendle and they couldn't do anything.'

Sometimes she'd wonder aloud if the old woman who was known to live in a cottage beyond the woods was a witch. If so, she was the last one left. She had a black cat, that was sure, and someone said they'd seen jars on her shelves filled with all kinds of strange and wonderful things – perhaps potions and their ingredients. But it was probably just talk. You shouldn't pay too much notice. And no, we couldn't go and visit her.

It seemed the whole village came to the funeral when Bee died – everyone except the one-eyed Methodist from next door. I remember stepping out from a car that pulled up outside the churchyard, standing nervously under the roofed gateway to shelter from the rain amid an ocean of umbrellas and tears. I tried very hard to cry – my sister and cousins were inconsolable – but I felt dry inside: it was all too strange, too weird: life was still just starting; how could I begin to understand it was something that could stop? They cremated her, and buried her ashes in a small hole in the ground that bore no relation to the huge woman she had been. It wasn't Bee, in fact I knew it had nothing to do with her, with the spirit of the person who had been such a force of both natural and supernatural worlds, and who had marked us all in one way or another, seeming to touch us with an earthy, earthing vitality. Inside the church they sang her favourite song:

I'll live in you
If you'll live in me
For I am the Lord
Of the Dance . . .

Then we stepped outside and drove away again, far away from the rain and the songs and the stories. And Pendle Hill, its presence and deep rumbling energy, seemed to disappear from view, a shifting, weakening memory of another world – a slower, quieter, rougher-edged place to be that seemed ever more difficult to cling on to.

It was time to get back to the farm. I finished the drink, paid and walked out back into the intense light of the square. The same people, the same cars, the same smells and sights as before.

Everything had changed.

*

Real rain started falling, flooding the sky and the land beneath it. Down in the valley below, the first pools formed in the hollows of the dry riverbed, then slowly began to fill up, trickle out, join one another and link to form a tiny brook, then a stream, and finally a full torrent of water, gushing down through the rock and over the oleander bushes, past pine trees and poplars as it raced down to the sea: a river at last. Up at the house we looked out at a granite world, the clouds heavy above us and so close it seemed we could reach out and touch them as they smoked past and then sank down into the gorge. In between running around with buckets and pans as we discovered first one, then another, and another leak in our still-young roof, I watched as the land soaked the water in, darkening and softening as the hours and days passed. It was good rain: steady, not too heavy, persistent. A sudden downpour would scarcely register, skating over the surface, causing flash floods and quickly being lost down on the coast. This was exactly what we needed: hour after hour of simple *pluja* – rain.

There was little to do but watch and wait. We carried on with life as best we could, marvelling first at the sheer quantity that was finally falling; we laughed at the leaks: at least we knew now where they were. I thought about my trees and saplings drinking deep and long: this would keep them going for a good while into the summer. When this stopped we could expect no more – bar the odd exceptional summer storm – till late September or October. Two days passed, then a third. Still the rain fell. I lost count of how many buckets and pans of water we had to throw out before replacing them for the drips. We began to run out of dry firewood, the nights still chilly up on the mountain, especially now. The little power we had from the solar panels began to go, too: there was no sun to recharge the batteries. We started eating dinner by candlelight, going to bed early to stay warm and save on electricity. There was food enough to keep us going, and a wind-up radio and mobile phones to keep in touch with the world outside, but a growing danger of being cut off began to prey on our minds: the road to the village ran along the riverbed: if it burst its banks there would be no way for us to get out.

And yet still the water seemed to enchant us, coming after such a long time without it; it was as if we ourselves were soaking up something of its life and energy along with the soil and rock. The house was made of porous sandstone, and although the walls were almost a metre thick, I was curious rather than concerned to see whether the water would eventually soak through to the inside. In the older part of the house they were held together with nothing more than mud: heavy rain could damage the very fabric of the building. But even still I felt wonderment more than worry.

By the fourth day the rain seemed to ease a little, but still it fell: less persistent, but a drizzle kept the process of rehydration continuing between the heavier bursts. We started contemplating a temporary evacuation, but decided to see how things were in the morning.

We awoke to birdsong, and the streaming light of dawn breaking through the window. I got up and looked out: everywhere there was water, pools and puddles of it shining up like mirrors from the garden, the patio. The drip, drip of the leaks that had kept us company through the nights had stopped. We walked down to the kitchen and opened up the doors and windows on to the new wet world. Beyond the patio the bees were already buzzing merrily away from flower to flower while beads of light shone from every leaf of every bush and tree. I put on some boots and went out to explore, happy to feel the sun on my face after so many days trapped inside. The sky was clear and blue, the air almost still, with just a slight cooling breeze. I looked down towards the village in the far distance; the valley appeared to have changed its tone: greener, darker, denser. Tree trunks were sodden and almost black against the brilliant sunlight. The ground was soft underfoot, sinking in a way I had never known it to here, water oozing out at the sides where my feet pressed down. I had never loved water so much as now, had never longed so deeply for rain and been so entranced by it once it came. The sun could shine ceaselessly now for months: I didn't care. The odd shower over the past weeks had done little to break the drought. But now our mountain was sitting like a sponge, and life on the land could continue. There would be plenty of water in the spring, water in the river in the valley, water for everything and everyone.

I climbed up the slope to the *era* and over to the old oak tree. The drops falling from its budding leaves and the sound they made as they splashed on to the ground below made it seem as though it were moving, shaking itself dry like a cat after an accidental soaking. But there was another sound: something new. At first I thought it might be the wind blowing through the pine trees further down the slope, but it didn't make sense: the breeze that morning was very slight. No, it wasn't wind, but water. With a start, I looked up: over in the gorge, up above the Duende Stone that Marina had identified for us, cascading down the rocks, was a roaring white waterfall.

Half an hour later, with proper boots and some supplies in a rucksack, I set off to investigate. The waterfall was flushing down the gulley that split our land in two: a sharp fold in the mountainside covered in thick bush and tall oak trees that had been spared in the forest fire of several years before. At the bottom, where the track crossed over it, sat the Duende Stone. But I had never explored up there, despite meaning to do so at some point: there was always some other job or activity taking up my time. Now the moment had come. I felt compelled to head up and see the waterfall from up close, find where this river now coursing through our land was coming from.

A water mountain now soared up ahead of me as I trod along the muddy path. The sound of the trickling, gurgling, gushing stream echoed to the accompaniment of birdsong streaming from tree to tree. Small clouds of steam were forming and rising as the sunlight hit the surface and slowly warmed the sodden earth. Looking over at some of the terraces I had yet to work on, it was clear the showers had once again sent one or two of the stone walls tumbling as it dissolved the mud that held them together. But no matter: that morning belonged to the rain.

I climbed up the side of the enormous bulk of the Duende Stone and found a tiny path running up the side of the gorge. No one had been up here for years, though: it seemed the wild boar and the ibex trod this slope, forging a barely visible route through the gorse bushes and thick brambles. At times it was hard to see where it led, and I had to push through the dense web of needles to get past. It was quickly disorienting, with only the direction of the slope and the sound of the new-born river to one side to tell me roughly where I was.

The thick covering of the trees overhead filtered out much of the sunlight, and I soon entered a different world, one I had no idea existed so close to the farmhouse. Used as I was to the parched, sunburnt, rocky world that seemed to surround us, it felt strange to be transported so quickly to this dark, cold, protected corner. That morning everywhere felt damp, but this area gave the sense that here it was less unusual: lichens grew in yellow and grey splashes on the stones, while moss – something I hadn't seen in years, it felt; something I had never expected to see anywhere on our mountain – was growing in thick bunches up the northern sides of the tree trunks.

Halfway up the gorge I pushed my way through to catch a glimpse of the river. Pools waist-deep had formed in hollows, filled by smaller waterfalls splashing down and foaming before tipping over the edge to another, and then another, like an elaborate staircase. Insects darted about the surface, catching the odd ray of sunlight as it pushed its way through the leaves and branches above. This gorge had long been like this, had borne water from higher up the mountains down to the river below for thousands and thousands of years. I had grown so used to seeing it dry I thought the day would never come when it would revert to its older self. Water, I had told myself, hadn't flowed down here for years, and would never do so again, so dry did the land feel, so scarce the rain. Yet suddenly it began to make sense as a feature in the landscape: before, I had only been able to imagine this; now I was actually seeing and experiencing it. Life was surging from the rocks and from the land. If the fairies and earth-spirits of Marina's – and my grandmother's – world existed, I thought, this would be a place to look for them.

I carried on up the gorge, the climb getting steeper and more difficult the higher I went. Pulling myself up a small rockface by my hands and feet, I was able, finally, to claw myself out from the thick undergrowth and stand on a promontory. Far below sat the farmhouse, shining white in the sunlight. But just a few yards to the side was the waterfall, hurtling down from a lip of rock before crashing into a pool some way below. Great globs of water splashed over the area around, the water seeming to flow according to an irregular pattern. It felt young, new-born, flailing around in its new-found existence: vital and still unformed. The sound it made was tremendous, and I stood for a while soaking it in, the pounding roar resonating inside me as I stared and smiled.

To carry on further up the mountainside I would have to move away from the gulley and the waterfall to follow what seemed to be the only route up to the top. I wanted to see now where this water was coming from. For the first time I was finally close actually to climbing our mountain, and a driving curiosity was pushing me to see what lay on the other side. Once again I found myself fighting through the thick gorse as I tried to make out possible pathways. There were no terraces up here, no flattened stretches of land to make the climb easier, and I had to hang on to whatever shrubs and bushes I could to stop myself from sliding down the slope. Above, there seemed to be a section of the cliff-face that might just be climbable. Slipping and crawling over loose stones I headed towards it as best I could, hauling myself up by my fingertips, kicking at the rock as I tried to find footholds. The farmhouse was now little more than a speck below me.

Ten minutes later I pulled myself up the final few feet and stood to catch my first view of the world that existed beyond the top of the mountain. Stretching ahead, sloping down for about half a mile before rising up again as it soared towards the peak of Penyagolosa, was a great pine forest, a deep, dark green, red trunks surging like pillars from the ground. This was Scots pine, unsuited to the warmer climate just over the edge of the cliff I had climbed: it was a boundary between one ecosystem and another. I started to move in, enchanted by this new world. To the left I caught sight of a stream that must be feeding the waterfall. My feet squelched on the earth below as I walked towards it. Somewhere up here, I felt sure, there was a spring from which all this was flowing.

I pushed through sodden bracken and fern bushes and into the forest. The stream flashed as it flowed down a small incision in the land, sometimes spilling over its banks and creating a glassy sheen at the foot of the trees. I followed it as best I could, unable to see its course clearly from the density of the wood around me. Needles and cones were soft underfoot.

I got closer to the stream and began walking along a narrow ridge that ran along its side, too high for the water to reach. I was thankful there was no gorse up here, and it was a relief not to have to force my way through a prickly, uninviting shrubland.

Something lay across the path ahead and my legs seemed to stop instinctively before I even had time to register what it was. Everything froze as I looked down and saw a snake stretched out, barring my way, soaking up the sun where a break in the canopy allowed the light to shine through. It was a dull yellow, perhaps a metre long. It faced the stream, but one eye was watching me. Its tongue quickly spat out of its mouth and then sucked back in again. I felt an uncontrollable shaking begin to develop in my knees and started looking for ways to get past it, but the stream here was too wide to jump, while the undergrowth on the other side was too thick to get through. This was the only way forward, but the snake showed little sign of wanting to move. For a second I thought about leaping over it, but, although it was probably not poisonous, I didn't like the idea of it lashing out at me as I sailed over its head. Snakes: I tried to search my memory for some idea of how to deal with them that I might have picked up in the past. Arcadio had said something about burning rubber to make them go away: they didn't like the smell. But there was little chance of doing that up here in the middle of a very damp forest.

The snake was now starting to curl up, as though making a spiral out of its body, slithering into a tight coil, like a reflection of the knot growing in my mind as I tried to work out what to do. Something caught my eye to the side: a straight branch sticking out of the trunk of one of the nearby pine trees. I made a grab for it and broke it off: perhaps with a gentle push I might persuade the serpent to move out of the way. But the snake seemed to be one step ahead of me: as I hesitantly stretched out the stick, it whipped out of the coil it had made and darted towards the stream, where it disappeared into the grass on the bank. I waited for a moment to see if it would return, the stick still in hand, then cautiously walked over the spot where it had lain, ankles twitching lest it should dart out at me from the undergrowth.

I carried on up the slope, the stream still gurgling to one side. It was difficult to say for sure, but I had the impression of walking along a proper path now, widening and clearing as if it had still been in use within living memory. The air was damp and cooler up here, and tiny droplets of evaporating water were suspended in the still air, sometimes moving in waves like shoals of fish as they were caught by the occasional breeze, up and through gaps between the tight-packed trees.

And there, up ahead, I saw what looked like the beginning of a clearing. The stream, narrower now, the current gentler as the land began to flatten out, curled away to the right and was lost in the undergrowth; it had brought me this far: it was time to see what lay in this opening. The trees gradually thinned out as I approached until finally I found myself in a wide space, the sunlight a relief from the darkness of the forest. A track lay off to one side, while in front stood a *mas*: three or four low stone buildings with greying whitewash peeling from the walls. One of them was already a ruin, the roof lying in a pile of rubble at the foot of the walls, splintered wooden beams poking up at odd angles from the wreckage. Broken pieces of pottery lay scattered around the floor, canes tied together to form sheets for roofing sprawled in shattered shapes under lumps of masonry or plaster. It was a sight I had seen dozens of times now: an abandoned farmhouse left to rot and slowly be recaptured by nature. Something about this one seemed vaguely familiar, but I dismissed the thought: they were all so similar it was easy to confuse them.

I moved closer to the buildings, crunching stones and mud underfoot: the sound seemed to be blanketed by the enclosing, embracing forest. The peak of Penyagolosa must be visible from round here, but the only thing I could see above was clear blue sky. I felt as though I had entered some kind of bubble, part of, yet strangely removed from the ordinary world.

A rusted shell of a car – an old Renault 4 – was sitting by the side of one of the houses. The doors and windows were gone and the seats removed. One red plastic brake light remained at the back like an eye, somehow defying the relentless decay that surrounded it.

There was a sound, like a hoof beating the ground. I turned to look: a donkey was tethered to an iron ring bolted to a stone wall. Its head was bent and it was eating out of the hands of a very thin man with long, grey hair tied back into a ponytail.

'Hello,' he said.

He showed no sign of surprise that I was there: perhaps he had heard my footsteps.

'Come inside.'

Like a bolt, the memory hit me: I had been here before.

A flash of forgotten images, buried away where I had tried to hide them, a moment of madness, years – how many years? – before. A daytrip to the country, away from the city, and a village near the foot of a mountain. And a story – a story that somewhere up there was a man who lived alone in a *mas*. A crazy man, the villagers had said. Yet he knew the Secrets of the Earth, according to some.

And so I'd set off to find him, curious, laughing: lusting for adventure and hidden knowledge. 'Secrets of the Earth'? Who could resist that? And somewhere up that mountainside I'd found him, as they'd said, a hermit in a crumbling farmhouse. Long, grey hair tied back in a ponytail. Although he didn't look quite so old.

'Get out!' he'd shouted as soon as he saw me. 'Go!'

And without a word I'd set off back down the mountain again, back to the village, shrugging it off as just the ramblings of a loon. What did I want with secrets anyway? Probably all nonsense.

'You're right, he's mad,' I told the villagers on my return. And I'd left, and never gone back, just as he'd told me to.

The man led me to a sheltered patio outside the front of his house. I wasn't sure if he recognised me from all those years ago when I had first been here, but, if he did, he showed no sign of it.

'People are always welcome here,' he said with a smile. 'I have no secrets.'

Faustino had a quiet, unassuming ease about him. Of medium height, with long, slender limbs he looked as though he might easily snap in half, but was in fact immensely strong. His long, almost feminine neck stretched up to a neat, small head, a three- or four-day beard coating a protruding chin. A straight, sensitive nose sat between very pale, blue eyes that stared out gently from an open, lined face, their lightness contrasting with his dark Mediterranean skin. His smile was broad and frequent, with tiny dark gaps between each tooth when he grinned. This is how I always remember him in my mind's eye: a light, almost mischievous expression on his face as he fed his animals, watered and tended his plants, or else rolled himself a cigarette from his home-grown mountain tobacco. His hands, dexterous and strong, were swollen and almost purple, and hung like beetroots at the ends of his skinny arms, loose, dark clothes flapping over his seemingly fleshless body.

His house stood at the bottom of the small group of buildings that made up the *mas*. The door was open and inside burnt a large fire, flaming from a single thick log placed on the stone flags on the floor. Curled up together in an armchair next to it were a large, short-haired mongrel and a white Persian cat, with intense yellow eyes, both snuggling themselves as deeply as possible into a knitted patchwork blanket thrown over the back. Above them in a cage, with the door wide open, was a pale-blue songbird. All three seemed to be enjoying the fire, and barely raised an eyebrow as we appeared. I sat down on a long leather sofa pushed against the outside wall underneath the window, shaded by the patio roof. Despite the cold air up there, the heat from inside seemed to soak through the stone walls and give the place a welcoming glow. Wind chimes hanging from the rafters tinkled as a breeze caught them.

'You're in luck: it's a good day for walking – clear skies after all that rain,' Faustino said. His voice was nasal and deep. 'You can just make out the Columbrete Islands out to sea. Barbary pirates used to launch raids on the coastline from there.'

From his easy manner, and the curiously effortless way I seemed to slip into his world, it was almost as if he had been expecting me. Did living in the mountains make you like this? There was none of the formality expected on meeting someone in more ordinary circumstances: that could be dispensed with. I was welcome – at least today.

He went inside for a moment and I stared out at the view. The land cascaded down in waves before, in the far distance, reaching the sea, a great mantle wrapping itself around the globe. And beyond, lost on the horizon, small, rocky crags were just visible, tiny splashes of brown on an azure canvas. We were higher up than I had imagined, despite the steep climb to get here. To the east, the sea; Penyagolosa must be close behind us.

Faustino emerged from the house.

'Here,' he said, handing me an empty glass. Then he pulled out a bottle of russet-coloured liquid and poured some for me. 'It's truffle brandy,' he said, and helped himself.

I raised the glass and took in the smell: the usual brandy flavours were there but this time overlaid with something else: a familiarly powerful and very earthy scent.

'Chin-chin,' said Faustino, and we touched glasses.

'Do you live here alone?' I asked.

'People call me a hermit,' he said. 'Among other things.' He sat down in a wicker chair pulled up in front of the doorway. 'But I'm only on my own during the week. My wife lives down on the coast and comes up at weekends. So if I am a hermit it's really only part-time.'

We both laughed. If he laughed too much I feared he might snap in two.

'My wife doesn't like the mountains; I don't like the coast. So this is how we do it.'

'How long have you been up here?' I said.

He shrugged and smiled.

'I forget,' he said. 'Months, years – they don't mean too much up here.'

I sipped the brandy and felt it rushing from my stomach up to my head.

'And you don't get lonely?'

His pale-blue eyes rested on me.

'Once you've been here a while you begin to realise you're never alone. People live a more solitary existence in the cities. Being surrounded – or not – by others has little to do with it.'

He took a couple of large mouthfuls of brandy and started rolling a cigarette, plump, purple fingers nimbly prodding the tobacco into place and stroking it into shape.

'Do you like my well?' he asked, pointing at a small stone structure in a corner of the patio. 'Built it myself. It collects rainwater – enough to keep me going all year.'

He drew the cigarette up to his mouth, licked it, stuck it together, then lit it and inhaled deeply.

'We've got most of the things we need to survive around us. It's a matter of knowing how to collect and gather them.'

I drank my brandy. It made me feel warm and giddy.

'At first you've got your animals,' he said. 'Dog, cat, Dimoni.' The songbird sang out, as though on cue, at hearing her name. 'I let her out once in a while, but sometimes the cat goes for her. Can't help herself. She's happy, though, eating his seeds.'

I sank deeper into the leather sofa. The pine trees circling the house rustled in the breeze.

'They keep you going for a while,' Faustino continued. 'And they talk to you, in their own kind of way. Manage to make themselves pretty clear sometimes.' That broad smile again.

'And then there's the plants.' He paused, as though weighing up what he was about to say, with almost a kind of sniff of the air to see how I would react. 'And after a while you realise they're talking to you as well. Quietly, mind, so it takes a while to hear them, and then understand what they're trying to say. But they're talking.'

I had heard, of course, of people who talked to plants. But not, as far as I could remember, of plants that talked to people. Various alarm bells started ringing, but I decided to ignore them: it was too soon to start passing judgement.

'What are they saying?'

He looked at me and grinned, the grin eventually turning into a chuckle and a laugh. I felt he was examining me in some way. He bent down to pick up the brandy bottle from the floor, then leaned over and poured me some more. Sitting back in his chair, he gave me a fixed stare.

'The plants,' he said, 'the animals, and the stones and the fountains, are all telling the *cuentos de la tierra* – the earth-stories that spring from the land itself.'

Part IV

Fire

The Story of the Horse's Leap

Just south of the little town of Llucena you'll find a curious ravine, its vertical walls seemingly cut with a knife from the mountain through which it flows. These sheer limestone opposing cliff-faces, dropping over a hundred feet down to a rocky, dry riverbed, act as a gateway between the coastal flatlands and the inland mountains: from here on a clear day you can see the Mediterranean flashing deep blue out to the east, while behind you to the north-west the peak of Penyagolosa pierces the sky.

The ravine is known as the *Salt del Cavall* – the Horse's Leap – and the story goes that it was formed quite suddenly – as if by magic – many, many years ago. At that time a fierce battle was taking place nearby, the Moors on one side, the Christians on the other. Now as everyone knows, St James the Apostle often used to appear miraculously to help the Christians in their struggles against the Moors, and for that reason he is called *Matamoros* – the Moor-slayer. But on this day, despite the holy saint's presence, the Moors were too strong and they were beating the Christian army. The Christians, realising the fight was over, took to their horses and fled the battlefield, the enemy in hot pursuit. St James and a handful of knights tried to defend the retreating troops at the rearguard, but again the Moors' numbers were too great.

Finally, seeing that all was lost, St James spurred on his white horse and led the Moorish army away from the Christians. Closer and closer they drew behind him, until they almost caught up with him and dragged him down. But just when it seemed his horse could gallop no further, the apostle struck the ground with his staff and an enormous gorge appeared beneath him, stretching far down into the depths of the earth. His horse made a final leap into the air and landed clear of the ravine, but the Moors following close behind were all lost as they fell to their deaths at the bottom.

And they say that if you look carefully enough, on the top of the ravine you may find the footprint of the white horse's hooves, imprinted in the ground as it leapt into the air and carried the saint to safety.

JUNE

Now comes the season called summer, which is made up of three months, the first of which is known as Junius *in Latin,* Haziran *in Syriac and* Tirmah *in Persian. It is made up of thirty days. This is the month when the days stop growing longer and the nights shorter, and start going into reverse. It is also the time of the festival of* Al-Ansara [Pentecost]. *It is said that whatever is sown or cut on this day will not be infected with weevils. During the middle of the month, wheat is to be sown and sheep are sheared. Afterwards the males are placed with the females – and the same is done with the goats – for mating. Finally, all the measures we mentioned for the month of May can be applied in June as well.*

Ibn al-Awam, *Kitab al-Falaha,* The Book of Agriculture, 12th century

It's warming up now, and we've stopped lighting fires at night, sitting out on the patio instead and watching the waxing moon slowly cross the sky from left to right. All this night-time heat, however, has its downside: a remarkably loud crunching sound is coming from the beams of our new roof. It seems that we are infested with woodworm.

Or at least I'm hoping it's woodworm and not termites. All I can imagine is that during the short time the beams were lying down on the mountainside after the storm, something got inside them and is now feasting on them, and enjoying the warmer nights to do so. The noise they make is unbelievable as the grain of the wood gets pulped in their nasty little jaws. When I spoke to a man in the village about how to deal with it he could barely believe we could actually *hear* them. 'You must have very good ears,' he said. Perhaps woodworm always make the same noise; you just need the silence of the mountain to notice.

Anyway, I now have several tins of expensive and highly deadly liquid to brush on to the beams. It was either that or some toxic smoke bomb which would have meant blocking all the windows and doors and then letting it off before leaving the house for about a week. We'll see if this works. I was gladdened to find what looks like a tiny woodworm hole while applying a first exploratory coat. Termites, according to everyone I've spoken to, are much harder to kill. Perhaps in a week or so, when I've finished, we might be able to have dinner in peace again.

★

'I don't like it when people ask me how I am,' Faustino said. 'It always makes me wonder, Which part of me do you mean?'

After I'd found his *mas* up on the slopes of Penyagolosa, I'd been going back every so often, perhaps once a week, sometimes on my own, sometimes with Salud, who had immediately warmed to him. He preferred visitors during the week, leaving the weekends free to spend with his wife – when he was 'off-duty' as a hermit, as he put it. We'd go up just to spend time there: always taking something along – some food or some bottles of wine; and we'd end up chatting and drinking out on his patio, watching the sun drift slowly away and the first stars start to appear. He'd shown me a way of reaching his place by driving on a dirt track that wrapped around the hillside and entered the deep, dark forest: it would no longer be necessary to climb our mountainside and trek for hours across the fields on foot to go and see him.

And so we'd sit, and he would talk; sometimes the stories poured from him like rain, perhaps three or four in a row, while I listened, making the odd note, trying to remember them as best I could. Then on other occasions he wouldn't tell any, or just the odd anecdote, preferring instead to talk about people and places from the local area, as though filling me in on all that I needed to know about the mountainous world we had moved into.

'It's about reading the land,' he kept saying. *Se trata de leer el terreno.*

And I'd nod, as though I understood, although never quite sure if I did.

We'd sit down, either outside on the leather sofa on the patio, or else inside by the fire, Faustino wrapping himself in his patchwork blanket on the occasional cooler evening as he eased himself down beside his long-haired cat. He'd roll a cigarette, and then, as if it were the most natural thing in the world, start telling a story.

'San Vincente Ferrer is one of the most important figures in this area – a local saint, born in Valencia in the fourteenth century; they said he could speak in tongues, and that he performed endless miracles in his journeys around Spain and Europe preaching the gospel. Perhaps the most incredible of these was when he was staying with a family in the town of Morella. The mother was holding a baby in her arms while she was making broth for their guest that evening. But as she was stirring, the baby fell into the cauldron and was boiled to death. The poor mother was distraught, but San Vincente simply dipped his hand into the liquid, fished out the baby, gave him a shake, and within moments he was alive again and screaming like any healthy child, without a scratch or burn on him. Or so says the story.

'These lands had only recently been conquered from the Moors then, and there were plenty of Muslims and Jews still living in these parts. Often Vincente would arrive in a town just as a pogrom against the local Jewish community had started, but, by use of his miracles, he was always able to bring the violence and killing to an end, and in thanks the Jews flocked to him and begged to be converted. Some say it was Vincente himself who organised the pogroms beforehand, and that his "miracle" was simply to call his thugs off. But no matter: people at the time thought he was the real thing.

'His fame spread; he rose high in the church ranks. The Angel of the Apocalypse, they called him, as one of his main arguments for conversion was the imminent threat of Armageddon. This was the time of the great Schism of the West and the last of the Avignon Popes. Vincente was great friends with our own Avignon Pope, Papa Luna, who lived down on the coast at Peñíscola, but the two eventually fell out. That's when Vincente went on his travels again, preaching the end of the world. He died at Vannes, in Brittany, shortly after. But he's a local saint: there's barely a village or town in the area that doesn't boast a spot somewhere where San Vincente Ferrer came and preached.

'This story about him is one of my favourites:

'San Vincente was making his way down to the sea to catch a boat to France, where he was due to meet his friend, Papa Luna – I'll tell you more about him later. It was a nice sunny day and after a few miles San Vincente saw a plume of smoke rising up from a nearby wood. There, in a clearing, he found a charcoal-burner.

'The two men greeted each other and San Vincente asked: "Tell me" – for although his day's work miracle-making was finished he still had time and energy for some preaching – "have you heard of Jesus?"

' "Oh yes," said the charcoal-burner.

' "And do you pray to him every day?" asked the saint.

' "Yes, indeed," said the charcoal-burner, and he quoted the prayer he repeated at bedtime: "Oh Lord Jesus, may I never worship you, and ever offend you."

'San Vincente was horrified. "My child," he said, "you've got it the wrong way round. It should be: 'May I *ever* worship you and *never* offend you'."

' "Oh, I see," said the charcoal-burner. And he scratched his head. "Could you say it again for me?"

San Vincente did as he was asked.

' ". . . Ever worship . . . never offend," repeated the charcoal-burner after him.

' "Say it like that every day," said the saint, "and your soul shall be saved."

'And San Vincente went on his way, following the path to the sea where he was due to catch his boat.

'Now a few minutes after he had gone, the charcoal-burner started thinking about what the stranger had told him. But he couldn't remember the right words for the prayer.

' "Oh no!" he cried. "I'm almost certain to get it wrong again. I must run after the man and get him to tell me how it went."

'And he set off down the mountain after San Vincente. But by the time he reached the coast, the saint's ship was already far out to sea. So the charcoal-burner simply took off over the waves, running as swiftly as he could over the surface of the water. "Stop, stop, come back!" he shouted.

'A few minutes later the sailors on board San Vincente's ship began to hear the sound of someone's voice behind them. They turned round to look and were amazed when they saw the figure of the charcoal-burner chasing after them, skipping over the waves as though they were rocks and stones.

' "I must talk to the holy man!" cried the charcoal-burner.

'The ship's crew were used to San Vincente himself carrying out miracles, but they'd never seen anything like this, so they called the saint out on deck to see what was happening. Just as San Vincente appeared, the charcoal-burner ran up to the ship.

' "Oh, kind sir," he called out when he saw him. "You must help me. I can't remember how the prayer went. Could you say it to me again once more?"

'But San Vincente, seeing how the charcoal-burner stood there on the water, leaned over and said, "It's all right, brother. Carry on as you were saying it before. I can see no harm will come to you."

' "I see," said the charcoal-burner. "Goodbye." And with that he turned round and ran straight back across the waves towards the shore. And before long he was back in his clearing in the forest and working his furnace once again. And he carried on saying the prayer as he always had done until the day he died.'

★

This morning, as I was stepping into the old part of the house, something on the chain curtain hanging over the door to keep flies out caught my eye. Stopping to check, I found myself looking at a praying mantis, perfectly camouflaged. I've seen them about in the garden a few times, bright green as they crawl around the undergrowth at the base of the fig trees, or occasionally the odd light-brown one, perhaps in an area of dry grass. But this one was a perfect silvery metallic grey, blending in seamlessly with the chains on which it had decided to rest. It was only because it was sticking out a little from the chains themselves that I managed to see it.

There is something disturbing and fascinating about these insects: long and leaf-like, they seem so fragile, awkward almost, with those unwieldy front legs, until you imagine them devouring their sexual partners with bloodthirsty skill and speed: those huge globular eyes scouring the area around for yet more prey. I stood at a respectful distance for a while, watching, waiting to see if it would move. But it looked settled in its new environment, the silver sheen it had taken on making it a perfect trap for any unsuspecting spider crawling around the doorway. I wasn't quite sure what to tell Salud: that a natural predator of all the insects that made her life a misery up here had just arrived? Or that this predator itself was probably going to scare the bejesus out of her? Best not to say anything, I think. The chances are it's so well camouflaged she won't even see it anyway.

The land is gradually falling asleep around us as the heat increases. Summer is almost like a negative image of winter here – the plants, trees and animals all seem as though in suspended animation, waiting for the worst to come and go, longing for the cool of autumn, for a last burst of life before the frosts arrive. There are few flowers left, except for the occasional flash of colour from the oleanders down on the valley floor – Arcadio says they were used traditionally to cure scorpion stings: cuttings were tied around the affected area to prevent the poison spreading.

The onions have come up well, and we have been using them in our cooking. Occasionally they taste a little of soap, probably from the drainage water we used to irrigate them. Still, no matter: they're *our* onions, which is what counts. Beside them, the lettuces have sprouted well and the few that haven't already been eaten are about to start bolting. They have a rich flavour, like iron. I should have planted more. Next time.

Perhaps with a proper watering system some of the deadness of summer could be alleviated, but the sun is so intense, and the air so dry I wonder how effective it could be. I've thought of planting potatoes some day, but they would need a good flooding of water to grow properly. I've probably done things the wrong way round – planting first, then thinking about how to water everything after. Still, irrigation can be the next stage. But I have my doubts: there may be too much land for our little spring to be able to cope: I doubt if it produces more than a thousand litres a day. Perhaps we can set something up for next summer. For now, like the rest of the world around us, we seem to be sliding into our own form of heat-induced hibernation.

★

'You mentioned Papa Luna,' I said. 'San Vincente's friend. Who was he exactly?'

A cloud of smoke billowed from his lungs as Faustino exhaled, the cigarette glowing between his swollen fingers. From his lap, his white cat opened her eyes and looked at me, her yellow irises slashed with black, shining pupils.

'Round here Papa Luna is greatly loved, perhaps even more than San Vincente,' he said. 'Our very own pope, besieged down on the coast, defying the rest of the known world, outliving all his enemies, refusing to give in to the pressures of all the kings and dukes and lords of Europe. A very stubborn, and a very Spanish pope. You know the expression *seguir en sus trece*?'

I nodded. It was an idiomatic phrase that meant something like 'to stick to your guns'.

'Comes from Papa Luna, see? He was Pope Benedict XIII, in the early fifteenth century, and he refused to give up his position. Once a pope, always a pope was how he felt about it. So he "stuck to his thirteen", there in exile in his castle down in Peñíscola.'

I had been a couple of times to Peñíscola, towards the northern end of the Castellón coastline: the town that had served as the city of Valencia in the shooting of the Charlton Heston classic *El Cid*. It was a perfect fortress, perched on a village-sized lump of rock jutting out into the Mediterranean, with only a tiny strip linking it to the mainland. Once a magnificent site, with splendid castellated walls and fine stone Gothic buildings, today it has been all but destroyed by the mass tourism beast, the beachfronts on either side of this peculiar little peninsula now awash with holiday flats and hotels. The old town itself, meanwhile, is flooded with shops selling beachballs and suntan lotion, with fast-food joints offering 'Papa Luna' pizzas and hamburgers with 'Knights Templar' ketchup.

'Papa Luna was from Aragon originally,' Faustino said, 'and was a descendant of the last Moorish kings of Mallorca, but as he lived out his last – and most important – days round here the usual regional prejudices are put aside and he has been embraced as a local. He became head of the Church during the times of the Great Schism of the West from 1378 to 1417, when several men were competing for the title of pope. Papa Luna was one of the Avignon line of popes – and effectively the last. He's remembered for many things: laying the foundations of a united Spain, ordering the building of Saragossa cathedral, and establishing the University of St Andrew in Scotland. Some Scottish students in Paris who supported his cause wanted a place of their own to study, you see, away from the politics of the Sorbonne. Scotland stayed loyal to him until close to the end, but eventually followed the rest of Europe in declaring him "anti-pope" and joining the other side. Only Peñíscola and the local area refused to betray him.

'It wasn't as though the other popes claiming the title were particularly holier than him. One of his rivals in Rome, Pope John XXIII – not the recent one; this one dates back six hundred years – was actually deposed for murder, rape, sodomy and incest, among other things. Oh, yes, piracy as well, I think was the other one. No, it's just that in their attempts to resolve the question of having two – and sometimes even three – popes at the same time, the only solution anyone could come up with was for them all to stand down and for a new one to be named in their place. But Papa Luna – his real name was Pedro de Luna, of the Luna family – just didn't think a Church Council had the power to make a pope resign, and so he refused to go. At first he had a good number of supporters – half of Europe was on his side. But the years passed and little by little his patronage shrank, till even his friend San Vincente Ferrer – not a saint yet, you understand; that bit came later – a man Papa Luna had saved from the Inquisition years before by burning the papers that incriminated him, turned against him and made unpleasant predictions about children one day playing football with his head for his obstinacy. There was a great argument between them in Perpignan and Papa Luna left in a huff. He jumped aboard his boat to set sail in the middle of a storm. The captain of the ship was reluctant to draw anchor, fearing they might sink. "If indeed I am the true pope," Papa Luna told him, "then the sky will clear and we will be able to sail unhindered." And so it was: the storm broke, the sun came out, and Papa Luna sailed straight down the coast to Peñíscola, a hideout that had been given to him some years before by the Knights of Montesa.

'And there he stayed, safe from attack, defying the rest of the world which, in his view, had come under the sway of heresy. He was the real pope, and while he was there, Peñíscola was the centre of orthodoxy.

Noah's Ark, he described it as. Others might call him the anti-pope, and accuse him of being a magician – they said he kept two demons in a little box: the God of the Winds and the Revealer of Hidden Treasure; he only needed one more, the Prince of Sedition, and the Vatican would be his. But Papa Luna refused to give in, or even die, to help the dispute. There were attempts on his life, but always, as if by a miracle, he was saved. Once, some attendants in the pay of Pope Martin V's legate gave him some sweets laced with arsenic. Papa Luna took one bite of them and was immediately sick, his guardian angel forcing him to vomit out the toxins before they could do him any harm.

'So he lived out his last years in virtual self-imprisonment, surrounded by his library of over a thousand books, occasionally leaving Peñíscola to come up here to the mountains, but usually staying in his safe hideaway. A moderate man, some say a vegetarian, and greatly loved by the local people. When he visited Morella on one occasion, the town was infested with flies, but Papa Luna put a curse on them, and there's never been a fly seen there since.

'And so it went on, until, in 1423, at the age of ninety-five, he finally died, having outlived five of his rivals. The church bells rang out spontaneously, while mourners noted how his body smelled of flowers. Some of his followers tried to carry on for a while, and one of his four cardinals was named pope, but after a few years they realised it was a lost cause, and in the town of San Mateo, just inland from the coast, the Avignon line rejoined the rest of the Church.

'Not that they don't insist round here that he really was the true pope – *our* pope. They say that when there's a full moon you can see Papa Luna's ghost walking the ramparts of Peñíscola shouting *¡El verdadero papa soy yo!*. The waves that beat against the rocks below the castle, you see, are actually sea-spirits of the people who followed him into exile, and whenever Papa Luna is annoyed a great plume of sea spray shoots up from a tunnel running underneath the castle that they call the *Bufador*. The worst instance, as you can imagine, was when an Italian took his name – Benedict XIII – on becoming pope back in the eighteenth century. As Papa Luna had been declared an anti-pope, the name was free for future use, you see.'

*

Arcadio was still waiting for the hospital to call him in for his eye operation.

'Keep putting it off,' he said. 'Got more important cases to deal with.'

It suited him, fearful as he was, that they should take their time, but all the while it extended the stress of waiting for it all to be over with. Still he carried on as usual, driving around the valley with impaired vision in only one eye, scouting around his almond groves, checking out his beehives. He'd come up every now and again, and we'd sit under the oak tree for a while drinking wine from scratchy tumblers, sometimes talking, at others simply looking out over the valley and watching the birds. There were some new arrivals now, migratory birds that came up here to spend the summer. On a couple of evenings now I'd heard the distinctive triple call of a hoopoe, or a *pu-put*, as Arcadio called it.

'They never hunt those,' he said. 'Smell awful, like carrion, even before they're dead.'

One afternoon he pointed down at the little brown balls, like nuts, that always littered the ground beneath the oak tree. I hadn't paid them much attention before.

'Got plenty of oak-galls here,' he said, picking one up and crushing it in his short, thick fingers. A thick, yellowy powder fell out and was caught up by the breeze.

What exactly were they?

'Insects try to get inside the oak,' he explained. 'Burrow into the wood. So the oak protects itself by making this *galla* around it. The tree keeps itself clean of bugs, and the bug gets a place to lay its eggs.'

I held one in my hand. It was a dull, almost greyish-brown colour on the outside, with a hard, rough surface. Inside, though, there was a soft, powdery sponge.

'See the little hole?' Arcadio said. 'That's where the insect gets inside.'

I turned it over, then looked up at the branches above: there must have been hundreds, perhaps thousands, of them, jutting out from almost every twig, like Christmas decorations, but where the lights had been switched off.

'Can you use them for anything?' I asked. It seemed nothing here, no plant or stone, was without its value. In Arcadio's world they were bound to be a cure for stomachache, or fevers, or something.

He paused for a moment, rolling one of them between the palms of his hands.

'I've heard they once made ink out of them,' he said. 'Never done it myself, so I can't tell you what else you need.'

Ink! An idea in me began to stir.

'Not a great one for writing, me,' he grinned. 'Only went to school for three months, back when I was seven. Father wanted me working in the fields, so he pulled me out and brought me back to the *mas*.'

I looked at all the oak-galls lying around, and the great quantities still hanging from the branches above. There was probably enough here to start an ink factory. I would have to find out how to make it. It was probably something to do with tannins – I imagined the oak-galls were stuffed with them.

I already knew what I wanted to use it for. Faustino's stories played on my mind, repeating themselves over and again as I worked on the land, did repairs on the house, cooked meals, or as I was going to sleep. I'd repeat them to Salud to keep them fresh and help memorise them, jotting down a few notes, like a sketch, of the outline. But with ink from the oak-galls I would write them down properly. It seemed only fitting that ink made from the local earth should be used to record his earth tales.

Perhaps, I thought, Faustino would know about making ink from oak-galls. But I didn't have to ask. The answer came, curiously enough, from Jordi, the postman.

'They used to make ink like that during the Republic, back in the thirties,' he said. For some reason – I can't remember why – the topic of oak-galls came up in conversation during one of our chats when I went down to collect the mail.

'The government was keen to increase learning and education,' he said. 'Built schools all over the place. The levels of illiteracy back then were scandalous.'

'And they used oak-galls to produce ink?' I said.

'Cheaper that way. They wanted to help the children learn to write.'

I jotted down the basic recipe from what he could remember of it and hurried back to the *mas* to try it out. It went like this.

The 'inkiness' of the ink came from the tannins in the oak-galls, as I had suspected, but the trick was extracting them and then turning them into something with which you could write. For this process, the two other main ingredients were some rusty nails and some vinegar.

On my first attempt, as an experiment, I crushed five or six oak-galls in a bag with a hammer, and then poured the powdery mix into a jar with about half a litre of white-wine vinegar. Then I added the rusty nails. Apparently, the acetic acid of the vinegar on the nails produced iron sulphate, which reacted with the tannins.

I let it sit for a few days, occasionally checking to see whether anything had happened. Eventually, after almost a week, I took it out to see whether the process had worked. It smelled very sharp, and quite unpleasant. I fished out the nails with a fork, drained the ink into a container, and then threw away the pulp of the oak-galls that had sifted to the bottom.

I didn't have a large amount, nor did I have the right kind of pen for writing with. So, not being able to find a feather, I whittled a piece of wood into a sharp point and dipped it into the ink.

I wouldn't have won any handwriting prizes with what came out, but the marks made on the paper were definitely ink-like, and blotchy, the ink growing distinctly darker as it dried. After a few attempts I managed to scratch out a few half-legible words. After all the hundreds of thousands I had written with ballpoint pens bought for ten pence at the corner shop, or picked up accidentally from God knows where, not since I had written my first letters in primary school had I felt such joy at the simple act of making words on a page. The fact that you could barely read them, and that they made no sense, was irrelevant. My own ink from my own tree was making those marks.

A proper pen, paper and some blotting paper. It was time to start writing down Faustino's stories.

★

It was midsummer's eve, *la noche de San Juan*. I drove up with Salud through the mountains on the now familiar trail to Faustino's place, up behind the farm and towards the peak of Penyagolosa, across empty, rocky fields and through pine forests full of mistletoe. The sun stood over the western horizon, a purply light hovering over the hills and sierras far into the plains of central Spain beyond. Jays, their brightly coloured wings flashing in the lengthening shadows, struck out in threes and fours as we bumped along.

When we arrived, we found Faustino face-down on the floor. He didn't move when we called through the open doorway. For a moment we were unsure what to do. Was he praying? Perhaps he'd smoked too much home-grown tobacco. The dog and the cat were nowhere to be seen, while his songbird was hopping about frantically inside her cage. The door at the back of the kitchen was open, and it looked through to what seemed to be a study, or library: bookcases covered the walls from floor to ceiling, while hundreds of books were piled in towers, loose papers with handwriting on them scattered about the place.

I looked back at Faustino.

'Oh, my God,' Salud started. 'You don't think . . .'

'Faustino!' I called. There was no response, his body motionless on the ground.

I stepped through the doorway and walked towards him, my heart pumping. God forbid he should have had some kind of attack up here. Very gently and slowly I lowered my hand to feel him and see if he was all right. When my fingers were no less than an inch from him he jumped up with a start.

'Oh!' he said, looking up at us as though we were something odd and exotic. 'You're here already.'

He pulled himself up and on to his feet, and smiled, his pale-blue eyes like sapphires.

I thought it best not to say anything, but Salud was more concerned.

'Are you all right?' she said. 'Is there anything you want us to do?'

For a moment I thought he might snap at her, but he simply beamed back.

'I'm fine, my dear. Very kind of you to ask.'

He pulled his hair tight into the rubber band that held his ponytail, then tripped over to a wooden cupboard at the back of the kitchen and started pulling out some glasses. Salud gave me a look.

'Drink?' he said. 'Tonight is an important night.'

We drank an aperitif, clinking glasses in a triangle like an alcoholic version of the Three Musketeers.

'To San Juan,' Faustino said.

'San Juan,' we echoed.

Faustino clapped his hands.

'Right. To work.'

I pulled out some lamb chops we'd brought, placed them on a wire rack and started cooking them over the open fire, clearing away a patch of embers to one side. Faustino pulled out a large pestle made from a single lump of marble and started crushing cloves of garlic in it with a wooden mortar, pouring in the occasional drop of olive oil as he quickly pressed and stirred.

'The best garlic mayonnaise – *all i oli*,' he said, 'has to be made fresh just before eating. That way it doesn't oxidise and change its flavour.'

Salud leaned over to offer to do it for him: she was still worried about him. But now he seemed to sparkle with life, without the slightest indication that he'd been lying face-down on the cold stone floor only moments before, dead to the world.

'Open the wine,' he said to her. 'The corkscrew's in the drawer.'

It was never made clear if he recognised me from that first time when I'd gone to see him, so many years before, when he'd chased me away from his *mas* in no uncertain terms. I felt it best not to bring it up, not to ask. The fragile bond that had grown up between us so quickly might be lost or broken. But part of me couldn't help wondering if I really would have understood or absorbed anything of his stories if he'd told them to me back then – a simple, adventure-seeking day tripper. Having lived up at the farm for the past few months, I had the feeling of starting to sink roots into this earth myself. Before, it would have meant little to me.

A smell of lightly burnt lamb fat wafted through the room as I turned over the chops. The dog and cat came in from outside to join in, curious at the cooking sounds and scents.

'I've got some watermelon for later,' Faustino said.

'Ah, my favourite.' Salud's eyes lit up.

'It is the tradition to eat it tonight. Part of the San Juan festivities.'

Down on the coast, we were used to the usual midsummer

celebrations, where bonfires and fireworks were let off on the beach, the whole city, it seemed, heading out to the seashore to set up barbecues and dip their feet in the water at midnight for good luck. The traffic jams up and down the coastal roads stretched for miles. Up here in the mountains, however, in the vicinity of Penyagolosa, a mountain linked to St John himself, they did things differently.

'Here it's all to do with magic and magical rituals,' Faustino said, still beating away energetically at the *all i oli*.

'Some say the mountain was originally sacred to the ancient Celtic god of light and the sun, Lug, or Lugus. So Penyagolosa would have been something like Penyalugosa – Lug's Mount. But the consonants got switched round. When the Romans came, they associated Lug with their god Mercury, but whether from there, once the Christians took over, he became St John . . .? Perhaps.'

Often the link between pagan deities and Christian saints was fairly clear, he said. The feast of the Virgin Mary was held on 15 August, while the ancients had celebrated 13 August as the day of the goddess Diana – also a virgin. The parallels between the two were emphasised by the fact that the moon was the symbol for both, while Mary was said to have died at Ephesus, the site of the great temple to Diana/Artemis, one of the Seven Wonders of the Ancient World. In the end, however, there were almost certainly elements of many ancient goddesses in the character of the Madonna. The link between Lug/Mercury and St John, on the other hand, was more difficult to determine.

'The Christian saints are a colourful and elemental enough pantheon as it is,' he said, 'without working out all the time who they might be derived from. These mythological characters have always been with us, and although they may change their names and appearance every so often, they never go away. John the Baptist is fascinating in himself, perhaps even more so than either Mercury or the little-understood Lug.'

According to local legend, he said, everyone who had witnessed St John's execution was condemned to dance Salome's dance for the rest of eternity. And they could only be seen, out up on the mountain, on that very evening. But anyone who caught sight of these grotesque, whirling figures would be sent mad, or die of fright on the spot, unless they called out in time for protection from St John himself.

'So we'll be staying in tonight, then?' said Salud with a laugh.

I remembered the bonfires of the feast of Sant Antoni, back in January, and how Concha and El Clossa had hinted at connections between the Christian and the pagan midwinter festivals. I wondered if Faustino knew anything about it.

Fire was an obvious symbol of light and the sun, he explained, but was commonly associated, like water, with purification. The dates didn't exactly coincide, but the Roman purification festival *Februa* was held in the middle of the following month, to which it had given its name. So there might be a link there. Back then young men dressed in skins had beaten the local girls with sticks to make them fertile, much as they did today during Sant Antoni. But also *fiebre*, or fever, came from the same root, the idea that the burning and sweating of a fever purified the body in some way. This in turn made one think of 'St Anthony's fire', an old name for ergotism. Which brought us back to the midwinter festival of Sant Antoni.

'So they're linked,' I said.

'Are they?' he said with a smile. 'I don't know. All we've done is make a circle. That's easy. The ancient Iberians used to bless their animals at sacred sites in the mountains, so perhaps that's part of the festival's origins as well.'

The lamb chops were ready. We sat at the table, some salad in a bowl, a bottle of wine, bread, dollops of Faustino's fresh *all i oli* placed at the edge of our plates, and the chops piled high on a tray in the centre. We dived in, gobbling them down with sticky, greasy fingers. The *all i oli* was so strong I thought I was going to hallucinate.

Afterwards, Salud cut chunks of sweet red watermelon and we cooled our mouths. Faustino threw the bones to the dog, picking off some remaining strands of meat and feeding them to the cat. She miaowed contentedly, her heavy purring filling the room as she ate. The dog sat in a corner, cracking the bones apart with his teeth.

'Sorry, Dimoni,' Faustino said to the songbird in its cage. 'Nothing for you.'

The bird sang out and fluttered its wings. It already seemed to be falling asleep.

'Dimoni?' Salud asked.

'She's a little devil,' Faustino said, and gave a chesty laugh.

We cleared away the plates and tidied up before heading out to the covered patio. Salud and I sat on the old leather sofa; Faustino drew up a wicker chair. He pulled out a buckskin pouch where he kept his tobacco and started rolling another cigarette, carefully and lovingly moulding and forming it in his fingers before putting it in his mouth, lighting it and breathing in. After a few moments he let the smoke pour out thickly through his nostrils and seemed to relax deeply into his chair.

'Keep it all in special boxes, one for each month,' he said. 'Make sure I don't run out that way. Have to ration it otherwise I'd smoke a whole year's supply in a week.'

He laughed again, the laugh turning into a cough that seemed to catch hold of him and shake his skinny frame until we thought it might crack. His face went bright red, pale-blue eyes staring out in near panic. Salud rushed up and got him a glass of water. He took it from her and drank, then smiled again.

'Who said laughing was supposed to be good for you?' he said.

I sensed that Salud could feel it, too: a desire born out of concern and sympathy to ask if he was really all right, if there was something we could possibly do; and an understanding that if he was truly ill the last thing he would want was for us to know the details, or to act as nursemaids. We kept a respectful, if uncomfortable, silence.

Faustino finished smoking. I got up from the sofa and walked to the edge of the patio. The sun had already gone down behind us some time ago, but there was still a faint light in the sky, and a landscape of shadows stretched out into the distance. A very occasional light was visible here and there where villages or the odd inhabited *mas* stood.

'That must be where the pelegríns of Les Useres come up from in April,' I said, pointing out to the south-east. We hadn't seen El Clossa since that day. After Concha's commune fell apart he had been keeping his head down. Usually we'd have bumped into each other at some point by now – either in the village, or else out and about in the countryside.

'Did you do the pilgrimage this year?' Faustino asked. I nodded.

'Good,' he said. 'It's important, the pilgrimage. The people here haven't lost their connection to the earth. And although it's specifically meant for the village of Les Useres, it's important for everyone in this area, passing through or near so many of the other villages on its way to San Juan. Further north, in the village of Catí, there's another similar event the following weekend. Although that can turn into a bit more of a drunken orgy than this one: they're probably linked to old springtime fertility rites.'

The crucial point, he insisted, was that it was all to do with rain. April was traditionally the wettest month up here, whereas on the coast it was October. We needed the rain for the crops and for the land itself to come to life briefly between the death of winter and the sleep of summer. Water was the most important element, the one that was most lacking, and the one that alone could make the earth sing.

'Those gorges and gulleys and empty riverbeds,' he said. 'They can lie empty, waiting for it to rain all year. And then, if all goes well, for perhaps just a few weeks, or days even, if enough rain falls, they come into their own, the land begins to make sense. You know,' he said looking me in the eye, 'it was the waterfall and the stream that brought you here.'

I still remembered the thrill of that morning when I'd first seen the water cascading down our mountainside, and my scrambling walk up and over through the forest, until I'd eventually ended up here. The waterfall had only lasted for a couple more days, but for that brief time it was as if it had always meant to be, as if in those two or three days the landscape had reached a point of fleeting perfection.

And so the spring pilgrimages were a necessity: a call for the heavens to open and bring the rain that the land so needed to keep the delicate, fragile cycle in motion. Without rain, without water, there was no life.

Without quite knowing how, I understood at that moment that by 'life' he didn't just mean the word in the strictly biological sense. There was more to what he was saying than a simple, natural truth.

He got up and brought out more truffle brandy. On more than one occasion, now, I'd had the feeling of slipping into a different world when at his house. But whether it was the powerful alcohol, or else something about him, the place and the stories he had to tell, I could never say. Rather than a simple *mas*, it sometimes felt more like a castle in a fairy tale, high up in the clouds, away from the world of day-to-day existence. Perhaps it was just the brandy. But I could sense it as soon as I arrived, before even drinking a drop.

'Tonight, however,' he said when he'd filled our glasses, 'isn't about rain or water. It's about making contact with the underworld.'

He sat down in his chair again and began his story.

'Tonight is the night when the great *Avenc* can appear on the slopes of Penyagolosa, right where we are now. A deep, bottomless, fiery chasm that opens up suddenly and closes again, never appearing twice in the same place. Who knows? Perhaps we'll see it here before the night is out. The *Avenc* always swallows up an animal – usually a sheep or goat that has wandered off from the rest and is never seen again. Once there was a shepherd here who saw one of his flock vanish as the *Avenc* gaped open on the night of San Juan. He rushed up to the edge of the hole and looked down, but saw nothing but a strange orange glow. Curious, he threw down some shears attached to the end of the rope to see if he could touch the bottom. But down and down he let the rope fall, until he had no more, but still the shears hadn't touched anything. So the shepherd started to haul it back up again, but this time it was far heavier than to start with. Eventually, as he strained and pulled the rope back up, just as he was getting to the end, he saw that a giant featherless chicken had bitten on to the shears and that he was bearing its weight as well. With a shout he let go and the rope and the monster fell back into the *Avenc.* Now the shepherd didn't stop running till he got back to the village, where he told them everything that had happened. But the villagers just laughed. The shepherd was insistent, though, and so the next day a group of them went out with him to find the bottomless chasm he said had opened up the previous night. But when they got to the spot they found that there was no great hole, as the shepherd claimed. Although they did find the rope, with the shears attached to the end of it.

'Everyone laughed at the poor shepherd, and said he had obviously fallen asleep and dreamed it all. But strangely enough, exactly a year later, on the Night of San Juan, but in a different part of the mountain, a similar thing happened when a man lost his mule down a mysterious hole in the ground that seemed to open and close, swallowing the poor animal up. Now the local people don't laugh when they hear such stories, and they put it down to the *Avenc*, which thankfully only appears once a year.

'Some say the chasm is a passageway to the Underworld itself, and that flames shoot out, burning up anyone nearby caught unawares. And that horrible beasts can appear, dragons and dinosaurs, breathing fire through their nostrils. Nobody, they say, should be on the slopes of Penyagolosa on the Night of San Juan, for they might never see the light of the following day.'

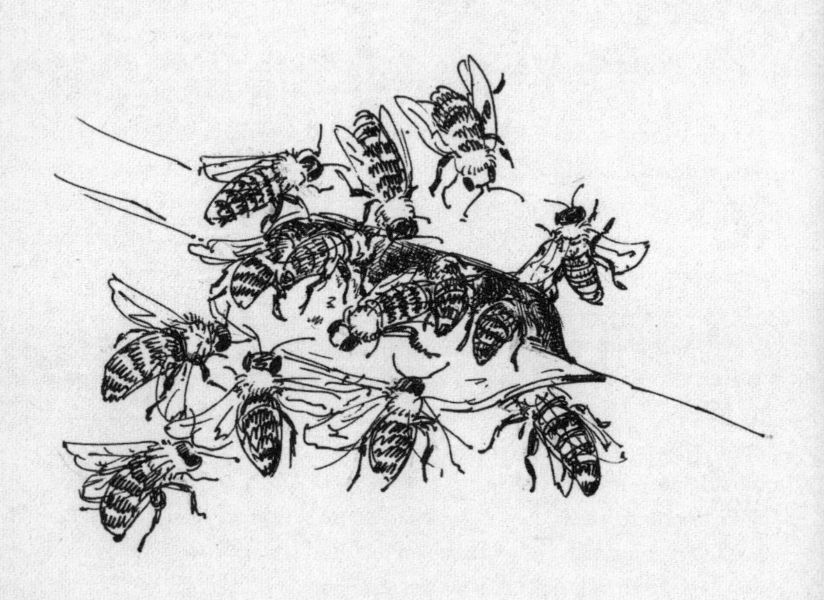

The Story of how the Rosemary Flower turned Blue

People tell the story of how one morning, Mary, the mother of Jesus, was walking alone through the mountains when it started to rain very heavily – one of those sudden showers that blow in from the coast, and then just as quickly blow away again. As there were no houses or shelters in sight, she ran as quickly as she could to an overhang in a nearby rockface.

After a few minutes the rain stopped and the sun came out again, but Mary's sea-blue cloak had got wet, and so she looked for somewhere to lay it out to dry for a few minutes. The gorse bushes, with their bright yellow flowers, were too harsh and prickly and told her they would not be the place to hang out her cloak. The holm oak trees, with their bright green leaves shining wet in the sunshine, offered to help, but their branches were too high for Mary to reach.

Then the thyme spoke up from down below.

'Lay your cloak on me,' it said.

'You are very kind,' said Mary, 'and your scent is sweet, and your mauve flowers very pretty, but I fear you are too close to the ground, and my cloak will almost certainly get dirty and muddy if I lay it on you.'

It was then that she caught sight of another bush nearby that she hadn't noticed before. It stood alone, neither prickly, nor too high, nor too low to the ground. Its flowers were pale white, with almost no colour at all.

'Who are you?' asked Mary.

'I have no name,' said the plant, 'nor pretty bright colours for my flowers. But you may lay your cloak on me, if you like, and in this sunshine it shall be dry in a moment. And I shall scent it with my perfume, for it is the only thing I have to give.'

So Mary lay her cloak over the bush, and in less time than it takes to tell, it was dry again. And when she placed it once more over her shoulders, she breathed in the wonderful refreshing scent the plant had imbued it with.

'Thank you,' she said. 'But it is not right that you have no name, nor colour for your flowers.' And so, as she spoke, the pale flowers of the bush began to turn blue, just like the cloak that a few moments before had been lying on them

'And from henceforth,' said Mary, 'you shall be known as Rosemary.'

And so she went on her way. And from that day on, the bush has always had bright blue flowers, and gone by the name of *ros mariae*, the Dew of Mary.

JULY

The Latin month Iulius *is known as* Tamuz *in Syriac and* Mordadmah *in Persian, and is made up of thirty-one days. It is a time for harvesting seeds: from the marshmallow, the safflower, lemon balm, lettuce, basil, garden cress, purslane, melons, cucumbers and gherkins. Pomegranates begin to ripen and dates start turning red. It is a good time to work the land around the base of olive trees, as the dust thereby produced is good for the olives themselves. This should be done just before, during, or shortly after sunrise, as the dust at this time of day will be cooler. According to the* Agricultura Nabatea, *any cracks that appear in the ground during this time should be filled or covered over to prevent the heat of the day from reaching and adversely affecting any tree roots. It is said that this is not a good time for planting trees or seeds because of the hot weather, although in Seville I have seen orach sown at this time of year, and cabbages and chard are transplanted.*

Ibn al-Awam, *Kitab al-Falaha*, The Book of Agriculture, 12th century

Following Ibn al-Awam's advice, I got up early this morning to churn up some of the soil around the base of the olive trees. Although I didn't quite make it for sunrise itself, it was still early in the day and the worst of the heat had yet to make itself felt. Great weeds have built up over the past weeks and months, so it gave me an excuse to take some of those out at the same time. Most of them look like some variety of fennel, great skinny stalks stretching up to around six or seven feet. The green flowery heads give off a pleasant scent when I crush them between my fingers, but digging around in the ground I've yet to find nice bulbous bits for eating that I'm used to finding in the markets. Perhaps this is some other kind of variety.

I tried not to dig too deep around the olive trees, for fear of damaging the roots, but a hoe is perfect for this kind of work, angled as it is so that it just scrapes up the top layer of soil. I still marvel sometimes at how versatile this simple, ancient tool can be.

There was plenty of dust, all right, as the ground is becoming increasingly dry again, and I had to break away a couple of times from the cloud I'd created just to be able to breathe properly. Quite what good this is doing to the olives beyond killing any competing weeds I can't say. Perhaps the dust coating makes them less appetising for the birds, or protects them against disease, or the sun. Anyway, we'll see next December if it has worked. Already there seem to be far more olives on the trees this year than last. Whether they'll hold out till harvest time is another matter, though. Last summer a freak hailstorm wiped them out. There's a saying: *Aguas por San Juan quitan vino, aceite y pan* – If it rains around midsummer, there'll be no wine, oil or bread. The sun has been shining constantly now for the past three weeks, so at least we're all right on that score.

If the soil feels so dry, though, it's not just because of the lack of rain. The downpours of April and May and then a few more into early June drenched the whole area. It's the intensity of the sun itself, I think, which drains the land of its moisture. Perhaps not the most earth-shattering observation, but being up here you can almost feel the liquids being sucked out by the harsh white light of midday – not only from the soil and plants, but from your skin and body. The flies have made a dramatic comeback, and buzz hyperactively around our mouths in search of a precious drop of moisture. And I can almost sympathise with them while swatting them dead – there's so little of it up here. The only place in the world where I have come across such fast, death-defying flies was in the Sahara. It makes me realise how vulnerable this landscape is: an annual downpour or two is all that keeps it from turning into desert. Any change for the worse in the weather patterns and in a matter of five to ten years it would be unrecognisable.

Still, with my eyes fixed on no further than next spring, I've planted some iris bulbs near the house – perhaps my last gardening act before the autumn, and the new farmer's year. I was surprised when Arcadio told me a couple of months back that now was a good moment to plant them – I would have thought November would have been a better time, and that's certainly what it says on the packet. But I've come to trust him. If he says summer is better, then a summer planting it shall be. Once I'd buried them in the soil, I gave the bulbs a thorough, late evening watering, with sharp mental images of them brightening up the hillside next spring.

*

I hadn't seen Arcadio for a while: I knew he'd been called some time around now for his operation as part of the national rush to get things 'done' before the great August holiday, when almost everything – including hospitals, it seems – either closes down or works part-time. I looked out a few times to see if his green Land Rover was heading our way from further down the valley, but there was no sign of him. I would have heard, I thought, if something had happened. It was a simple operation, and, although I knew he was frightened, there was surely nothing that could go wrong.

The days passed, though, and still he didn't show up. Eventually I decided to pop over on my way down to the village one day. Although I knew where he lived, he had always been the one to come up and see me: it was a strange experience going to his house.

Arcadio had a *mas* among a group of other houses just off the road, near the bank of the river. A small, old dog was sitting by the door when I drove up, barely raising its head as I walked over and parted the chain curtain to knock on the door. A few plants lined the whitewashed steps, and fresh light-blue paint had been brushed around the doorway and windows in the traditional fashion.

There was a long pause, and I was about to walk away, assuming no one was there, when I heard movements inside. Finally, the door was opened and there stood Arcadio.

'*Home*,' he said with a smile when he saw me. He looked tired, and his slippered feet shuffled along the floor as I followed him into the house.

The room was dark and bare, a cold, tiled floor and unadorned walls. He sat down next to a small round table with a lace cloth covered by a glass top and pointed for me to pull up a chair. A jug of water stood next to a vase with some drying herbs stuck in it.

'*M'han deixat fet pols*,' he said. 'They've screwed me up.'

The shutters were down on the only window: it kept the heat out, but it felt miserable. I wondered if he'd been told to protect his eyes from the sunlight as they recovered from the operation.

'What happened?' I said.

'Ah, the operation went fine,' he said. 'Took out the cataracts. I was only in there for half an hour.'

He got up and shuffled to the kitchen, where he opened the fridge, took out a bottle of cold wine and poured a glass for me.

'Not having one yourself?' I asked. He shook his head.

I tried to look in his eyes to see if there was any noticeable difference from before, but in the poor light it was almost impossible to see.

'So your eye's better now?' I asked.

He chuckled. 'That's the problem. I can see too well.'

He scratched the side of his nose and laid his hand out on the table.

'Can't drive any more,' he said. '*Me dona por* – I'm frightened.'

For years the cataracts had been growing slowly in his eyes, and he had simply grown used to them, driving up and down the same old tracks and roads as he had done for so many years. He knew this valley better than anyone. He didn't need eyes to be able to move around. But now that they'd been given back to him, the acuteness of this new-found sense had thrown him. He couldn't drive up the valley any more: it was too dangerous.

'That bend past the turning to the watermill,' he said, 'where there's a long steep drop on the other side . . .' He waved his hand in the air to signify how frightening he found it now.

'Must have driven along there thousands of times,' he said. 'Don't remember it being like that. I tried to do it a week or so ago and had to turn back.'

That in itself must have been a hair-raising experience: there was virtually no room to make a U-turn there.

'Almost makes me want to go to the hospital and ask for my cataracts back,' he said pouring himself some water.

I offered to come down and pick him up myself. It was tragic that by giving him back his sight he should have been left off worse than he was before. What would he do if he couldn't carry on with his everyday routines? The mountains didn't feel the same without him pottering around pruning his almond trees, inspecting his beehives, and keeping an eye on things. But he refused.

'My daughter's on at me again to move into the village. Says I'm getting old and she can't look after me properly if I stay out here.'

He paused for a moment and looked towards the door, as though expecting someone to arrive any minute.

'Don't like the village,' he said. 'Too many people.'

From his body language, though, it seemed that for the first time he might actually be contemplating the move he had been fighting. In the past the *masovers* used often to move into the village in old age to live out their last years in some degree of comfort after a lifetime struggling just to survive in the harsh *mas* environment. But now there was a proper tarmac road linking Arcadio's house to the village; he had electricity, running water, a mobile phone. The only other thing he needed was some degree of autonomy and the ability to get around to check on all his fields and scattered pieces of land around the valley. But that was slipping away from him. It was the first time he'd come into contact with modern medicine. It had given him back his sight, but had taken something vital away from him at the same time.

'I'd have to sell the Land Rover,' he said almost under his breath. Then he raised his eyebrows a little and looked at me. 'Interested?'

*

We were woken up this morning by the sound of something alive scrabbling around inside the house. As I drifted into wakefulness, it became it clear it wasn't a mouse – the sound was too loud – and that whatever it was was desperately trying to get out again. Salud got up first and went to check and told me it was coming from the fireplace. We have a black iron stove there: it seemed a bird had flown down the chimney and got stuck there, where the flue joined the casing. After much heaving and pulling I finally managed to open it up to let the poor thing out. At first nothing happened, then with a great flapping of wings, the blackened bird came flying out, dashing itself against the doors and windows of the kitchen. It looked like some kind of harpy, its claws outstretched, its eyes bright yellow against the unnatural tone its feathers had adopted from the soot inside the chimney. It flew so fast and frantically I couldn't see what kind it was: perhaps a thrush. Eventually, though, we managed to herd it towards one of the open windows and it flew away. I only hope it can clean itself and survive.

Living on our own up here, with so much contact with a natural – and sometimes supernatural – world, these things start to feel like omens.

⋆

Jordi rang up to say that a large box had arrived for me and was taking up space inside his tiny office. I drove down to the village and found him glum-faced, sweat patches spreading from under his arms as he sorted the mail.

'Air conditioning's packed up again,' he said. 'And the holidays are coming.'

Surely, I thought, that was something to look forward to, particularly for one so workshy.

'What am I supposed to do over the whole of August?' he said, pleading. 'I need something to keep me busy. Can't just sit on the beach the whole time.'

'Why don't you come back up to the village,' I suggested, 'and do some moonlighting. Taking the post out to the *masos* so we don't have to drive into the village, for example.'

'Can't do that,' he said. 'Years of strikes and workers' blood went into winning us our annual holiday.'

I unburdened him of my package and took it eagerly back to the farm. I had been waiting for this to arrive for over a week.

I opened the box: inside was a brand new bright copper still. With its bulbous form and curiously shaped lid, it looked like the dome of a Persian mosque, or Russian Orthodox church. I lifted it out and placed it on the table. It was a thing of beauty, wonderfully crafted, with little brass handles. For a few moments I simply stroked it, following the smooth contours with my fingertips. It was impressive enough just to sit as an ornament on some shelf or windowsill. But it was also fairly large, and was clearly meant to be used. Salud wanted me to make some essential oils using the herbs from the mountainside, but I was more tempted by the thought of employing it to make some mind-numbing and preferably illegal hooch. For a man with his own mountain, and now a still, there were no limits. It was time to think big. Perhaps we could even start a business – use fresh water from the spring, rosemary and thyme for a bit of flavour, all natural ingredients. People would buy it in bucket loads. Organic Mountain Moonshine. Acquavita de España. Webster's Weed Killer. Possible names for the potion I was going to make had already started to form in the back of my mind.

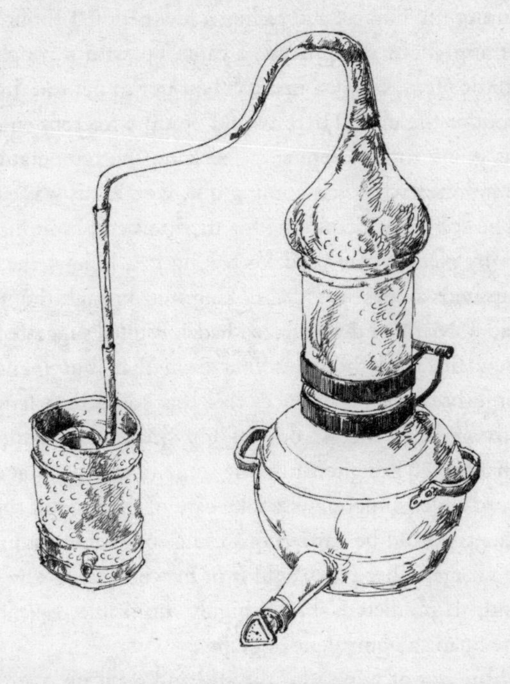

But first I was actually going to have to produce something. The instructions that came with the still were basic, so I had to fish around for other sources of information on how to use it. I remembered a few experiments as a thirteen-year-old in the chemistry lab at school – in fact, probably the only thing I *did* remember from those classes. The whole process had been dressed up as a means of testing the different evaporation points of alcohol and water, but in reality was an excuse for our curiously small chemistry teacher to stock up on his supply of booze for the next end-of-term party. Along with the obligatory admonitions that what we were performing was against the law, we'd make pints of the stuff for him, only to see him siphon it off and place it in the locked cupboard at the back of the class 'for disposing of later'.

From all this, two useful facts had stuck in my mind: 1) the evaporation point of ethanol, the good stuff, was 78 degrees, and 2) the evaporation point of methanol, the stuff that made you blind, was about 65 degrees. Still, I had something to go on.

After scouring my library, and calling a few people I thought might know something about the process, I came up with a rough idea of what I had to do. It was only a first try: best not to get too fussy about what came out at the end. There would be time for refinement. The problem was going to be keeping a check on the temperature. That way I could monitor what was coming out: whether it was ethanol or methanol. The still hadn't come with a thermometer built in, so I had to improvise by placing one used for baking in a hole at the side and bunging it up with a cork, the dial poking out through the middle so we could read it. Many of the sources I had consulted suggested making my own brew first and then distilling from that, but I knew from previous home-brewing experiences that this could be a lengthy and sometimes dangerous process: one of my friends had ended up in hospital with a busted gut after drinking some of my 'beer' at a party. I decided instead to let someone else take care of that side of things: our first experiments would be carried out using some cheap wine picked up from the village, where they sold it in five-litre jugs. The resulting nectar would, I predicted, be a highly drinkable *aguardiente*, or firewater, the Spanish equivalent of grappa.

I emptied the jug of wine into the still and set it up over the hob. Again, I had been told that this was best done outside, with logs of holm oak for firewood as this kept a constant, long-lasting heat. But it was late July: not only would making a fire be uncomfortable at such a hot time of year, it was highly dangerous. At the first sign of smoke the local firemen would descend on us. I sealed all the pipes with flour paste and then placed the cooling spiral and its container to one side with a pipe flowing in and out to keep the water circulating and prevent it from overheating.

If all went well the hooch would pour out of the bottom of the cooling spiral and drip down into a pan I had set on a chair just beneath it. I kept a cup to catch the first drops – the head – which would be thrown away. The still came with a special compartment which allowed you to place herbs above the evaporating wine, the steam catching some of their essence and thus flavouring the liquor. At the last moment I decided to add some, rushing out of the door and grabbing a few handfuls of thyme and some of the fennel stalks that sprang up all over the place.

I lit the gas, put it on a low flame, and sat watching the thermometer. For what seemed like a very long time it didn't move. Then slowly it began to rise. The still was making an incredible sound, like a wheezing kettle, as it heated up. The beautiful copper colour of the outside was quickly being dirtied by the flames, but I liked the idea that we were actually using it rather than treating it as a decoration: this was what it was meant for.

After a lengthy wait the temperature finally began to move towards the magic figure of 78 degrees. I expected it to pause just before, at around 65 degrees, for a moment, when the first drops might start to form and spill out from the end of the cooling spiral. This, in theory, would be methanol. But nothing emerged at this stage, and still the thermometer kept moving up. So no poison, then. What would eventually drip out of the tube should be highly drinkable ethanol, flavoured, I hoped, with some of the herbs I had thrown in to steam with it.

The thermometer hit 78 degrees and nothing happened. Then 80, 85 . . . Still nothing. Finally, as it got close to 89 degrees, the first drops began to appear at the end of the tube and started dripping into the pan below. A strange smell began to fill the kitchen, and Salud quickly reached for all the remaining windows that weren't already open. I was so excited, though, that I barely noticed. This was just the beginning, I thought. In years to come people would talk about this historic day when the first bottle of *Maestrazgo Moonshine*, as I had decided to call it in the end, was made. We could even write a little story about it and put it on the back label, along with claims about it being made from a secret recipe handed down over the ages, and how we only used local ingredients, with no pesticides or E numbers, or any of the other things we were supposed to jump up and down about these days. The fact that the basic ingredient was someone else's plonk was a minor detail. We could get round that.

After about twenty minutes of evaporation, around half a litre of liquor was now sitting in the pan. I reasoned that the temperature was showing higher than it should because it was measuring the heat at the bottom of the still, nearest the flame of the hob, and not on the surface, which was where the alcohol would be evaporating. Or at least that was the only way it made sense. But now the temperature was rising again: we'd got through the ethanol and water was starting to evaporate instead. It was time to turn everything off. I took the pan and poured the contents into a bottle, then left it on the table to cool while I cleared away. It was at this point that I noticed that the smell in the kitchen was really quite strong, and not entirely pleasant. There was something sharp and yeasty about it. I only hoped it would blow away soon, or else my new career as a distiller of fine liquors could be short-lived, at least if Salud had anything to do with it.

Once the hooch had cooled to room temperature, I screwed on the cap and placed it in the freezer to cool some more. It would bring out the best of it, I told myself, if we drank it at the right temperature. Too warm and we could hardly be surprised if it was undrinkable.

After dinner that evening I brought it out, carefully picking up a couple of shot glasses from the cupboard and placing them on the table in front of Salud. She smiled nervously.

'Do I have to?' she said.

'This is a great day. How often have you drunk home-made *aguardiente*?'

'Too often,' came the reply.

'It'll be fine,' I said, and unscrewed the cap.

The liquid flowed out thickly, like vodka. Good sign, I thought. Then I raised the glass to have a sniff. To be honest, I couldn't detect anything of the herbs I had thrown in to flavour it: all that hit me was a choking waft of alcoholic fumes.

'Ho, ho,' I said, 'looks like we're in for a fun evening.'

Salud's eyes were watering just from the smell of it. We looked at each other as though for the last time before jumping off a cliff.

'Here we go,' I said. 'To our first thousand bottles.'

'I'm not sure if I should,' she said sniffing it again suspiciously. 'Remember what happened to Miguel when he drank your beer . . .'

'It'll be all right,' I said. 'I've learned from my mistakes.'

We raised our glasses, counted to three, and then knocked it back.

*

The mule was a bad-tempered animal which seemed to like nothing more than to nip viciously at Faustino as he led him along the path. His purple, swollen fingers looked as if they were painful enough, but Faustino simply laughed, looking for crumbs of something in his pockets to try to assuage him.

'It's still too hot,' he said calling over to me as I followed behind them. 'He thinks we should wait another hour or two to let the sun go down.'

It was already past six in the evening, but I was more on the mule's side on this one. The heat of mid-afternoon still sat over us like a heavy cloud in the lifeless air, while every stone and rock was hot to the touch, radiating the energy of the sun absorbed over the course of the day. I wiped away drops of sweat forming on my temples – the first of many to come.

'Don't worry,' Faustino said to the mule. 'It'll be fine once we get under the trees, and then we can cool ourselves down when we get to the spring.'

I tried to keep my distance from the mule's hind legs: if he wasn't satisfied with biting chunks out of Faustino's fingers he was more than capable of taking a kick at me in his rage. The empty plastic water jugs Faustino had slung over his back made a deep drumming sound as they beat against one another with each step.

We crossed a grassy field – now quickly drying out in the intense summer light – and made our way down from the *mas* and towards the edge of the pine forest that stretched away down one side of a long, straight gorge. A mere half an hour from here, Faustino had told me, was a secret spring that no one knew about, where he grew his tobacco plants.

'So I can water them easily.'

As soon as we stepped into the shade of the forest the temperature dropped, and within minutes I could feel the sweat on my brow begin to dry. The mule calmed down a little, and merely shook his head from time to time as the occasional fly buzzed around his eyes.

'You'll be glad of the exercise,' Faustino said. 'Don't get out enough.'

The pine trees soared high above our heads: straight poles with an umbrella of foliage at the top forming a dark, green canopy to filter out the sun. The forests of the slopes of the Penyagolosa were well known for being rare ecosystems. There were supposed to be more than a thousand varieties of plants up here – more than in the whole of Ireland – and many of them unique to the area.

'Some people say this forest is *encantado* – enchanted,' Faustino said, as though reading my thoughts.

'Is it?' I asked. If anyone would know it would be him.

He turned round and grinned at me.

'Don't you find it enchanting?'

It was a special place: cool and still, and with that peaceful, contemplative quality that some forests have, sometimes captured and refined, you felt, in the great Gothic cathedrals, or in the mosques of the Islamic golden age.

'When I die,' Faustino said, 'I want someone to bring my ashes up here, pack them in an almighty firework and then set it off from somewhere inside this forest.'

The mule stopped in its tracks, shuddered and then brayed loudly, its pained voice echoing around the trees.

'It's all right, Bruno,' he said, patting the side of the animal's face. 'You can come along as well if you like. We can't let you end up in the dog-meat factory. They wouldn't take you anyway: you're too old.'

The mule blew hard through its nostrils and then reluctantly began to move on again.

'That's it,' Faustino whispered to him. 'Of course,' he said turning towards me again, 'they'd never allow it. It would be a fire risk, they'd say. I'll probably end up getting toasted in the usual fashion and put in a neat little box somewhere.'

Silently I wondered how long he had left. He talked about it as though it was something he expected to happen in the fairly near future. Again I looked at his skinny form, the gaunt, drawn look in his face, his mysteriously swollen hands. The appearance of frailty about him was in such contrast with the essential vitality that seemed to radiate from him, and his physical strength. Anyone else who looked that weak should be lying down in hospital on a drip. Yet when I was with him he never stopped. Was knowledge of impending death giving him so much energy, some kind of psychological charge? Or was it simply that he wasn't that ill in the first place?

We continued down through the trees along the side of the gorge. The pine trees were beginning to thin out and gnarled oak trees with oversized leaves took their place.

'*Roure reboll – quercus pyrenaica*,' Faustino said as he walked up to one and stroked the bark, giving the name in both Valencian and Latin. 'One of our very own varieties of oak. You can tell it by its large leaves.'

The area had first come to botanists' attention, he said, thanks to the research carried out two hundred years before by Antonio José Cavanilles, a Valencian natural scientist and leading figure of the Spanish Enlightenment. He'd spent time up here as part of the research into his magnum opus, *Observaciones sobre la historia natural, geografía, agricultura, población y frutos del Reyno de Valencia*, a botanical portrait of the old Kingdom of Valencia, the first of its kind to be done in Spain. Thanks to him we had a clear idea not only of the natural habitat of two centuries ago, but also a brief description of every town and village, with a rough idea of how many people there were and the crops they grew.

'Cavanilles used to say he could only come up here to Penyagolosa between June and September,' Faustino said. 'Because for the rest of the year it was like midwinter up here. The top of Penyagolosa,' he went on, pointing instinctively in the direction of the peak, invisible from where we were owing to the density of the forest, 'was covered in snow all year round.'

It was very different from today, when we were lucky to get one coating a year in midwinter perhaps. Two hundred years on, this was most definitely a hotter part of the world than it had once been.

'It's lucky for me the place is heating up,' Faustino said. 'I wouldn't have been able to grow my tobacco up here otherwise.'

We stepped from the shade of the forest and out into a field. We were in a kind of dell, and the heat seemed to have been trapped there. Bits of dirt found their way through the gaps in my walking sandals as we cut across dry, scratchy long grass.

'Down here is the perfect spot for it,' he went on. 'It's warm and sunny, as you can see. Look, it's south-facing. There's a constant supply of water. And, what's more, no one else even knows it exists.'

From somewhere below I could hear a trickling sound. Wherever his secret plantation was, it was probably somewhere close by.

'Water's important, you see,' he said. 'It always has been.'

Many of the old oracles of the ancient world, he said, were next to natural springs or rivers: Per-Wadjet, Delphi, Siwa. All the old theatres in Shakespeare's London as well.

'You should know that: Holywell, Clerkenwell, Sadler's Wells – all near sacred wells. And then there are all those folk tales about the fountain of eternal youth, etcetera. There's often something making a link between stories and water.'

I'd travelled to the Siwa oasis many years before as a student learning Arabic in Alexandria. It was strange hearing him mention it now. For a moment I was there in the Western Desert again, riding in the back of a rusty, baking old bus along the Egyptian–Libyan border to visit the place where they said the oracle had once named Alexander the Great the son of the god Amun. It had been a place of stories and mysteries, water simply bubbling up through the barren rock in places with names like 'Cleopatra's Bath'. The oasis was still unspoilt when I went there, with a unique Berber culture which up until a hundred years earlier had allowed homosexual marriage. The locals told me stories of incredible treasure still buried in the nearby hills from the time of Alexander and before, but the secret of finding it had long been lost. My visit, however, had coincided with the first forays of a tourism development team from Cairo, driving around the sand in a golden Mercedes with plans for hotels and golf courses where at that time stood ancient salt-mud ruins. I hadn't been back since, but reports I'd heard suggested the place had changed beyond recognition.

I was brought back to the present by the sound of Faustino's voice.

'The ancient oracles used to be sacred to the earth, or the earth goddesses,' he said, 'before they were handed over to Apollo.'

He stopped the mule and turned to look at me. We were caught in the blazing sun; I rather wished we could find a shady spot before pausing in our walk like this.

'There was a sacred laurel at Delphi,' he said. 'When the oracular power was transferred to Apollo, the god started chasing after Daphne, Gaia's daughter. But she fled, and as she ran she called that her mother might save her. And so the earth opened up and swallowed her, leaving Apollo on his own. And where she had vanished a laurel bush stood. Apollo was angry, and he commanded that if Daphne wouldn't be his wife, then the laurel would forever be his tree. And he plucked a branch of it there and then and crowned himself with it.'

The thought came to me that if he knew about the stories behind the plants, he might know something about their supposed healing properties as well. The heat was beginning to make me dizzy and I could feel a headache developing at the back of my neck.

'Headache?' he said with a look of surprise when I mentioned this to him. 'Take an aspirin!'

And he turned and walked away. After a pause I followed after him. If we were indeed near the spring at least there I might be able to cool down a little.

We skipped down some rocks at the side of the gorge, and suddenly there in front of us was a small field with bright green, unmistakeable plants growing in bushes, like a small wood. Next to them was an archway built into the side of the mountain, from which a steady flow of water was spilling out down a channel and into a small, round pool made of stone, perhaps ten feet across. At the edge of this another channel had been made and was carrying water in the direction of Faustino's plants.

I'd never seen home-grown tobacco plants before. It wasn't anything a farmer in Virginia would waste his time with, but for one man's supply it was nothing to be ashamed of. The plants were already almost as tall as we were and were branching out in thick bunches of leaves. There must have been about twenty or more of them, each giving off a heavy odour in the late afternoon sun.

'They'll easily grow another half a metre or more before harvesting,' Faustino said. He looked serious all of a sudden, the farmer tending his precious crop. The mule started drinking from the pool while he got down on his hands and knees and started checking the irrigation channels running to the base of each plant. The whole thing was kept very neat, I noticed, as though he came down here quite regularly. There wasn't a weed to be seen around the plants themselves, while the irrigation channels ran in perfectly straight little lines. I took a step forward to get a closer look.

'Mind where you're treading,' Faustino barked without looking up.

I'd been a smoker in the past, but had given up after picking up a nasty chest infection some five years before. Still, there was something jolly about this little corner of an illegal field: the sense of freedom and a complete lack of state or police interference. In a landscape so devoid of man it seemed churlish even to think of 'laws'. Some other, deeper laws of behaviour and civilisation were the norm in this kind of environment: the very absence of the modern world seemed to call to a deep-rooted, more essentially human sense of right and wrong. And there was clearly nothing 'wrong' in an old storyteller growing a few plants to help him pass the winter nights if he wanted to.

Once again, Faustino seemed to be reading my mind.

'And to think they say it's illegal,' he said. 'How can you make a plant illegal? Can you imagine making oak trees illegal? Or artichokes? Or parsley?'

He scraped at the soil plug in the channel at his feet and the water flooded through to irrigate another one of his plants.

'There ought to be a law against making things illegal,' he said.

I sat in the shade cast by a rock higher up the side of the gorge and sniffed at my hands where I'd rubbed them through the leaves of his precious plants. Could you tell something about the quality of a plant from its smell, I wondered, as you could with a wine? Perhaps there were tobacco 'noses' out there sniffing and sampling and discussing tasting notes as we spoke.

Faustino finished with his plants and came over to the pool to rinse his hands. I watched as the water circled the base of each bush, bubbling and foaming a little before soaking gently into the soil. He would leave them like this for a few minutes to get a good watering before we set off again, he said. I put my hands into the pool as well: the water was cool and fresh, small eddies showing where the tiny current pushed it along and down towards the irrigation channels. Small-leaved plants grew in bunches at the edge, like moss, while flies and other insects buzzed about, catching the few precious drops that splashed out and landed on the surface of the rocks. I cupped my hands and brought the water up to my overheated face, splashing it on to my hair and letting it run in delicious streams down my neck and under my shirt to my shoulders.

'You can drink this if you like,' Faustino said. '*Está muy buena* – it's good water.'

One of the things I'd always loved about the Spanish was the way something as simple as water could be appreciated so highly. As a child growing up in the overly damp British Isles, water was simply something that fell out of the sky – usually too much of it. You certainly never heard anyone describing a particular type of water as being 'tasty' or 'good'. It was just 'wet'. Here, though, particularly if it came straight out of a mountain, and hadn't passed through a bottling factory on the way, it was treated with an almost holy reverence. I took a few grateful gulps. Faustino was right: it was wonderful. No wonder his plants looked so happy.

We sat on the edge of the pool enjoying the coolness of the spot and watching the water spilling out and on to the land below our feet. For a long while neither of us spoke.

'Watering the land,' Faustino said after a time, 'is like gathering and telling the stories. They come from the land, but have to be poured back into it to make things grow. If we don't take the water that's coming out of the mountain here it will drain away. Some plants will be able to benefit from it, but not many. But if we take the water and use it to irrigate the land, then we can do a lot more.'

The sun was finally falling behind the hillside at our backs, and the shadow crossed the small patch of the field by the spring as he spoke, slowly creeping up the other side of the gorge.

'You have to find and look after the stories, otherwise they'll be lost.

And you make sure other people hear them, so that maybe one day they'll tell them to someone else.'

He leaned back and put his hand into the water again, making a whirlpool with his fingers.

'It's important to go out and find the springs,' he said. 'The land is drying up.'

*

I sat on the terrace outside the house looking out over the valley. The sun had passed behind the Picosa and a cooling breeze was blowing in from the sea. It was an exceptionally clear afternoon for summer, when the cotton-like haze tended to blur the outlines of the horizon. In the south, beyond the village and the hills that rose up behind it, the summits of the next mountain chain – the Sierra de Espadán – could just be seen, a purply, jagged outline that stretched from right to left. We had driven through the area and explored its tiny villages a number of times. It had been one of the last bastions of Moorish Spain, home to the Moriscos, the 'little Moors', who remained in Spain under Christian rule long after the fall of Granada in 1492. Forced to convert to Christianity and forbidden from speaking Arabic, they had become one of the forgotten peoples of history. After the fall of Granada the Moorish intelligentsia and nobles had mostly gone into exile, fleeing across the Strait of Gibraltar. Those they left behind were mostly farmers and artisans, tolerated by their Christian masters only for their skills and usefulness to the economy, and looked down upon as tainted by their co-religionists in the rest of the Muslim world.

Over the course of the sixteenth century, the Moriscos were increasingly seen as a thorn in the side of Spain, a country that had already rid itself of its Jewish community and was doing its best to homogenise itself into a Catholic superstate. After a rebellion by the Moriscos of Granada was brutally put down, the Kingdom of Valencia became home to the most significant concentration of these hangers-on of Al-Andalus. Attempts had been made to convert them fully, even to join Islam and Christianity in some way, concentrating on the common themes of both religions in a manner that might be acceptable to them. But the Moriscos failed to assimilate en masse. They developed their own written language, Aljamía – Castilian Spanish written in Arabic characters – and built up a sub-culture based in part on the folk magic and customs they managed to keep from the eyes of the Inquisition.

But the threat of war and of invasion by other Muslim powers – principally the Ottoman Turks – meant the tide was turning against the Moriscos. In 1609 the decision was finally taken to expel all 300,000 of them from the country. After a nine-hundred-year presence in Spain, the last of the Moors were given just three days to pack their bags and leave. Ships were chartered to take them to Oran and into North Africa. Anyone not complying with the order would be killed.

They said the expulsion had started right here, in the Sierra de Espadán, in Argelita, the next village along from ours as you headed south. Four hundred years ago, the land I could now just see from my terrace was the last home of one of the greatest cultures in history: Moorish Spain. There were hardly any *masos* in that area: the Moriscos had always preferred to live in or near the towns and villages. The cultural differences between one valley and the next, between Moors and Christians, had been left like an imprint on the land itself.

I wondered how much of the Morisco traditions had seeped into the local folklore. Theirs had been a mostly oral culture, so it was probably impossible to say. But it seemed fitting that they, too, should once have been hiding out in these hills. It was as if a local theme were developing: the last Cathars, Papa Luna, Juana la Pastora, the hermaphrodite anti-Franco guerrilla leader. All these people had been fighting rearguard actions, trying to survive against the mainstream and the tide of history. And they had all found temporary sanctuary up in these hills, while the rest of the world went on its way. All of them with beliefs they held dear, that they wanted to protect and safeguard. I remembered Faustino's tales about the Moors burying treasure just before they were expelled from their lands by the Christians. It was a running theme, a template of a story you found all over Spain. Perhaps here in these mountains there really was treasure of some sort: the memories and legends of the past, buried deep in the land: the earth-stories.

Something stirred in the back of my mind: a blurred memory long forgotten; a connection. I dashed inside and started rooting around my bookshelves. Somewhere in there was a tattered old Arabic dictionary from my university days, held together now with sticky tape. Within a second it leapt out at me, and I started flicking hurriedly through the pages. There was a word there, a word that had caught my attention many years before but that had long since slipped from my memory.

Arabic was a fascinating, if devilishly hard language. One of the most interesting things about it was how words were grouped around a triliteral consonantal root. For example, words with the sounds K, T and B were all about writing in some form. So KiTAB meant book, maKTUB meant written, maKTaBa was a library, etcetera. Quite often, though, words which on the face of it had no connection at all were also grouped around the same root. Usually you had the sense that there was no link there. The word LaBaN, 'milk', for example, seemed to have nothing to do with LaBiNa, 'brick' or 'adobe'. But occasionally you stumbled on examples where the consonantal link between the words had a deep resonance, as though there were a hint of a code, with some poetic truth buried deep in the language, like a puzzle, to be explored. One example was the root HBB, which formed HuBB, 'love', and also HiBB, 'seed'. AYN produced 'eye' and also 'spring' or 'fountainhead'. Another echoed Faustino's story about Apollo, Daphne and the laurel tree: the root GhWR had the sense both of falling, a cave, swiftness of running and 'laurel'. There was another one of these curiously linked words, though, one that had always seemed to speak of a truth I couldn't quite grasp.

The dictionary opened on the page I was looking for, and there it was: the root RWY. I glanced down quickly at the meanings of the words made up of this combination.

RaWiYa: to drink, be irrigated, tell a story
RiWAYa: a tale, story, novel
RiWa'i: a writer, storyteller
RaYYan: well-irrigated, lush, verdant
taRWiYa: reflection, consideration

Faustino's words of a couple of days before back at his tobacco plantation came back to me: gathering and telling the local stories was a way of watering and irrigating this dry, endangered land. He might not have been the first to perceive the link, but here there seemed to be proof of some kind of the truth of what he had said.

I thought of the work we had put into the land over the past year, the scrub we had cleared away, the trees we had planted and tended: hours of sweat to try to make a small change in this abandoned landscape. There was magic here: people had always said so, but now it was as if I could see it properly for the first time myself. Not the magic of Marina and Concha, with their rituals and witchery, nor even the fairies and *duendes* that had seemed to make an appearance in our lives over the past months. The life that seemed to vibrate from the rocks and earth round here came from the stories that flowed through it: stories that were a vital part of the landscape, and without which it would be impossible to understand the area to which we had come to live. Learn to read the land, as Faustino said, and you started to get a sense of how the land and the stories that came out of it were one: neither could properly exist without the other. And in a world where we lost our understanding of the land, where we abused it, where we built golf courses and airports and miniature Eiffel Towers, the tales dried up: there was no one to gather and nurture them, no one to listen to them. Crowd it out with so much other noise and you would fail to hear the earth-stories as they were whispered by the stones and the trees, the rivers and mountains. They needed silence; for men to sense their presence, then to weave them into legends and folk tales to be passed on, and on. Some were living stories, such as the Pelegríns of Les Useres. Others came from the history of what had happened here: the Cathars, the Moriscos, Papa Luna. Some seemed to explain the world around: the colour of rosemary flowers, why clefts and gorges appeared where they did. And then there were others that just seemed to exist of their own, inexplicable; perhaps the better for it. Yet they were as much the part of the landscape as the others, more so, even.

Where they had come from, and who had first told them, mattered not. They resonated with the land and the land resonated with them. They were the earth-stories of Penyagolosa.

The Story of the Three Pieces of Advice

After many years away, a merchant who had become rich travelling the Seven Seas decided it was time to return to his wife and home. But before making the journey back, he went to see a hermit who lived in the mountains, to seek his advice. The hermit was known for his wise words and good counsel, but all he said to the merchant was:

Never leave a straight path.

Never get involved in other people's affairs.

Always sleep on a decision before doing anything important.

Now the merchant was a bit disappointed when he heard this.

'Fine advice that was,' he thought to himself. 'I could easily have come up with that myself.'

And he went on his way, heading for home.

Not long after he came across a group of travellers who were going the same way and he decided to join their company. After they had gone a few miles they came across a fork in the road. Up ahead stood a great mountain, the path winding up its slope until it seemed to disappear in the mists. To the right was another path, much flatter and going around the mountain instead.

'Come on,' said the merchant's companions, looking at the alternative path. 'Let's go this way. It'll save us an hour at least on our journey.'

Now the merchant was about to go with them, but at the last minute he remembered the hermit's words.

'Perhaps there was something in them,' he thought. And he decided to carry on straight and up over the mountain.

He walked and he walked and he walked, and the path seemed to be even longer than it had looked from the bottom. But eventually, as all things come to an end in this world, he found himself down once again on the other side of the mountain. There he found his companions. But they were all sitting by the side of the road, their heads in their hands. Some were almost crying.

'What ho!' cried the merchant. 'Why such long faces?'

'We should have listened to you and gone up over the mountain,' one of them said. 'Soon after you left us a group of thieves attacked us and stole all our baggage, and they whipped and beat us all the way here.'

After picking themselves up and cleaning their wounds, the group were once again back on the road, and come nightfall they found an inn in which to spend the night. At dinnertime they sat down at a table and waited to be served.

But the innkeeper and his wife were having a terrible row that evening, and they were throwing pots and pans at each other in the kitchen rather than preparing the travellers' food.

'We should go in and do something,' one of the travellers said. 'Someone's going to get hurt.'

They all got up to intervene, but the merchant stayed where he was, remembering the hermit's second piece of advice: not to get involved in other people's business.

When the travellers confronted the innkeeper, he got so cross with them that he forgot all about the argument with his wife, picked up a big stick and chased them all out of the inn. And they all had to sleep outside in the cold, with no dinner.

Sitting on his own, back inside, the merchant began to realise the hermit's words were more valuable than at first they had seemed.

The next day the merchant arrived back at his home village, and he saw his old house. But before going up to meet his wife he decided to hide in some nearby bushes to see what he could see.

Shortly after, his wife appeared at the door with a young priest. And as she said goodbye to him she gave him a kiss.

Now the merchant was furious with rage and he would have run in there and then and killed his wife on the spot. But he remembered the hermit's last piece of advice: always to sleep on something before making a decision. So he walked up to his house as though nothing had happened, and his wife received him with open arms.

His wife was so shocked to see him that she was speechless, and it was only the following morning that she found she could speak again.

'Yesterday,' she said as the merchant was waking up at her side, 'was the happiest day of my life. First because Fate brought you back to me – you who I haven't seen nor heard from for so many long years. And secondly because our son came to visit me from the seminary, where he is training to become a priest.'

Giving thanks once again for the pieces of advice, the merchant decided that the hermit must have been none other than King Solomon himself, whose wise words had brought him safely back home.

AUGUST

The month Augustus *in Latin is called* Ab *in Syriac and* Shahrivarmah *in Persian, and is made up of thirty-one days. The dew begins to return, the heat lessens and mornings become fresh. This is the season for harvesting almonds. Peaches can be eaten now, and dates and jujubes start to ripen. It is said that wood will not rot if it is cut after the third day of this month. It is the time for sowing rice, and for harvesting carob, safflower seed, cress, coriander, sesame, melon and gherkin. In order to speed up the ripening of grapes, work up the soil around them and the dust settling on them will have this effect.*

Ibn al-Awam, *Kitab al-Falaha*, The Book of Agriculture, 12th century

The nights are very hot. Surprisingly, the older part of the house, with its thick stone walls, can actually feel warmer at night than the newer section. The stones seem to absorb the heat over the course of the day and then radiate it in the hours of darkness. Thank goodness for modern insulation: it seems to be doing the trick. I would sleep outside, where the air can be tolerably cool, but the very idea is enough to send Salud into apoplexy. 'We'd get eaten alive!' She's probably right.

Still, we stay up late, adjusting our existence to the weather and the seasons. It's too hot to do much through the day, and everything just slows down to a relaxed and gentle pace: more out of necessity than anything else, as any physical exertion in this kind of heat can be lethal. Builders are always the first casualties of any heat-wave, quickly followed by the elderly, despite the custom of taking siestas during the hottest hours. But there's clearly something unhealthy about toiling away under the sun when it's almost 40 degrees. So in the interests of my own longevity I have decided to join in the national tradition of doing precious little until it begins to cool down again – which shouldn't be until mid-September at the earliest. I limit myself to watering the trees after sunset and preparing salads for dinner, our bodies, like the plants, craving fresh, watery food over anything else. The pomegranate tree has only given us half a dozen fruits after the heavy pruning I gave it in the spring, but the juice is sharp and refreshing in the morning, with just a teaspoon or two of sugar added to take away some of the bite.

It is the time of year of the *Lágrimas de San Lorenzo* – the tears of San Lorenzo, the spectacular meteor shower that falls through the night sky. San Lorenzo is actually 10 August, but the meteors have come a couple of days later this time. Still, they've coincided with a new moon, so there's no other light to filter out the streaks of yellow, white and gold as these rocks from outer space hit the atmosphere and burn up. Why San Lorenzo should have been crying in the first place, I can't remember. Ah, yes, he was the one who was barbecued to death by the Romans, famously telling his executors that he was done on one side and they could turn him over. Enough to bring tears to anyone's eyes. Put on a nice show for it, though.

We stayed out on the patio for a couple of hours gazing up at the sky and trying to spot the meteors. It's not exactly easy, as they're so fast that the moment you say, 'Ooh, look, there's one', it's flashed and disappeared. After a while we stopped and just tried to keep our eyes on the section of the sky where they seemed to be most concentrated. Eventually, with practice, we saw some that did cut across the darkness at the very spot where we were looking. It was a relaxing experience: as though you had to empty your mind and let it happen rather than trying to catch them all the time.

It was late when we finally went inside. The anti-mosquito candles we'd placed around us like a barrier could only do so much, it appeared. Salud scratched at her arms as she closed the doors shut.

'*Malditos bichos* – damn bugs.'

⋆

I went for a walk around our land at dusk one evening. Our first full year up here was almost at an end; had we managed to achieve much in that time? Everywhere I looked I was struck by all that still needed to be done: great tracts of land I'd wanted to clear but which were still under the tyranny of the gorse; walls that had fallen down and needed rebuilding, but so far out of reach it would take an effort of will and strength just to walk through to them; fields I had ploughed after a fashion with the rotovator but which were now once again awash with weeds. The sheer vastness of what we had up here, and the amount of work for just one man overwhelmed me once more. Was it absolute madness all this? How could I possibly have expected to 'farm' forty acres of rocky mountainside on my own? The idea was insane.

I skipped up the track to inspect my truffle-tree plantation. Only half of the two hundred I had planted up here had survived the boars' onslaught. Those that remained appeared to have rooted in well enough, but were still little more than three of four inches high, while the wild flowers that had sprung up around them were up to my waist in some places. If I wasn't careful the oaks and holm oaks I'd put up here were going to get choked and lost in the returning thicket. It was simply too hot now even to contemplate doing anything about it. It would have to wait till autumn, in between the almond and the olive harvests, if I had time.

I carried on walking up the slope, to one of the old pine trees, sitting down with my back against its trunk, sensing the temperature of the air slowly, slowly begin to fall as the sky darkened and the birds circled and screeched in the hollow below. Down to the left stood the farmhouses, where Salud was switching on the first lights. It no longer amazed me to think the power to generate the electricity came from the sun. You quickly grew used to it, then began to understand the intensity of the energy that beat down on us daily. Living with it, feeling it on your back, watching it bring things to life, then destroy them.

So much I had wanted to achieve, and so much still to do. It was a start, I told myself. We had done what we could. Perhaps we might have accomplished more, cleared more land, planted more trees, built up more walls, laid out a great irrigation network to make better use of the water coming out from the spring. All these ideas for transforming the mountains had been at the front of my mind when we started. Now I had come to understand what such projects entailed.

Yet despite this, despite looking down on the farmland and ticking off all the areas where I had seemingly fallen short, I noticed that an overall sense of failure was missing. I felt content up there, the scent of pine needles drifting around me in the heaviness of dusk. I had come with ideas about how I would change the land, how I would do things with it: great plans. And they were good ideas, ones that I might realise yet. But while I had managed to get some things done over this time, the direction of influence had always been the reverse. This land, this mountain, had done more to me than I to it. Working on it, touching it with my hands, feeling its pulse and rhythms, its cycles and transformations. I had put down roots of my own, had made contact with something I had barely known before, or perhaps had forgotten: a sacredness of the land; an earthing, strengthening, vivifying gift of this silent sierra, something that had existed in my childhood, standing next to my grandmother in the shadow of Pendle. This was the real story of my year on the mountain.

★

There was a sharp bend in the track.

'Pull over here,' Faustino said. 'I want you to see something.'

I found a space at the side underneath some ivy dripping off the trunk of a tall pine tree. The road continued steeply down the side of the mountain and was lost in the greenery. In front of us, just visible through the trees, the peak of Penyagolosa soared into the sky. We were on its north face now, and a coolness encircled us, wrapping itself around my limbs, bringing delicious relief from the heat. This was where I needed to come when it all got to me, I thought. I would remember this spot, when my head seemed to boil and my body ached from the sustained overheating of late summer, and I would just sit here in the shade of the trees, enjoying, revelling in the sensation of feeling . . . not quite cold, but cool, yes, definitely cool.

We were high up now, at well over a thousand metres, but there was something unique about this little corner, as though the sun never actually reached here at all. It felt like a miracle at such a scorched time of year.

Faustino was walking away from the track and into the forest. I followed behind him, wondering what it was he wanted to show me.

'There,' he said proudly, stopping and pointing up ahead. I saw nothing: a small clearing, perhaps, but nothing noteworthy. Pine tree after pine tree stretched in all directions. There was nothing else there.

Faustino had been acting strangely since I'd arrived at his house an hour or so earlier. I'd come to expect sudden changes in mood in him, but this time he seemed dulled, somehow, as though weighed down by something he was unable to talk about. We'd chatted for a bit, but it had seemed forced, and I'd been on the point of leaving, feeling uncomfortable there, when he'd suggested we go for a drive.

'Who knows?' he said. 'Maybe I'll fall into the *Avenc* and end up dying on this mountain after all.'

If that was his plan I wasn't too happy about him taking me with him, but we'd come in my car, and as we cut our way through the forest higher up the slopes of the mountain to the north side and into this cooler, lighter air, he'd seemed to cheer up a bit.

And now he'd brought me here, to this edge of a small clearing, and was pointing for me to look at something where there was nothing but a grassy mound. For a moment it seemed as though the moment I had always feared with him had finally arrived: the moment when, having walked a fine line between being some kind of a visionary and some kind of nutter, the barminess would win the day. What did he expect me to see? A golden bull protecting some long-hidden treasure? Some vision from one of his stories?

'Don't look at me as if I'm some kind of lunatic!' he said. 'Come closer. Look.'

I came out into the clearing. The trees around looked normal, the grass was normal, up in the sky the odd hovering clouds looked normal. My eyes turned back to the ground. Something down here? I climbed up the side of the mound and scouted about. Something caught my attention: a branch was lying at the top. I went over to take a look and found myself staring at a small hole in the ground. The edges were made of cut stone. I knelt down and peered into it: all was darkness, as though a great cavern opened up beneath.

'What's this, the *Avenc*?' I said. It was the strangest thing: a square hole about the size of a football, clearly man-made, leading down to some kind of cave, and it was here, lost in the middle of this forest. It was too small to crawl through, but it seemed someone had placed the branch there to stop people falling into it. It needed a marker, otherwise you would walk past it and never notice it at all.

Faustino was smiling, and started to laugh. But the laugh caught in his throat and he started coughing, great wheezy gasps echoing from deep in his chest as he almost bent double and his face turned purple. I ran down towards him, but he managed to stop by the time I reached him. He spat something on to the grass, then looked up, his eyes bloodshot and watery.

'This,' he said, pointing at the mound and the hole in the top, 'is the ice house of Penyagolosa. And it's one of the best preserved in the country.'

He started walking down the edge of the mound and into the forest again.

'This way,' he said. 'You'll be able to see it better from here.'

I followed him, past a honeysuckle bush to the other side of the hillock. We were ten or twelve feet lower down here. The air felt even colder.

'Through there,' he said. 'Can you see that gap?'

I looked at a thicket he was pointing to and saw there was some kind of way through. I crouched and lowered myself in. The ground was soft and slightly muddy, as though it had rained recently. Pushing my way through I came out into a vast stone hall. The sight of it almost took my breath away. A double-barrelled vaulted ceiling rose to around fifteen or twenty feet above my head, light streaming in through what was presumably the hole in the ground I'd seen above just a couple of moments before. The walls were made of perfectly cut, smooth limestone, the crossed archway of the vaulting in a perfect straight, white relief, like a hot cross bun in reverse. The hall was square, each wall roughly seven or eight yards long. The floor was of mud, although whether there were stone pavings underneath was difficult to say: I picked up a stick lying around and pushed it in to see, but it just sank until it broke in my hand. The place was in very good condition, and had obviously been built by master craftsmen: this wasn't the rough and ready workmanship of the *mas* builders. But it was clear it had received little attention since it had been abandoned. For a moment I was grateful for the lack of tourist development round here: an architectural gem was buried underground on the very slopes of the highest mountain in the area. Anywhere else the place would have been plagued with tour buses and mobile cafeterias selling tea in polystyrene cups to day trippers up from the coast for a bit of relief from the monotony of their beach holiday. Here, though, you would only find the place if someone actually brought you to the very doorway.

Faustino walked in behind me and looked up at the ceiling, and the beam of light shining like an arrow through the hole at the top.

'That's where they used to throw the snow in,' he said. 'Then it would be compacted down at the bottom.'

There had once been scores of these *neveras*, or ice houses, dotted over the hills and mountains. The Romans, then the Moors, had a tradition of gathering and storing snow and ice for use in the summer, but it had really taken off from around the sixteenth century.

'This one was built in the seventeenth century,' he said, tracing the round arches in the air with his finger.

The ice-men, *nevaters*, would work through late winter and early spring shovelling the snow from the mountainside and dropping it in from the top. Then it would be compressed by foot, like the pressing of grapes, until it turned into ice. Different sections were made by placing a layer of straw and soil as a kind of packing, before more snow was placed on top and the process would start again. Once the summer came the *nevaters* would become transporters of this precious material down to the cities and the coast. The Valencia area had been one of the biggest consumers of ice in the past, as its doctors, once the most famous in all Spain, had used it to treat all kinds of ailments, from inflammations to haemorrhages and fevers. The ports had also been a place of great demand for the ice, to help preserve the fish brought in in the mornings, while the rest of the population enjoyed the frozen drinks and sherbets to cool themselves down in the summer sun.

'The *nevaters* would set off from here after sunset and travel by night so as to lose as little ice through melting as possible,' Faustino said. 'The boxes were packed with more straw and felt to stop the heat from the mules ruining it. They used to follow the *camí dels nevaters* – the ice-men's route. Passes down very close to your *mas* before connecting with the river and ending up down on the coast.'

Some of the ice hadn't even finished up there, he said. Much of it was taken to the port and exported in special ships to the Balearic Islands, or North Africa.

I looked up at this great man-made cave. It felt like a crypt of a church or cathedral: the last thing on earth I would have expected to find here in the middle of this underpopulated land of abandoned farmhouses and empty pine forests. And here thousands of tonnes of compacted snow must once have sat, a great refrigerator serving the people of the coast. The ice that had cooled an overheated brow, or been drunk in the shade of a patio flavoured with lemon and sugar and cinnamon, wouldn't have been plucked from a nearby freezer plugged into a wall. It would have started its journey right here, trekking through the night on horseback, past our farm, heading for its final destination, perhaps even on the other side of the Mediterranean. All this water, travelling so far.

'It's an amazing thought,' said Faustino.

It had all come to an end towards the end of the nineteenth century and the beginning of the twentieth, when artificial means of creating ice had been introduced. No one had use any more for the ice from the mountains: they could make it themselves. And so the ice-houses had been abandoned one by one. Many had been lost or forgotten, some had fallen down, but a number were still to be found around the mountains in good condition, a testament to a different, distant way of life.

We stepped out through the small entrance and into the forest again. It had grown quite chilly in there and I was almost thankful to come out to a more normal temperature.

'The sad thing is,' Faustino said, 'that even if you wanted to go back to those old ways, there wouldn't be enough snow to make it viable any more. Yes, it snows up here in the winter, and how. But not like it used to. Not enough.'

He coughed again, and spat.

'Think of all the ice that they could gather and store up here back then. Keeping it safe until it was needed and then taking it out and distributing it, pouring it out like rain. The land needs more of it, more than ever, but we're running out. We have to look after what we've got, use it well.'

It didn't need saying, but I knew that by talking of 'water' and 'ice' he was also referring to his stories. They were what moved him most, even if he would never have admitted it. If there was a link between stories and water, then this ice-house would mean much to him. I imagined the trail of the ice-men, trekking over the mountains and down to the coast, like ancient camel routes or the Silk Road, streams of stories, legends and folk tales rushing under the feet of the merchants with their wares as they crossed the land. This place had once been a fountain, a source, for the people in the cities, a direct link between themselves and the mountains that rose in the west. The connection had been lost. Now the fountain itself had all but dried up.

Faustino walked back to the top of the mound and sat down near the hole. Fishing into a pocket he pulled out a hip flask and took a swig.

'It's not a good idea to have a smoke out here,' he said looking around at the dead, dry wood and pine needles on the ground. 'Not at this time of year.'

He handed the flask to me and I sat down next to him. It was odd to think there was a bloody great vaulted hallway right underneath us. But for the hole in the ground, which was almost covered in grass anyway, there would simply have been no way of knowing. I lifted the flask to my mouth and drank. Truffle-flavoured brandy powered its way down into my belly: it felt like smoke was pouring from my ears.

Faustino stared out into the trees. Something was on his mind, but it seemed best to let him be for the time being. He was the kind of man who only ever said what he wanted to say: there was no point trying to push him at all. We sat like that for some time, watching the occasional bird dart in and out among the trees, listening to the breathing of the forest as the sun moved overhead, lengthening the shadows that crossed over us, protecting us from its rays. It was a good place to be, to sit and do nothing. So much could happen by simply keeping still. My mind wandered, dreaming of the ice-men and their watery trails. Where else had they gone from here, I wondered. Inland, perhaps? North and south, as well as east to the coast? It felt like a hub of some sort. My imagination flew, and I could see trails spreading out in all directions from where we sat, crossing the landscape like a vast spider's web, droplets of water like dew glistening along each path. And each droplet was a story, the stories spreading out, soaking into the land to give life, then slowly joining together again like beads of mercury to form a lake, a sea. And there the water stayed, waiting, waiting . . . until the process could begin once again.

After a time Faustino stirred a little and I was brought out of my reverie. He shuffled where he sat, then took another drink. I could hear the brandy sink through him as he gulped, his Adam's apple twitching down his long, fragile throat.

'It's time I was going,' he said, not making a move. 'Time to leave.'

He looked at me with his piercing blue eyes.

'There are plenty more stories out there,' he said. 'I've hardly told you any. If you want to hear more it looks like you'll have to go out and find them yourself.'

He put the hip flask back in his pocket and got to his feet.

'My wife is very ill,' he said. 'She can't come up here to the mountain any more. I have to go down to the coast and look after her.'

I got up and stood next to him.

'It worked for a while, her coming up here at weekends, but it's come to an end. I was never a very good hermit anyway,' he said. 'Only ever did it part-time.'

'You're going for good?' I said.

He nodded.

There was an awkward moment when neither of us seemed to know what to say. I had never met his wife, and was never really sure if she existed. Was he really as close to death as he sometimes looked? Perhaps the story of looking after his wife was really a way of talking about himself. He would never say what was wrong with him, and sometimes when his energy had surged you felt he was healthier and stronger than most people. Yet there was always an air of terminality about him, a sense that he wouldn't be around for much longer. Whether we would find him dead in the *mas* one day, or else he'd disappear, I could never tell.

'I'll drive you back to your house,' I said. 'I've got to go that way.'

He waved his hand. 'I'll walk,' he said. 'It's not far. There's a shortcut if I go this way.'

I waited for a moment to see if he wanted to add anything else, perhaps an invitation to come down and see him on the coast if ever I was around those parts. But he remained silent.

'You can always . . .'

'Right, okay,' he said, turning to leave. '*Hasta la vista!*'

He didn't even give me a chance to shake his hand.

'Nice day to walk to the top of Penyagolosa,' he called out as he disappeared into the trees. 'Just keep going straight.'

I watched his back, the streak of grey where his ponytail fell down his shoulders, the light, almost skippy walk, with his paper-like frame, his feet barely making an indentation in the ground.

He turned down the path, not looking back, and was gone.

★

The wedding was set for the end of September. Salud and I headed back down to Valencia for a few days to work on the preparations. The city was blissfully deserted and tranquil at this time of year as most people were still away on holiday, and for a while we simply revelled in the change from our country life. When it was like this the city was idyllic, with just enough spark and life about it to stimulate without smothering you in its noise and overcrowding. The streets were almost empty, many of the shops closed. On one afternoon we jumped in the car and just drove around the place, taking in some of the sights, free now from the walls of cars and smog and stress that ringed them throughout the rest of the year. I loved Valencia: I had been living there for some seven or eight years, but I was glad I now had somewhere else to call home.

First news of the fire came on the twenty-eighth of the month. Somewhere around Les Useres, the village of the Pelegríns, a blaze had taken hold in the fields nearby. One of the beauty spots, a wooded gorge, had been reduced to ashes. The strong Ponent from the west, blowing hot, dry air from across the Spanish plains, was fanning it, making it hard to bring under control. I consulted a map: although uncomfortably close, the fire was blowing away from our farm. For the time being I stayed put.

The next day the news seemed to improve. Salud switched on the radio as soon as we got up and the reports spoke of the fire being almost under control. The firemen expected to be able to put it out over the course of that day. But the temperatures were rising – already 40 degrees up there – which was making their job more difficult.

I'd been used to 40-degree heat down on the coast: there were usually a handful of days some time in August when the thermometer hit this unbearable temperature. But I hadn't ever expected it to reach so high up there in the mountains. The Ponent, as ever the ill wind, was bringing more pain and destruction.

We followed the news over the rest of the day. It seemed we were all right: everyone was confident that in a matter of hours it would be extinguished. And besides, it was still moving away, not towards, the farm.

I was woken up the following morning by the phone ringing: it was Concha.

'*Cariño!* Where are you?' she said frantically.

'What's happened?' I said.

'The fire.' She was almost gasping. 'It's moving towards Penyagolosa.'

'Are you sure? I thought it was going in the opposite direction.'

'It's been started deliberately,' she said. 'Burn all the land so they can build on it afterwards. They've been wanting to do this to Penyagolosa for years.'

Salud was already listening to the radio. Her face had dropped.

'The wind changed direction overnight,' she said. 'It's moving towards our village. Completely out of control.'

Minutes later I was in the car driving as fast as I could back to the farm, a feeling of panic gripping me by the throat. For over an hour it was as if I were unable to take a single breath, my body suspended in a taut, brittle state as I battled with visions of the farm and the mountainside going up in smoke. It had always been there: the threat that one day, just as had happened some fifteen years before, the whole area might disappear in a forest fire. I had had to live with the idea: now it was becoming a reality.

I sped up the motorway and reached the turning to head inland. Coming over the top of a hill the whole of the sierra stood in front of me and my first vision of the hell that had come to our little patch of the country. Helicopters moved silently from this distance like flies over the plumes of smoke that streamed up into the air from four, five, six different points on the scorched mountainsides. Even from here it was clear that a large area had been affected. But above it all sat a vast black cloud, as though a thunderstorm were blowing in and was about to break over the flames. It was so big and dense it took me a while to realise that this was no rainstorm about to save us all, but the accumulated smoke from the fires that were now eating away at the land, sitting like a fat, evil genie smiling down at the destruction beneath.

I drove on, the black, death-like blanket blotting out the sun as I drew closer. Planes and helicopters were now flying low overhead, dashing to the nearby reservoirs with their buckets and then racing back to the mountains, a trail of spray spilling behind them in an elegant curve. Fire engines charged up and down the small country roads, while policemen stood in groups at strategic points, watching the smoke through black binoculars.

Just before arriving at the village I caught sight of the flames for the first time, bright orange and red against the deep green of the pine trees they were consuming. Old farmers with walking sticks stood at the edge of the road and looked up helplessly at the spreading inferno.

The village was awash with soldiers and members of the emergency services, but I pushed through and kept on to get to the farm. The air was thick with smoke and breathing started to prove difficult. The whole of the area to the east of our valley was on fire: it was only a matter of hours before it reached us.

Still hardly able to breathe from the panic and now the poor air, I finally reached the chain at the bottom of our drive. But I couldn't open it: someone had tried to force the padlock and now there was no way of getting it open.

I stood breathless for a moment. Flakes of white ash were falling all around like snow. The fire was moving in on us. I had to get up to the farm, if only to see if there was anything I could do. And yet now, at this crucial moment, my way was barred. There was no time to think who it might have been: thieves? Hunters? Perhaps one of the teams of forestry officials, looking to see if there was any water up there to help fight the fire.

Cursing whoever it was, I jumped back in the car and sped towards Concha's. Driving up over the far side of the valley, I stopped for a moment to look back in the direction of the blaze. And panic became cold fear. The whole of the landscape on the other side of the Talaia mountain was on fire, and the first flames were becoming visible as they reached the crest of the ridge just behind. It was moving towards us and it was coming very quickly. There was no time to lose.

I found Concha on her own, quietly tending her garden, coughing as the smoke caught in the back of her throat.

'The last time there was a fire round here,' she said, 'I stopped it right here at the edge of the house by clearing out some brambles that had grown up there. Would have taken the house with it otherwise.'

She seemed strangely calm, if a little pale. The experience of having lived through this before showed, I thought. Was I overreacting? I had seen the flames, and it looked very much as though they were about to engulf everything I had worked on over the past year. An icy determination had virtually possessed me: I had to get up to the farm, no matter what. I explained about my broken padlock.

'Take the metal cutters,' she said. 'Pau kept a pair. He left them behind when he went.'

She helped me find them: great heavy pincers of the kind used by firemen or professional burglars.

'Are you sure they'll work?' I said.

'Pau always said they could cut through a chain like butter,' she said.

'You can't stay up there, *cariño*,' she added as I was driving off. 'There's only one way out. If you get caught up there . . .' She raised her eyebrows. The back wheels of the car kicked up stones and dirt as I sped away.

Pau was right, and it was worryingly simple and quick to cut through the steel of the padlock loop. Within less than five minutes I had managed to open the chain and was speeding up to the farm.

The view was terrifying. The whole of the eastern half of the sky was black with smoke, stretching from the Talaia all the way to the village. A squadron of planes flew in low from the west, passing so close I could almost see the pilots before they crossed the valley and moved over towards the centre of the blaze. Much of the land was already turning an odd grey colour with the amount of ash that was falling, while the smoke changed the sunlight to a dirty, grubby shade of orange. I tried to take a deep breath as I worked out what to do. The house, the farm, everything was under threat. I had to do something, however small, as a gesture, as a way of telling myself that whatever happened I had at least tried the best I could to save our mountain home. Concha's story about saving her house the last time stayed in my mind: I would clear some of the bushes and debris close to the house. If the flames did pass this way, then at least we could keep some kind of distance between them and the actual house. I thought of the wooden beams holding up the roof, the wooden floor. There was much to burn here. Anything I could do to reduce the risk must surely be of help.

The trees and bushes close to the house suddenly changed from being pleasing, shading garden features to dangerous, treacherous beasts sitting waiting for their moment to come. There was so much to do, too much to do, and so little time. I scrabbled around for a few moments picking up bits of rubbish, scraps of firewood, weeds and building materials that had been left lying around waiting for another day to be cleared away. That day had come, but after just a quarter of an hour I was finding it hard to breathe, my pulse surging in my veins like a ticking clock.

Sweating profusely, I stopped for a moment and looked up. The black cloud still hung overhead, great eruptions of smoke bellowing angrily from behind the mountain. At the bottom of the valley helicopters swirled and groaned as they cut through the air.

Down in the hollow, where the road came up to the farm, a car was approaching. I caught a flash of it before it disappeared behind a pine tree. God forbid that the police should come here to evict me, I thought. I've only just arrived and I need more time. I carried on clearing away as though I hadn't seen anything. Whatever I could do would be of some help. But even now, amid the panic, awareness of the sheer futility of what I was doing faced with the scale of the fire raging just a few miles away was beginning to sink in. A blaze like this would engulf the house in minutes.

I heard a familiar clatter from behind, and a voice.

'It's a big one, this time.'

It was El Clossa, skipping down towards me. He pulled out a bottle of wine, half full.

'Here, drink some of this.'

I gulped it down, hungry and thirsty.

'There's nothing to eat,' I said. 'I didn't have time to stop for any food.'

He put his arm on my shoulder. 'Clearing up? I'll give you a hand. Oh, by the way,' he added. 'There was another car behind me. Might be someone else coming. Looked like a green Land Rover.'

I ran up to the *era* in time to find Arcadio pulling up next to El Clossa's car.

'Thought I better come up and see how you were,' he said opening the door and getting out. His expression was the same as always: still, calm, unmoved, despite the fire and smoke.

'I thought you couldn't drive any more,' I said.

'Pah!' he snorted. 'They weren't going to get me moving to the village.' He looked at the car and placed his hand on the bonnet. 'I'm getting used to it again. Just do a little bit every day, get further and further each time. That bend near the top still gets me nervous sometimes, but I just shut my eyes and pretend I've got my cataracts back. That way it doesn't bother me.'

There were probably few people in the world, I thought, who could genuinely claim to drive better with their eyes *closed*, but I was standing next to one of them now.

'What do you reckon about the fire?' I said. If there was anyone who could predict what might happen over the next few hours it was probably Arcadio. Heaven knows how many fires he'd seen in his time here.

He looked in the direction of the house, where El Clossa was bending down and picking up a few tools to be stored away.

'Clearing up?' he said. I nodded. He shrugged, then frowned. 'It might help.'

The cloud seemed to be thickening, more ash falling on our heads.

'I'm going down to check my almond trees,' he said. 'It would be a shame if we lost those this year. Looked like we were going to have a good crop.'

He climbed back into his car and wound the window down.

'Can't stay here long,' he said. 'Might not be much time.'

Looking back on that day, so much of what I did and the decisions I made now appear frankly stupid, but the emotions that gripped me proved so strong it was only days later that a clearer idea emerged of how I might have gone about things. After Arcadio's warning I went back to the house and carried on clearing away as best as I could with El Clossa's help. It was hard work, with only half a bottle of wine between us to keep us going, and the heat of the day and smoke from the fire draining us of almost all our energy. Eventually it seemed there was nothing else we could feasibly do. The area immediately around the edge of the house was now relatively clear, but as El Clossa warned me, when the fires burned with this intensity, they could jump.

'It's not just a slow, steady advance,' he said looking me straight in the eye, as though aware I was in some kind of trance-like state from the panic. 'Once the fire reaches the top there,' he pointed at the Talaia, just on the other side of the valley, 'it'll start coming down that side and then jump across to here before it even reaches the bottom. I've seen it happen – a bunch of trees that's separate from the rest of the *incendio* will just burst into flame spontaneously.'

I was thankful he didn't say it outright, but I knew he was telling me to get out of there while I still could. And in the meantime he was risking himself by coming here to help me. I'd missed his company since the commune had broken up and he'd kept to himself. It meant a lot to me that he should have turned up that day.

Still, two powerful and deeply rooted impulses were at loggerheads within me: the urge to stay here on my property and defend it, at whatever cost, and the instinct of survival. There was so much of me on this mountain and in this farm now, though. To leave it behind to be burnt to a cinder felt like leaving a child. For the first time I could understand the stories of people dying in forest fires because they refused to leave their homes. It made no sense from the outside: how could anyone be so stupid. Yet now I was close to doing the same myself. What little rational thought was left to me was clear about what I had to do. But even so there was something I needed to do first before I could abandon the place for good.

El Clossa left and I drove behind him, heading for the village. His last words to me rang in my brain. 'You can't stay here tonight,' he'd said, gripping me by the arms and almost shaking me. 'Whatever happens, do not stay the night here.'

It was already getting dark as I reached the village. The streets were lined with old widows in black staring up at the hillside from which the fire was moving towards them. I dashed into the ironmonger's just as they were about to close and bought a new padlock.

A couple of women and an old man stopped me as I came out. They knew who I was and where I lived, although I couldn't remember ever having seen them before.

They wanted news. What was it like up there? I told them what I'd seen, about the smoke, the flames, and how it was coming down very quickly this way.

'It's all going to be wiped out,' the old man said. 'Hasn't been a fire up here for fifteen years, it was bound to happen.'

One of the women leaned up and kissed me on the cheek.

'Good luck,' she said.

I charged back up to the house. In the darkness the flames glowed ominously from the next valley. The helicopters and planes would be on their last flights: there was nothing to be done now except wait until the first light of dawn and start again.

Back at the house I forced myself to imagine that by the following morning none of this would remain. I looked at the walls my friends and I had built, at the roof we'd put on, not once, but twice. At all the windows and doors my father had made for us, the great pine table. All the debris of a life lived up here over the past months: books, scraps of paper with recipes, a carpet given to us by a friend, a weathervane that was still sitting by the fire waiting to be attached to an outside wall. And all about to be lost. There was no time; I had to go: the flames were visible now from the house. But I had to take something with me, save something from the coming flames. I couldn't just let this all disappear. There was so much I wanted to take: I'd take it all if I could. But I had to run.

I arrived back in Valencia late that night, exhausted and shaking. Salud came down into the street to help me unload.

'How does it look?' she said. I shook my head, barely able to say anything. She opened the back of the car and started pulling out some of the things I'd brought with me.

It was only when I caught the expression of surprise and confusion on her face that it began to dawn on me.

'The chainsaws,' she said. She peered into the car to see what else there was before turning back to me.

'And the strimmers.'

I nodded.

'Is that it?'

I nodded again.

'You don't think . . .' she started, then stopped. 'Come on.' We picked up the things and carried them up to the flat. Seeing these power tools suddenly placed on the floor in the spare room gave me a jolt, and for a moment I seemed to come out of the trance that had gripped me since the morning.

'What,' I said turning to her, 'am I going to do with a couple of chainsaws and strimmers if the fire does reach our land? There won't be anything left to saw or strim.'

I couldn't believe I'd been so stupid. Of all the things I could have picked up and brought with me. Salud put her arms around me and sighed.

'We'll just keep listening to the radio,' she said.

★

Time passed: it felt like an age. The trees darkened, a twilight world forming under the shade. It was cold, finally cold, but for the first time the air on my skin was unwelcome. I needed to shake myself awake. Standing on the mound of the ice-house, in the middle of the small clearing, it was as though Faustino had never been there. Had I found this place by accident on my own? How on earth had I got here?

I looked up through the break in the trees. The peak of the mountain was visible up ahead, inviting me to climb. How long had I waited for this moment? The day when I would finally reach up to touch the keystone of this wondrous landscape that had taken me in. So many times I had said to myself that the next day, or the next, I would climb

Penyagolosa, yet every time I had failed to carry out my promise. Today, though, I would succeed.

I leapt off the mound and headed straight into the trees. The peak was no more than a few hundred metres above where I was now. In an hour, perhaps less, I would be at the summit.

After a few minutes the forest came to an abrupt end and I stepped out on to the rocky north face of the mountain. A handful of juniper bushes were dotted about, poking through the rough gravelly earth like traffic bollards. The air was suddenly warm again and I looked out to the west, and the view of the slowly sinking sun drifting over the high Spanish plains in the distance: there was just time to get to the top of the mountain and back again before it got too dark. Behind me, the Maestrat, the land of the Templars and Cathars, stretched to the north and east, great chains of barren hills slicing through wide tracts of fields falling away to the coast where they were captured by the deep blue of the sea.

I pushed on up the slope, my feet slipping in places, finding a path as best I could. The summit seemed so very close: if I ran I could be there in just a second. The forest and the coolness of the ice-house were now fading memories. How long had I been down there? I should have been sailing up here always, lifted by the breeze and carried to the point I had been circling all this time, yet never reaching in to grasp.

The climb seemed to go on and on, always continuing on the same line, the same degree of slope. It had been an optical illusion, perhaps, the sensation that it was barely a stone's throw away.

I was sweating now, my legs tiring a little. They had grown stronger over this year, slowly getting used to the constant up and down: whenever I wanted to work on the land, get the water, pick some herbs for dinner. This was steep, though, and the summit was further than I had anticipated.

To the east the view of the sea grew wider as I rose higher and higher. The day was clear, although the haze of a summer evening cast a blanket over the landscape, blurring some of the view. The sun was dropping mercifully low, however, and an orange, honey-glow was settling on the rocks and stones.

The gravelly earth came to an end and I found myself on a well-worn path. Even the bushes had disappeared now and I pushed myself on to the top, lungs bursting, sweat trickling through my eyebrows. After a few more minutes the peak itself came into view. Perched on the top was a tiny building – a lookout for the local foresters. I forced my way up the final stretch, panting heavily now, yet so close. Finally, I scrambled up the last few yards to the top. I walked up to the foresters' lookout and peered through the window: no one was there; I had the mountaintop to myself.

From the summit I could now look down towards the south of the mountain. The Cabeço Roig stood some way down to the left, a great dome, like a giant mushroom. Beyond it, at the far edge of the massif of which Penyagolosa was the heart, sat our farm, out of view from here, yet nestling in the slopes of the valley that cut its way through the land before stretching away towards the coastal plains. Back towards the top of the valley the village of Xodos perched on the edge of its outcrop of rock. It had been some time since I had been to see the Truffle King. Within a few months the cold would have returned and he would be out with his dog sniffing for black nuggets of gold. Just beyond the village, further towards the coast, a cloud of yellow dust was visible, coughed up by the diggers working at the site of the new airport. This was a privileged moment: not long now, and these clear, silent skies would soon be filled with budget flights spewing out their sun-seeking fumes.

To the south, the mountains of the Sierra de Espadán, one of the last corners of Moorish Spain, rose up proudly from the plains, stretching up and back towards the banks of the Millars River. I held out my hand, trying to trace the contours of its hills and mountains with my fingertips.

This was my vantage point: here I could finally see the land I had been exploring and digging my hands into over the past months, laid out at my feet like a magic carpet. Where else would we go together, I wondered, this landscape and I. The adventure had only just begun: there was so much else out there to discover.

I had to get back down the mountain again before it got too dark, but I sat for a moment on the edge of a rock, staring out at the great world circling around the mountain like a spinning top. Whole areas I barely knew or had yet to explore seemed to shine out like jewels. I felt I might melt into the rock myself here and become one with the earth.

Something near my feet caught my eye: a shell. It looked like an ear. I bent down and rubbed my finger over it: an ancient mussel, once living in the sea, now fossilised and set here at the top of a mountain in stone for millions of years. It was buried in an amalgam of stone and grit, but by chipping away underneath for a few moments I was able to break it free and lift it up. It was no more than the size of two of my fingers. I wondered about the world it had seen when it had been formed and lived in an ancient sea. What convulsions and changes had it been through to end up here, on the summit of Penyagolosa? What stories did it have to tell?

I lifted it up and brought it close to my ear. Perhaps, if I listened . . .

BEGINNING, AGAIN

The last of the guests had gone, and Salud and I were alone again in our *mas*, the debris from the party scattered around the kitchen and terrace outside. We stood by the door, watching as the trail of cars slipped away down the mountainside, down to the riverbed and then away along the valley and back to the village and beyond. The sun was slowly working its way towards the peak of the Picosa: soon the evening shade would settle over us, the temperatures quickly dropping now we were in late September. Quiet and peace descended once again on our little world. My thumb twitched over the ring on my left hand, testing it, feeling its smoothness, its roundness, trying to get used to this new, strange element.

Neither of us moved, breathing in the still, fresh air, the silence penetrating our skin as the noise of music, shouting and laughter of just a few moments before slowly ebbed from the walls and sank into the earth. A robin was fluttering between the branches of the olive trees on the terrace below. Before long it would be time to harvest them again.

After a ceremony near Valencia, we'd had a more informal party up at the *mas*, friends from the local area joining us as we toasted our new status as a married couple. Already, only a few hours in, it felt as though something had changed, despite my expectations that everything would carry on as normal: something to do with a wholeness that perhaps had not quite been there before. Salud, I knew, felt the same.

'*Bueno, ya está*,' Salud said. 'That's it.' Preparations for the wedding had overtaken us over the past month, all done in haste at the last minute, as ever with us; I'd even had to write the speech for the official marrying us in the seconds before the actual ceremony – it was his first time and he was a bit nervous, he told me, having been out drinking till five the previous morning. Still, it had gone off smoothly. Or at least that's what people told me. Now a happy exhaustion came over us: for the time being we could ignore the call of the clearing and washing up behind us. The view of the valley in front, as so often before at this special time of day, had captured us and seemed to carry us to a different world.

I looked over towards the Talaia on the other side of the valley, and for a moment I shivered as I remembered the great ball of black, billowing smoke that had risen from it only a few weeks past. The sense of fear and panic had gone now, but an echo of it still remained. One day we might not be so lucky. The firemen had managed to put the blaze out the night I had left here, saving our valley, and the village with it. But just in time. Ministers from Madrid had been helicoptered in to oversee the operation; over 6000 hectares of mountainside had been burnt. It had been the biggest forest fire of the summer on the Spanish mainland. And they had stopped it right on our doorstep. From here you would never even know that it had happened, but I'd driven over to the other side of the Talaia since; a weird, blackened landscape, the trees and bushes reduced to stumps of charcoal. Thankfully – and I didn't know how – the sanctuary of Sant Miquel de les Torrocelles had been saved, but much of the pathway for the Pelegríns of Les Useres had been wiped out. It would be a very different pilgrimage to Sant Joan next year.

After glistening for a second on the mountain peak, the sun finally dipped out of sight, and we were struck by a wall of cold air. Time to get back inside. My eyes fell on some of the glasses of the home-made hooch I'd been pouring for our guests. Most of them were empty, but a few had only been half-drunk, it seemed. It was powerful stuff – I could already feel my own liver complaining from drinking too much of it. Perhaps my dreams of setting up a moonshine empire would have to wait. Might have to work a bit more on the recipe first.

Slowly, reluctantly, we began to pick up the pieces. It had been fun: a guitar had been produced at one point, a few tunes were played. Salud had been persuaded to dance for a while. Concha had sung more of her folk songs, El Clossa beating out the rhythm for her with his crutches. They'd both seemed happier than I'd seen them for a while. The commune was slowly fading to memory: we didn't talk about the others any more.

I nibbled on some of the spare bits from the *jamón* I'd been slicing over the afternoon as plates, cups and cutlery were placed in the sink with a clatter. Perhaps we could leave the worst of it till the morning. Right now all either of us wanted to do was fall into a heap on the sofa.

I looked across at the now empty space of the kitchen; it was as if something had caught my eye.

'What was that Concha was saying to you as she left?' I said, suddenly remembering what I'd wanted to ask her.

Salud smiled, and carried on picking up the mess.

'*Nada,*' she said. 'Nothing.'

I kept my eyes fixed on her until she looked up again, the smile breaking out into a laugh.

'You know what she's like,' she said.

'What was it?' I said.

'Something about the future.'

'Not more ghosts this time.'

She shook her head, then paused, bending down to wipe some of the crumbs from the table, catching them in her cupped hand before standing up to look me in the eye again.

'She said she could see children here.'

CODA: THE TREES

ALMOND

(*Prunus amygdalus*; *Ametller*, *Almendro* Valencian; *Almendro* Castilian.)

The first plant to come fully into bloom after midwinter, the almond is seen as a symbol of hope and the coming of spring. After the phylloxera disaster of the end of the nineteenth century, many local farmers moved from grapes to almonds as their staple produce, so that nowadays in February and March the hillsides south of the Penyagolosa are awash with delicate white and pink blossom, glistening in the low winter sun. Many of the trees have been abandoned as the farmers and *masovers* have left the countryside for the towns. But occasionally you catch a glimpse of a well-tended grove on a distant hillside, pink-orange soil laid bare by careful ploughing against a background of thick green.

Almonds are linked in mythology to the complicated stories of the Phrygian goddess Cybele and her lover Attis. It was said that Attis was conceived after Nana, the daughter of a river spirit, placed an almond in her breast. The almond came from a tree that had grown up from where the hermaphroditic daemon Agdistis had had his male genitalia cut off by the Greek gods. Attis would later castrate himself, thus giving rise to the Cybele-worshipping eunuch priests of Phrygia. Attis – and after him Mithras – is usually represented wearing the 'Phrygian cap', later commonly worn by the descendants of freed slaves in Rome; it subsequently became a symbol of liberty in the revolutionary movements of the eighteenth and nineteenth centuries: the French Marianne is portrayed to this day wearing a soft red conical cap.

Locally, almond milk, made by pounding almonds and honey

together in a mortar and pestle and then adding water as required, as well as traditionally being a common refreshment is said to cure coughs (it is said to be more effective if the skin and shell of the almond are mixed in). Bitter almonds, despite being poisonous (they contain hydrogen cyanide), are supposed to help prevent drunkenness when eaten just before a night out. Perhaps a memory of this can be found in the common local custom of eating a plate of roasted, salted almonds with the first cold beer of the evening. If the barman himself has prepared the nuts it is quite common to come across the odd bitter specimen or two, usually resulting in the order of an immediate refill to help wash away the unpleasant taste.

Ibn al-Awam recommends a special fertiliser for almond trees, mixing animal dung with almond shells and leaves; your 'farm workers' should then urinate on this mixture until it rots and turns black, after which it can be mixed in with the soil around each tree.

CAROB

(*Ceratonia siliqua*; *Garrofer* Val.; *Algarrobo* Cast.)

Locally, the saying is that the carob tree needs to be able to 'see the sea' if it is to survive, a reference to the fact that temperatures below minus five can easily kill it. For that reason this small, compact tree is often found in the east-facing foothills with a cutoff point of roughly 500 metres above sea level. Traditionally it was cultivated to produce animal feed, particularly for pigs and horses, but in times of famine – most recently the period immediately after the end of the Spanish Civil War in 1939 – the seeds were often eaten by humans as well. There are still many to be seen in the area, despite the reduced demand, often huddling alongside similar-sized olive trees. The carobs can be quickly recognised by the richer green of their leaves compared to the light grey tones of the olive.

Carob trees, along with holm oaks, are said to provide the best shade in which to hide from the midday sun. Ibn al-Awam says that mosquitoes will never come near carob wood.

The 'carat' system of measuring gold and precious stones comes from the ancient tradition of weighing gold against carob seeds. Eventually this was standardised so that a 'carat' equalled 0.2 grams.

Carobs are sometimes referred to as 'St John's bread' as supposedly the Baptist lived off the seeds when he was in the desert.

Carob is said to be very effective against diarrhoea, while a syrup made from carob, lemon juice and honey is used locally for coughs.

CYPRESS

(*Cupressus sempervirens*; *Ciprés*, *Xiprer* Val.; *Ciprés* Cast.)

Spain has inherited from the Greeks and Romans the association of the cypress with death and the Underworld. Almost every graveyard you see – usually placed on the outskirts of a town or village – is filled with towering, dark-green cypress trees, hundreds of years old. As with the yew, it has also become a symbol of resurrection and eternal life – the ancient Persians associated the tree with Mithra, the god of light, while no Persian garden – *pairi-daeza*, hence 'paradise' – was complete without cypress trees. For the Phoenicians the cypress was sacred to the goddess Astarte, who later evolved into the Greek Aphrodite. Eros's arrow was said to be made from cypress wood, while, according to some traditions, Christ's cross was supposedly made from a mixture of cypress and cedar. The cypress was also Hercules' tree: he himself planted a cypress grove at Daphne.

Cypress cones have traditionally been used as a cure for sciatica and rheumatism; in some local villages it is deemed sufficient simply to carry an odd number of them on one's person, in a trouser pocket, for example. As a cure for haemorrhoids, others suggest boiling the cones in water for ten minutes before drinking, or applying externally via a sitz bath. Similar concoctions are said to be useful against migraines and chest problems. Cypress cones can also be left in wardrobes as a defence against moths. For the same reason, wardrobes and chests for keeping clothes were traditionally made from cypress wood – cut in winter during the time of a waning moon: not only did they keep the clothes inside safe, but the wood is impervious to woodworm. Beds were never made from cypress, however, as this was said to cause impotence.

ELDER

(*Sambucus nigra*; *Saüc*, Val.; *Sauco* Cast.)

Many *masos* in the area had an elder near the house as both an important medicinal plant, and also because it was thought to ward of the evil eye. A great number have now died, and it is no longer as common a tree as it once was. But the memory of its medicinal properties remains among the older generations. Locally, elderflower water was used to reduce bloating and as a cure for conjunctivitis, while elderflower tea was meant to cure bronchial problems. Pulp taken from younger branches of the tree were used to help heal burns. Pipes were also made from elder wood.

There is no hint in the Penyagolosa area of the elder being an 'unlucky' tree, as it is often regarded as being in the Northern European tradition.

ELM

(*Ulmus*; *Om*, Val.; *Olmo* Cast.)

As elsewhere, elms here have suffered greatly over recent decades, their presence ever diminishing in the face of the Dutch elm disease pandemic. Elms would often be seen in public squares, or in the countryside, often forming a transitional ecosystem between the dry mountainsides and the wetter areas around a river or lake. Some specimens remain, but the famous elm that stood outside the Sant Joan hermitage at the foot of the Penyagolosa has now died.

Elms were highly valued for the hardness of their wood, and the fact that elm wood was impervious to decay when kept permanently wet. For this reason it was commonly used for shipbuilding and bridges: Achilles used an elm trunk to make a bridge and escape the flooding waters of the Scamander and Simois rivers, enraged at his having slaughtered so many sons of Troy.

Applied externally to the skin, creams using elm pulp are used to help the healing of ulcers and wounds. Ibn al-Awam insists the trees should never be pruned, as this can hinder their growth.

HOLM OAK, HOLLY OAK
(*Quercus ilex*; *Carrasca* Val.; *Encina* Cast.)

The holm oak ('holm' being an old English word for 'holly') is the nearest there is to a national tree of Spain: it is estimated there are close to seven hundred million of them in the country – about fifteen for every Spaniard. It is a strong, slow-growing evergreen, with small, roundish, prickly leaves whose shape and size are similar to the holly's (Q. *ilex ssp. rotundifolia*), or smooth, longer, thinner leaves almost like an olive's (Q. *ilex ssp. ilex*). Traditionally its wood was used in the making of ships, resulting in a dramatic reduction in its numbers over previous centuries. It makes exceptionally good firewood and was one of the main sources of material for traditional charcoal-burners. It is particularly suited to dry conditions and likes limey soils, making it ideally suited to much of the Mediterranean basin.

The acorns of the holm oak, along with other oaks, are used to feed the pigs that produce the finest hams. There is even a categorisation system for *jamón serrano*, where acorns replace stars. A 'five-acorn' ham is the best you can get.

The shade of a holm oak is often regarded as one of the coolest places in summer, its shade as sought after as that of the carob tree, and for this reason they are often found planted near *masos*, offering farm workers a corner in which to escape the intensity of the sun. The acorns of the holm oak, made into a tea, were traditionally used as a cure for haemorrhoids.

For centuries the acorns were ground down and turned into flour in times of famine. Pliny the Elder says this was common in Hispania in the first century BC: 'Sometimes . . . when there is a scarcity of corn, they are dried and ground, the meal being used to make a kind of bread. Even to this very day, in the provinces of Spain we find the acorn during the second course: it is thought to be sweeter when roasted in ashes' (*Natural History*, Book XVI, ch. 6). This dependence on acorns among rural communities in Spain continued well into the twentieth century. Ibn al-Awam gives a recipe for making bread from ground acorns, but quotes Rhazes as saying that it can be harmful to the liver.

Similar in appearance to the holm oak is the kermes oak (*quercus coccifera*; *Coscolla* Val.; *Coscoja* Cast.), a smaller, bush-like evergreen plant with similar, holly-like leaves. It is often seen growing around the base of the holm oak, producing a thick covering rarely rising above one metre from the ground. In *The White Goddess*, Robert Graves suggests the original 'holly' associated with the Holly Knight who battles every year against the Oak Knight was in fact the holly or kermes oak. Apart from the similarity of their leaves, the 'scarlet-oak', as it was also known, is host to the berry-like kermes insect from which red dye was made in ancient and classical times. There are associations and echoes of the Oak Knight and the Holly Knight in both Gawain and the Green Knight, and John the Baptist and Jesus respectively. The Green Knight enters Arthur's court brandishing a holly branch, while, according to Matthew's gospel, Jesus wore 'kerm-scarlet' when dressed as King of the Jews.

JUNIPER

(*Juniperus communis*; *Ginebre* Val.; *Enebro* Cast.)

Forest fires have wiped out most of the oldest specimens of this conical tree, but younger ones can be seen sprouting all over the countryside, especially at the colder, higher altitudes, where they poke out of the rocky soil with the promise that one day, some years from now, this will again be a proper juniper forest such as the ones that stood there in the past. It is a prickly plant, its little spindles flashing like stars in the sunlight as you brush past it, savouring the distinctive aroma that rubs off on to your hands, reminding you of sharp perfumes, incense and gin. It is a slow grower, and its wood, along with its cousins the *savina* (*juniperus phoenicea*) and *càdec* (*juniperus oxycedrus* – Spanish cedar), was prized by local builders for its sinewy strength and resistance to woodworm and other invertebrate threats. Now it is illegal to cut them down.

According to classical legend, juniper was one of the ingredients Medea used to send the dragon guarding the Golden Fleece to sleep. Locally, it is regarded as being effective for treating fevers: pieces of the root are cut up and then boiled until the water has been reduced by about half: the fever will be stopped almost immediately. The juniper berry is said to give long life, either by an individual eating three or four a day, or by drinking the juice in an infusion. Placing them in your mouth and chewing very slowly is also supposed to help fight respiratory infections. The oil from the berry is supposed to cure toothache, although it can also damage and even break the tooth it is meant to be treating.

LAUREL

(*Laurus nobilis*; *Laurel*, *Llorer* Val.; *Laurel* Cast.)

Common to the entire Mediterranean area, the laurel is a regular flavouring agent in most regional cuisines. Locally, it is used in meat stews such as a *tombet*.

The laurel is usually associated with Apollo, to whom the Pythian Games were dedicated: similar to the Olympics, they are the origin of awarding a laurel wreath to the winner of a sporting event; victorious Roman generals were also garlanded in this fashion. The story of how the laurel became sacred to Apollo refers to his unsuccessful wooing of Daphne, a mountain nymph, priestess of Gaia, Mother Earth. The laurel, which until that point had been eaten by priestesses of Gaia at the oracle of Delphi, now passed over to the young god, who became the overseer of prophesy.

In the apocryphal gospel of Pseudo-Matthew, the laurel plays a role in the miraculous pregnancy of St Anna, mother to the Virgin Mary. Despairing in old age of never having a child, she sees a swallow's nest in a laurel tree and prays to God that she might become pregnant. St Anna is particularly important to Gypsies, who celebrate her feast day on 26 July. This is reflected in an Andalusian folk song:

Entre los árboles todos
se señorea el laurel;
entre las mujeres Ana
entre flores el clavel.

Among the trees,
The greatest is the laurel,
Among women, Anna,
And among flowers, the carnation.

Medicinally, the laurel is used to stimulate appetite. Laurel berries mixed with juniper berries and left to soak in wine are also supposed to help women regain their menstrual cycles.

Ibn al-Awam says the laurel is good for keeping snakes at bay, as they dislike the tree intensely. A branch of laurel hung near a crying baby is also meant to help calm him, he says.

MASTIC

(*Pistacia lentiscus*; *Matissa* Val.; *Lentisco* Cast.)

Mastic is the original chewing gum, said to be good both for teeth and gums, as well as the stomach. In the Eastern Mediterranean, small cuts are made in the branches of the bush to collect the sap, which is then used in making toothpaste, perfumes, hair and skin lotions, as well as modern chewing gum and varnish. This practice is less common in the Western Mediterranean, where traditionally it is used more in infusions to cure gastric problems, as well as rheumatism and haemorrhoids. Locally, mastic baths are said to sooth aching feet, while a mastic mouthwash was used before extracting teeth to prevent heavy bleeding.

Often found in or around areas of holm oaks, it usually grows no more than a metre in height, with small, round, red berries, turning black as they ripen. It is less resistant to the cold, and is rarely found above 1000 metres.

MISTLETOE

(*Viscum album*; *Visc*, Val.; *Muérdago*, Cast.)

Mistletoe has an important place in folklore here, although its pagan origins have been given a Catholic veneer. This venerated, parasitic plant is associated with St Lucy's Day (13 December, *La festa de Sta Llúcia*), the first day of Christmas, when schools traditionally break up for the holidays. The link with St Lucy – patron saint of the blind, but also of farmers and writers – is unclear, but may be to do with the symbolism linking the mistletoe (the 'Golden Bough') with the sun and light: because her eyes were cast out before her execution at the hands of the Romans, St Lucy is closely associated with all things to do with sight.

The custom is to take some mistletoe on 13 December and hang it up at midday over a door or a window in the house. It is then left there for the whole year, absorbing any bad luck that might otherwise have entered the home. Having dried out over a few months, the typical grey-green of the plant becomes a deep yellow, hence 'golden' in the pagan tradition. On the following 13 December it is cut down and burnt, thus disposing of the unwanted forces captured therein, and a new sprig is hung up in its place.

St Lucy's Day marks the first of a series of midwinter feast days with their own proverbs and sayings describing the lack of daylight.

Per Santa Llucia, un pas de puça
Per Nadal, un pas de gall.

Around St Lucy's, the day is about as short as a 'flea's footstep', while by Christmas it's the same as that of a chicken. However by the Feast of St Anthony, on 17 January, you can already tell that the light is on its way back: *A San Antón, a les cinc en sol* – there'll still be light by five o'clock in the afternoon.

MULBERRY

(*Morus nigra, morus alba*; *Morera* Val. & Cast.)

Long before oranges became the principal crop – and symbol – of the Valencia region, mulberry trees covered the landscape, providing as they did the necessary nourishment for the much-prized silk worm. Silk was one of the main industries on which the area's wealth was based, peaking around the eighteenth century, before witnessing a steep decline towards the end of the nineteenth century as a result of the cheaper silk imports coming from the Far East. Today mulberry farming for silk production has disappeared, but many towns still have Mulberry Squares, or Mulberry Streets, bearing witness to the importance this proud tree with its broad, heart-shaped leaves used to have.

According to classical myth, the colour of the berry – a deep blood red or purple – is a result of the deaths of the ill-fated lovers Pyramus and Thisbe, whose tragic tale was first told by Ovid, before appearing in *A Midsummer Night's Dream*. Agreeing to meet by night under a mulberry tree outside the town, Pyramus discovers Thisbe's bloodstained shawl and, mistakenly thinking his beloved is dead, plunges his sword into his heart. Thisbe, on realising what has happened, then does likewise and the blood of the two stains the fruits of the nearby tree, which until that moment had been white.

The story of how the silk worm – and hence the silk industry – first reached Spain reads more like a thriller. Yahya al-Ghazal – John the Gazelle – was a poet and astrologer living in Cordoba in the ninth century. The emir, Abd al-Rahman II, sent him as an ambassador to the court of Constantinople – then, along with Baghdad, the most important city in the world. The Byzantines had been trying to get hold of silk-making knowhow for centuries, being effectively cut off from the Silk Road by their rivals in Persia. By around the sixth century, however, they had managed to get hold of some silk worms – *bombyx mori* – probably from the hands of some Indian monks. They jealously guarded the secret, creating an effective monopoly of silk production in the Mediterranean. When al-Ghazal travelled to Constantinople in 840, he was sent with the aim of gleaning as much information as he could from the Byzantine court, and one of his objectives was discovering the secret of silk production. His hosts gladly showed him their mulberry trees and silk worms once he arrived, but made extra efforts to ensure none of the precious grubs were stolen. Al-Ghazal was too clever for them, however, and managed to smuggle some of the worms out with him, hidden inside a book, along with some mulberry leaves to feed them for his journey home. Once he got back to Cordoba a silk industry was established, and as a result for many centuries Spain was one of the world's most important producers of the material, eclipsing the Byzantines. Al-Ghazal, whose poetry is known for its simplicity and almost modern style in an age of mostly formal, formulaic verse, was also responsible for the valuable extraction of fig-tree seeds for propagation.

Ibn al-Awam says that silk worms can feed on mulberry leaves from the second year after planting; the tree, he insists, needs plentiful water.

The fruit is said to be effective against throat and mouth inflammations, particularly when mixed with honey to make a syrup: two parts honey to one of mulberry juice.

NETTLE TREE

(*Celtis australis*; *Llidoner* Val.; *Almez* Cast.)

A common tree in the area, suited to the dry conditions and capable of growing as easily on mountain terraces as in gorges or river banks. Sometimes referred to as the Lote tree, it is similar in looks to the much depleted elm, and often grows in the same areas as the few remaining specimens of that tree. The fruits of the tree – *llidons* – turn black when ripe and look like a small cherry. They are very sweet and much sought after. Ibn al-Awam says the wood is useful for making saddles and carriages.

Green, unripe *llidons* are valued in traditional medicine as an astringent and are used to reduce diarrhoea as well as heavy bleeding.

Dioscorides and other Greek writers referred to the *celtis australis* as the Lotus or Lote tree, associated with the 'lotus-eaters', or *lotophagi* of the *Odyssey*, who live on an island off the North African coast and eat a delicious, drug-like fruit. This has led some to conclude that the 'Lote-tree' mentioned in the Qur'an during Muhammad's night journey from Mecca to Jerusalem, and thence to heaven, is in fact the *celtis australis*. The tree in the text marks a boundary point of the seventh heaven beyond which no one can advance in their search for God. However, the Arabic word used in the Qur'an to describe the tree is *sidra*, which is the term for the Ziziphus – another contender for the mythical tree of the lotus-eaters – while the Arabic for *celtis australis* is *al-maysh*, reflected in the Castilian name for the tree, *almez*. The *celtis australis* may or may not be the tree of the classical tradition, but it seems unlikely to be the particular tree envisaged in the Qur'an.

Due to its strength, nettle-tree wood was traditionally used locally for making walking sticks and three- or five-pronged farmers rakes. One of the last masters of this ancient craft lived until very recently in the village of Aín, in the Sierra de Espadán.

OLIVE

(*Olea europea*; *Olivera* Val.; *Olivo* Cast.)

Ibn al-Awam quotes Abu al-Khayr as saying that olive trees dislike damp soil, much as their oil separates from water. Olive trees have been around in Castellón province for thousands of years, and some of the ones still standing date back to Roman times. Regularly pollarded and pruned, they have grown short and fat over the centuries, their stumpy, twisted forms found scattered over the lower hillsides, between the coast and the higher mountain ranges. Many have become celebrated. One, near the town of Atzeneta, has become so big and hollow that someone has built a door into it, so visitors can properly step inside and out.

The oil from the area is among the best in Spain, but as it's mostly made for personal consumption, it's very rare to find it on sale. Oil for export is left to the Andalusians of Jaén province much further south, who produce more than anyone else in the world.

Olive trees are sacred to the Virgin, a natural follow-on from their classical association with Athena. Smaller religious statues, such as figures of the Madonna, were usually carved in olive wood, while one of Mary's many official attributes is *oliva speciosa* – 'fair olive tree'. Perhaps for this reason many of the Madonnas miraculously discovered in the years after the conquest of the area from the Moors were found in or near olive trees.

Reflecting the wide range of medicinal uses of both the plant and its oil, a local saying runs:

La Verge Maria
quan pel món anava
amb oli de cresol
tot ho curava.

When the Virgin Mary
Walked the Earth
She cured all illnesses
With the oil from her lamp.

The healing properties of olive oil are widely known, and it can be used to cure almost anything from constipation to earache. The oil is known to have strong analgesic properties.

PINE
(*Pinus*; *Pí* Val.; *Pino* Cast.)

The most common pine tree in the area is the *halapensis* – the Aleppo pine, or *pí blanc*. The *sylvestris* and *nigra* – the Scots and Austrian pines – are found at higher altitudes, on the upper slopes of Penyagolosa, while the *pinea* – the stone pine, which produces pine nuts – is also commonly found. Pines have been used extensively in recent years in reforestation programmes, to the annoyance of some conservationists, who claim that the oak and holm oak are more suited to the landscape: pine trees grow more quickly, but burn easily, thus creating optimum conditions for yet more forest fires. Much of the countryside between Penyagolosa and the sea has yet to recover properly from a massive forest fire that swept through the area in the early 1990s. Nonetheless, pine-clad valleys and mountains can still be found, particularly around the River Villahermosa, where the heady smell of pine resin fills the summer air.

The pine was linked to Pan, 'the god of the wood', dancing and playing his pipes under the trees: he tried to seduce a wood nymph, Pitys, but she avoided his advances by turning herself into a pine tree. Pines were also sacred to Cybele, the 'Great Mother' goddess of the Phrygians.

Pine needles have traditionally been used in combination with rosemary and thyme to make a herbal tea said to be beneficial for bronchial problems. The mixture should be boiled only briefly and then left to cool, and should be taken twice a day. Pines are also said to cure warts: find a young tree and peel off its bark; when the tree dries up and dies the wart will disappear.

A legend tells of how a pine tree sheltered Mary, Joseph and the infant Jesus during the Flight to Egypt. Having nowhere to stay, they stopped en route under the branches of a bean trefoil. But selfishly the bean trefoil decided to pull up its branches and so the family had to move on, until a generous pine tree extended itself over them that they might rest safely for the night. Since that time the fruit and leaves of the trefoil have given off a vile smell, similar to rotting beans: some still refer to it as the Mediterranean stinkbush.

Locally, pine resin mixed with fresh beeswax is used to treat burns and lightly infected wounds.

STRAWBERRY TREE

(*Arbutus unedo*; *Alborç* Val.; *Madroño* Cast.)

Mention of the name 'strawberry tree' tends to invoke one of two responses: 1) 'You know strawberries don't grow on trees, don't you?'; or 2) 'I didn't know strawberries grew on trees!' The name in English comes from the bright red strawberry-sized fruits the tree produces, creating one of the most colourful sights of the year. The fruits, which go from yellow to orange to red as they ripen, are edible, but owing to their high tannin levels are not easily digested. They can, however, be turned into jam. Very ripe fruits often contain high levels of alcohol.

The leaves are used medicinally for their astringent, diuretic and antiseptic qualities. Some local herbalists say strawberry tree roots cut up and boiled can help against migraine and memory loss.

The town of Albuixec takes its name from an older version of the Valencian name for the tree, *alborç*. According to the legend, in September 1268 a priest from Valencia cathedral sent out a farm worker to plough some land in the area. But every time the poor labourer passed a nearby strawberry tree with his plough, the oxen pulling it would stop and kneel. After this had happened for a third time, he went to the tree to investigate, and there, in a hollow, he found a statue of the Virgin Mary, which had been hidden hundreds of years before. The Madonna is known as *La Moreneta*, for the dark-brown colour of her skin.

YEW
(*Taxus baccata*; *Teix* Val.; *Tejo* Cast.)

The yew is a fast disappearing tree in Spain, rarely planted or replaced. Place names attest to it once being very common – *Fuente del Tejo, Sierra Tejada* etc. – but being a slow grower and with a lingering popular association with the Underworld, it has become an ever rarer sight. As in some European countries, it is found in churchyards in northern parts of the country, where the Celtic influence was strongest; on the Mediterranean and most other parts the cypress is the tree of graveyards and resurrection. Locally, the most impressive yews can be found at the Sant Joan de Penyagolosa hermitage, where they line the route leading away towards the Carbó Valley.

Yew wood was traditionally used for making longbows, and Spanish yew was particularly prized for this, being considered straighter and stronger than other varieties. It was also common in ancient times for the poison from yew berries to be smeared on arrow points. The tree was sacred to Hecate, the triple goddess of sorcery, birth and death.

A Spanish expression for 'to flirt' or 'to declare one's love or attraction to someone' is *echar los tejos*, or *tirar los tejos*, literally 'to throw yews'. It comes from an ancient practice where young men and women would try to woo potential marriage partners by casting either yew branches or yew berries in their direction.

The yew trees I planted by the path leading down to the olive groves are still there, slowly taking root and producing new shoots. I sometimes ask myself if the spot is too exposed for them – they like a certain amount of shade, but a large pine tree to one side and a holm oak to the other should be enough to see them through. The ibex have nibbled on their branches a little, as they have on the cypress nearby, but they appear to have quickly moved on to sweeter plants. And so I water them during the hotter season, cleaning away the weeds that threaten to choke them in the spring, willing them on to survive and grow. I wonder if they will still be there a thousand years from now.

ACKNOWLEDGEMENTS

Many people have helped us over the past few years on the slopes of Penyagolosa, but our life at the farm, and the writing of this book, would be unthinkable without the involvement of three in particular: John Gordon, John Wildash and my father, John Webster. I am forever grateful to them. Many thanks also to Terry, Kevin, Dangerous Dave, Justin and my brother Chris for pitching in. Tanya, my sister, and my mother, Karole, were also incredibly supportive.

María José Soriano and José Crespo were extremely kind and hospitable throughout the period. Montse Arribas was a great source of information and inspiration, as were Rosa and Eduardo. Silvia kept us supplied with the local gossip, while María José gave us great gardening encouragement. Enrique, Toni, Gonzalo, Fidel and Jesús were also very helpful along the way, as were José at Molina in Xátiva and Jordi Martín.

Thanks also to Vincente and Tania, Vicentín and Cristina, and Marta and Alex.

My Spanish editor and friend Enrique Murillo was kind enough to correct some of my spelling of Valencian/Catalan words.

Thanks to my agent Natasha Fairweather for laying the groundwork for this book. Also to Alison Samuel at Chatto & Windus for believing in it from the start. And to Jenny Uglow: I don't think a writer could ask for a better editor. Many thanks also to Laetitia Bermejo for her wonderful drawings, and to Reginald Piggott, who managed to draw exactly the map I had in mind.

There is no full English translation of Ibn al-Awam's *Kitab al-Falaha*. However, a small selection taken from the book was translated by Philip Lord and published by The Black Swan Press of Wantage,

Oxfordshire in 1979 under the title *A Moorish Calendar*. Although I haven't quoted from it directly, it proved to be an invaluable aide in a number of instances when faced with some of the more impenetrable passages of Banqueri's Spanish rendition, and I would like to take this opportunity to express my gratitude to both the translator and the publisher.

INDEX

Locations are in Spain unless stated otherwise.

www.vintage-books.co.uk